THE EASTERN QUESTION IN THE EIGHTEENTH CENTURY

THE

EASTERN QUESTION

IN

THE EIGHTEENTH CENTURY

THE PARTITION OF POLAND AND THE TREATY OF
KAINARDJI

BY

ALBERT SOREL

STATE COLLEGE
LIBRARY

FRAMINGHAM, MASS.

NEW YORK

Howard Fertig

1969

First published in English in 1898

HOWARD FERTIG, INC. EDITION 1969
Published by arrangement with Methuen & Co. Ltd.

All rights reserved.

Library of Congress Catalog Card Number: 68-9661

8|70   BCL

PRINTED IN THE UNITED STATES OF AMERICA
BY NOBLE OFFSET PRINTERS, INC.

D
373
.S72
1969

PREFACE

Mr. Bramwell has asked me to write a few words of preface to his translation of M. Sorel's admirable study in eighteenth century diplomacy. This study was an early work of the greatest of living historians. My task seems somewhat superfluous in view of the preface in which M. Sorel himself has explained the scope of his essay. Till a comparatively late date the history of the 'Greatest Crime of Modern Times' was known only through Rulhière's famous *Histoire de l'Anarchie de la Pologne* (Paris, 1807). But the last phases of the 'Polish Question' were made clear to us when the late Professor von Sybel's *History of the French Revolution* appeared in English, and the Duc de Broglie's *Secret du Roi* has paved the way for the comprehension of the earlier history of the same question, and has explained the failure of France to assist her two old allies Poland and Turkey. The publication of the series of *Instructions données aux Ambassadeurs de la France* which is still in process of continuance, and on which M. Sorel has expended so much useful labour, is shedding increased light upon the intricate problems which agitated the minds of the states-men of the eighteenth century, and is illustrating only too faithfully the contention first sketched out in this essay, and afterwards brilliantly developed in the author's

Europe et la Révolution Française, that there 'was no
Europe,' no principle of public law, of treaty-making or
treaty-keeping, other than the interest of the moment,
and that the ease with which revolutionary France dictated her will to the Continental peoples was due to this
absence of principle in the Courts of Europe.

To follow day by day the exchange of diplomatic notes
between leading statesmen upon a question of first-rate
importance is always instructive, if at times a little tedious.
M. Sorel can never be tedious—few French historians
can—and he has never been more instructive or more
vivid than in the present essay. The characters of his
actors stand at full length upon the brilliant canvas—
Frederick the Great with his cynical foresight, far other
than the hero of battles, whom Carlyle drew—rather, as
he said of himself, the policeman of Europe ; Kaunitz,
with his objection to fresh air, his infinite conceit and infinite pedantry, yet also his infinite shrewdness ; the noble
Empress-Queen Maria Theresa, qui ' pleurait et prenait
toujours' only because her conscience, too, had to bow to
the Machiavelism of her surroundings ; above all, the
terrible Colossus of the East 'qui ne manque jamais de
suite dans sa politique' steered by the undaunted and
unscrupulous hands of the great Catharine.

Frederick is the Protagonist. He first suggests, at the
moment, the partition of Poland. Is he, then, to blame
for calling the Russians whom he so much dreads, whom
he has seen so close at Zorndorf and Kunersdorf, into
Europe ? Yes and no. Yes, because he does actually
call them in by his treaties of 1764 and 1772 ; no, because
if he omits to do so, they will come unasked, and swallow
Poland unpartitioned. Yes again, because he does not
take the only patriotic German course, and combine with
Austria to resist them ; no again, because such a combination with the Austria of 1770 is an impossibility. Not

that *prejudice* stands in Frederick's way. He is too 'detached' to feel anything of the kind. But the prejudices of Maria Theresa against Der Böse Mann, as she calls Frederick, can never be overcome, nor can Kaunitz nor Joseph ever long remain proof against the proffered seductions of Catharine. The King of Prussia then makes the best of a bad job, but it must be remembered that with the exception of the *reunion* (as he may fairly call it) of Polish Prussia to his own crown, he looks upon the rest of the business as a bad job. And if Frederick is really reuniting districts which have been German as late as the fifteenth century, Catharine, too, is in most places raising the Russian flag over a Russian-speaking people of the orthodox faith. No excuse of the same kind can be made for Austria. She is not only overstepping a huge natural boundary—the Carpathians—but no tie of history, language, or race binds her to the burgesses of Lemberg, or the salt-miners of Wielycksa ; while as to religion, she is of the religion of the very men who suffer most by the partition, viz., the nobles of Poland. And whatever political reasons Prussia and Russia may have for desiring a weak Poland, it is Austria's interest to create a strong one. She will find this out in 1791, and make an effort to effect it, but will then be too late.

M. Sorel—if one may venture to complain of any lacuna—gives us little indication of the method of life of the Poland that was partitioned—that strange democracy of nobles, called in the same breath a republic and a kingdom, which persecuted heretics with the fervour of a mediæval King, and ill-treated its serfs after the approved methods of Reginald Front de Bœuf. The lot of the average Polish peasant after the partitions was not a pleasant one to whichever of the rival Powers he might fall, but it was undoubtedly a better one than it had been under his native aristocracy. His master could, at

least, no longer enjoy the luxury of killing him for a fine
of a few piastres. . M. Sorel speculates little upon the
future of Poland, but that there is still a ' Polish Question '
may be occasionally discovered from the separatist news-
papers in Vienna.   I have read in one of these that the
' cry of Poland would continue to go up till it blended
with the last Hosanna,' which is a truly terrible prospect
for Eastern Europe, but the expression of which does not
show much confidence in the ultimate triumph of the cause.

That the truer interests of Austria lay in the other
side of the Eastern Question, the future of the European
and Christian provinces of Turkey, was in the eighteenth
century a self - evident truth.   The principle of self-
governing races had not then been overstrained to the
length of imagining Servian and Bulgarian ' nationalities '
and ' parliaments.'   Everyone was anxious to get rid of
the Turks, and all Western statesmen were anxious that
Russia should not alone, if at all, reap the benefit of their
expulsion.   But Austria was clearly not equal to the task
by herself, and the jealousies of the Courts of Europe
prevented then, as now, any concerted scheme for a new
map of the south-east.

MAGDALEN COLLEGE,
April, 1898.

AUTHOR'S PREFACE

SINCE the first entry of the Turk into Europe, there has been an Eastern Question; and since first Russia became a European Power, it has been her aim to solve this question to her own advantage. To become a European Power, she had to reckon with Prussia; for the solution of the Eastern Question, with Austria. Thus it came about that Prussia, who had no direct concern with Eastern | politics, was led to play a part in them, often a preponderating part, and that as Austria was concerned in all important matters of European politics, there was no political affair in Europe which did not have an influence in the East, or which was not influenced by the Eastern complications.

The ambitions of Prussia and Russia were in no sense opposed to each other. These two States became allied, and the alliance was continued, almost unbroken, for more than a century. Austria and Prussia were antagonists in Germany, Austria and Russia in the East. Austria was found in turn combating the ambitions of her two rivals, and associating her own with theirs. Hence we find an almost permanent alliance between Prussia and Russia, and intermittent alliances, now between Austria and Russia, now between the three States. I propose in these pages to show how the alliance between Prussia and Russia was formed in 1764, and how Austria, after at first opposing, was led to accede to it.

The circumstances under which these events occurred, and the characters of the individuals who were most actively concerned in them, are sufficiently remarkable to engage attention. Further, it has seemed to me not unprofitable to define clearly what were, on the eve of the French Revolution, the political usages of the three Courts which took so considerable a part in the so-called crusade in which the monarchies engaged against that revolution. Russia was of the three the most instant in preaching this crusade ; Prussia the most eager to engage in it ; Austria the most persevering in sustaining it. It has been much maintained abroad, and even in France, that the French Revolution and Napoleon I. upset the law of nations of the Ancien Régime, and substituted for a kind of golden age of diplomacy, where right ruled without a rival, an age of iron, in which might prevailed against all rights. In order to form a just judgment upon the work of the French Revolution and of Napoleon—to estimate to what extent they destroyed, innovated, imitated, or exaggerated—it is indispensable to know how, at the end of the Ancien Régime, the Governments most fully representative of that Régime used it amongst themselves, to know what was their conception of right, what their practice of diplomacy, whether with their competitors or with their allies. I conceive that the events set forth in this book are the best fitted to establish opinions on this point.

I have confined myself to my chosen sphere. I have not examined in detail the policy of France in the crisis which is the subject of this study. In the first edition of this book, I referred the reader, on this subject, to the *Diplomatic Studies* of the Comte de Saint-Priest, vol. i., ' The Partition of Poland.' A short time afterwards the second part of the Duc de Broglie's work, *The Secret of the King*, appeared. This work threw a blaze of light on the policy of Louis XV. in the Eastern Question and in the partition of Poland. I have made numerous references to it. The publication of the *Instructions*, undertaken by the Diplomatic Archives Commission, enabled me to follow out my indications upon many points. I have endeavoured to bring my essay, without altering its proportions, into conformity with the works which have appeared since its publication, that is to say, since May, 1878.

The reader will see that my account is almost entirely based upon diplomatic correspondences and documents. These documents, perhaps the most confidential and the most surprising that have ever been drawn from the archives, have been published in the last few years at Vienna, at St. Petersburg, and at Berlin. We may say that, upon the first and foremost episode of the Eastern Question in the eighteenth century, we possess the version of Austria, the version of Prussia, and the version of Russia.

The following are the titles of the principal works from which I have drawn my documents. They are:

FOR AUSTRIA.

Arneth : *Geschichte Maria Theresias I.*, vols. vii. and viii., Vienna, 1877 ; *Maria Theresia und Joseph II.*, Vienna, 1867.

Arneth and Geffroy : *Correspondance entre Marie-Thérèse et le Comte de Mercy-Argenteau*, Paris, 1874.

Beer : *Die erste Theilung Polens*, Vienna, 1873 ; *Die Orientalische Politik Œsterreichs Zeit* 1774, Vienna, 1883.

FOR PRUSSIA.

Œuvres de Frédéric le Grand, Berlin.

Duncker : *Aus der Zeit Friedrichs des Grossen*, Leipzig, 1876.

Ranke : *Die Deutschen Mächte und der Fürstenbund*, Leipzig, 1872;
Correspondance de Frédéric II. et du Comte de Solms, 1767-1772,
St. Petersburg, 1883.

FOR RUSSIA.

Publications de la Société d'Histoire de Russie, St. Petersburg,
1875-1888.

Martens : *Traités de la Russie*, St. Petersburg, 1875-1888.

Hermann : *Geschichte des Russischen Staates*, Gotha, 1867.

Rambaud : *Histoire de la Russie*, Paris, 1878.

FOR TURKEY.

Comte de Saint-Priest : *Mémoires sur l'Ambassade de France en
Turquie*, Paris, 1877.

Zinkeisen : *Geschichte des Osmanischen Reiches*, Gotha, 1863.

Hammer : *Histoire de l'Empire Ottoman*, traduite par Hellert,
Paris, 1839.

La Jonquière : *Histoire de l'Empire Ottoman*, Paris, 1881.

CONTENTS

CONTENTS

CHAPTER II.

THE REVOLUTION IN POLAND, AND THE WAR IN THE EAST.

(1764—1768.)

CHAPTER III.

THE ' RAPPROCHEMENT ' BETWEEN PRUSSIA AND AUSTRIA.

(October, 1768—January, 1769.)

CHAPTER IV.

THE PLANS OF FREDERICK THE GREAT AND THE PRO-
JECTS OF A TRIPLE ALLIANCE.

(February—May, 1769.)

CHAPTER V.

THE WAR IN THE EAST, AND THE MILITARY PRECAU-TIONS OF AUSTRIA.

(January—August, 1769.)

CHAPTER VI.

THE INTERVIEW BETWEEN FREDERICK AND JOSEPH AT NEISSE.

(August, 1769.)

CONTENTS

CONTENTS

CHAPTER X.

THE INTERVIEW AT NEUSTADT.

(September, 1770.)

CHAPTER XI.

THE MEDIATION.

(September, 1770—January, 1771.)

CONTENTS

CHAPTER XII.

THE PRELIMINARIES OF THE PARTITION OF POLAND.

(November, 1770—January, 1771.)

CHAPTER XIII.

THE OFFICIAL OVERTURES FOR PEACE AND PARTITION.

(January—June, 1771.)

CONTENTS xix

CHAPTER XIV.

THE AUSTRO-TURKISH ALLIANCE, AND THE PROJECTS
FOR THE DISMEMBERMENT OF TURKEY.

(January—October, 1771.)

Austrian diplomacy at Constantinople ; Thugut ; his position and his history - - - - 150
The Turks accept Austria's proposals for alliance ; the treaty of July 6 - - - - - 154
Negotiations for partition between Prussia and Russia - 155
Kaunitz's plans - - - - - - 157
Russia's reply ; Count Massin's proposals for partitioning Turkey - - - - - - 159
Frederick's fears - - - - - 161
Maria Theresa reassures him - - - - 161
Frederick upsets Kaunitz's plans - - - 162

CHAPTER XV.

AUSTRIA'S DIFFICULTIES.

(October, 1771—January, 1772.)

Austria's real position - - - - - 164
Deliberations at Vienna - - - - 166
Difficulties with the Turks respecting the alliance - 168
Kaunitz's interviews with Galytzin - - - 169
Frederick reveals the treaty of July 6 - - - 173
Russia's difficulties in Poland - - - - 174
Catharine's policy at Berlin and Vienna - - 176
Kaunitz and the French Chargé d'Affaires - - 178
Austria decides for the partition ; the 'graduated proposals' - - - - - - 180
Kaunitz abandons both Poland and Turkey to their fate 184

CHAPTER XVI.

THE PRINCIPLE OF THE TRIPLE ALLIANCE—THE EQUALITY OF SHARES.

(January—February, 1772.)

CHAPTER XVII.

THE DISTRIBUTION OF THE SHARES.

(January—May, 1772.)

CHAPTER XVIII.

THE CONSECRATION OF THE ALLIANCE—THE TREATY OF PARTITION.

(May—August, 1772.)

CHAPTER XIX.

THE CONGRESSES OF FOCKTCHANY AND BUCHAREST.

(May, 1772—March, 1773.)

CHAPTER XX.

THE TREATY OF KAINARDJI.

(June, 1773—September, 1774.)

CHAPTER XXI.

THE ANNEXATION OF BUKOVINA.

(September, 1774—July, 1776.)

CHAPTER XXII.

THE TRIPLE ALLIANCE.

BALTIC SEA

LIVONIA

R U S S I A N

Riga
R. Dwina
COURLAND AND SEMIGALLIA
WENDISH LIVONIA

SAMOGITIA
1772
Witebsk

Smolensk

Königsberg
Danzig
ERMELAND
WEST PRUSSIA
1772
EAST PRUSSIA
1772
PRUSSIA
LITHUANIA
Wilna

WHITE RUSSIA

E M P I R E

POMERANIA
Marienberg
Thorn
Grodno
R. Niemen
R. Beresina

SILESIA
R. Netze
1772
Posen
R. Warthe
R. Ustula
Warsaw
R. Narew
R. Bug
BLACK RUSSIA

R. Oder
Neisse
Lublin
R. Pritjet

Neustadt
MORAVIA
Cracow
Bochnia
Wielyczka
ZIPS
G A L
Belz
Lemberg
1772
C I A
VOLHYNIA
LITTLE RUSSIA
Kiev
R. Dnepr

UKRAINE

HUNGARY
Line of the Carpathian Mountains
PODOLIA
R. Bug

R. Sbrucz or Podhor
R. Dniester
Balta

TRANSYL-VANIA
BUKOVIN
1769
R. Pruth
BESSARABIA
Oczakow
Cherson
Kinburn

POLAND
at and after
THE
FIRST PARTITION
1772
From a rough drawing by C.R.L.Fletcher.

MOLDAVIA
T U R K I S H
E M P I R E
CRIMEA

The Russian frontier is ————
,, Prussian ,, ...
,, Austrian ,, ----------
,, Turkish ,, —··—··—

WALLACHIA
Galatz
R. Danube
BLACK SEA

THE EASTERN QUESTION IN THE EIGHTEENTH CENTURY

CHAPTER I.

THE ALLIANCE BETWEEN PRUSSIA AND RUSSIA.

(1756—1764.)

THE year 1756 witnessed a complete revolution in the federative system of Europe. The treaty of May 1, which the Austrian Chancellor, Count Kaunitz, regarded with reason as his political masterpiece, broke the chain of a rivalry which had existed for a century between the houses of France and of Austria. For this it substituted an alliance directed against the respective adversaries of these two houses : England and Prussia. Prussia sided with England, and supported her in her war with France and Spain. Russia turned against Prussia. The two Empresses, Elizabeth and Maria Theresa, joined hands in opposition to Frederick II. ' It being impossible,' as they said, ' for the peace of Europe to be assured, unless the King of Prussia is deprived of the means of troubling it, their Imperial Majesties will use every effort to do this service to humanity.'[1]

[1] Article VI. of the Convention of January 22, 1757, between Austria and Russia : Martens, vol. i., p. 207.

It was decided to reduce Prussia to impotence, and a vast bargain was made over the spoils of that kingdom, which should alter the face of the map of Europe.

Louis XV. promised Maria Theresa Silesia and the county of Glatz; Saxony received for her share Magdeburg and Halberstadt; Sweden received Pomerania. Austria promised France a part of the Low Countries, the rest to go to the Infant of Parma; she indemnified herself with the duchy of Parma.

These arrangements, concluded in 1757, were annulled in 1758. The two allies guaranteed to each other for the future only their eventual conquests. Austria pledged herself to give France an equivalent in the event of her obtaining 'any considerable advantages at the expense of the King of Prussia.' Russia, for her part, obtained from Austria a promise of the cession of Eastern Prussia, the Prussian province *par excellence*, the province which had given its name to the monarchy.[2]

The three greatest Powers of the Continent were thus in coalition against Frederick. He faced the storm. He had been up to that point audacious, fortunate, and adroit. But there was still something of the parvenu in this conqueror without scruples, something of the cynic in this crowned philosopher. By his stanchness under defeat, by the marvellous resources which his genius displayed in this unequal struggle of seven years' duration, the King of Prussia compelled the admiration of his contemporaries. For his friends and for his enemies he

[2] Treaty of May 1, 1757, between France and Austria : published by Frédéric Masson, *Mémoires de Bernis*, vol. i., p. 469. Treaty of December 30, 1758, between France and Austria : Martens, *Traités de la Russie*, vol. i., p. 226. Treaty of December 31, 1753, between France and Austria, *Instructions, Autriche*, p. 388 note. Treaty of March 21, 1760, between Russia and Austria : Martens, *ibid.*, p. 253.

became the Great Frederick. And yet there came a
moment when he felt himself lost. The Russians had
conquered Eastern Prussia—that is to say, the share that
had been assigned to them in the distribution. Frederick
had only 30,000 men. His brother, Prince Henry, had
no more, and the country was absolutely ruined in men,
horses, money, and provisions. Frederick wrote to Prince
Henry on January 9, 1762 : 'If all help should fail us, in
spite of the hope we still entertain, I confess that I do
not see what could delay or avert our destruction.' The
hope which he still held was that of a diversion from the
Turks. But he was wrong. M. de Vergennes, at that
time French Ambassador at the Porte, worked against
him, and the Turks made no movement. The help came
from another quarter, and certainly from the quarter
whence Frederick least expected it. Ten days after he
had written this alarming letter to his brother, on
January 19, the news reached him that the Czarina
Elizabeth was dead. Peter III., the new Czar, was a
fervent admirer of Frederick. He had hardly come to
power when he withdrew his troops from the coalition,
handed back to Frederick the province that Elizabeth
had taken from him, and signed with Prussia on May 5,
1762, a treaty of peace and friendship, with a promise of
alliance.[3]

The defection of Peter III. had saved Frederick. The
alliance was founded which was destined to bind Prussia
and Russia for more than a century, except for some short
intervals of rivalry, and for a few transitory conflicts. It
was based on grounds more substantial than the whims of
a Sovereign or the passing needs of a political combination.
It was the condition necessary for the success of the vast
designs with which parallel ambitions inspired the dynasty
of the Romanofs and that of the Hohenzollerns. Policy

[3] Martens, *Traités de la Russie*, vol. vi., p. 367 *et seq.*

was to maintain the fabric erected by a fanciful Prince,
and a proof of this was soon forthcoming. There was a
coup d'état, or, as the word then went, a palace revolution
at St. Petersburg. Peter III. was arrested, imprisoned,
and deposed by order of the Czarina, and assassinated by
her accomplices. The news of this deed was received with
the most lively joy at Vienna. ' I bow before the providence of God which has watched over Austria, over the
Russian Empire, and over Christendom,' wrote Maria
Theresa to her Ambassador in Russia, on July 29, 1762.
' This news came as a thunderbolt upon the King,'
Frederick records in his memoirs. The Czarina had in
truth shown herself very hostile to the Prussian alliance.
But both sides were too early with their reckoning, and
they reckoned without Catharine II. She replied to the
pious congratulations of Maria Theresa with much polite-
ness, and made no change in Peter III.'s treaty with the
King of Prussia.[4]

The fact is that Catharine, who was looking forward to
a very great reign, had quickly perceived that the prop
which she needed could be found at that time only in
Prussia.

The Seven Years' War was ended. France treated with
England at Paris on February 10, 1763 ; Austria with
Prussia at Hubertsburg on the 15th of the same month.
This bloody contest left Europe in the most profound
disorder. ' The peace which we have just made is neither
advantageous nor glorious,' said Louis XV. France felt
herself weakened and humiliated. An invincible antipathy separated Louis XV. from the King of Prussia.
With England it was a national rivalry always burning,
an impotent longing for revenge, a century-old hatred continually inflamed by wounded susceptibilities. England
was the *hereditary enemy*. The publicists of the time

[4] Martens, vol. vi., p. 2.

compared her relations with France to those of Rome with
Carthage between the second and third Punic wars.
' She has adopted the same principle of never allowing us
to recover ; of unintermittent watching of our harbours,
our yards, our arsenals ; of spying upon our plans, our
preparations, our slightest movements, and of stopping
them short by haughty insinuations or threatening demonstrations.'[5] With Russia it was a latent hostility,
scantily disguised under the cloak of official courtesy.
' This Princess,' wrote Choiseul, speaking of Catharine II.,
' this Princess, who, to the shame of our century, governs
an empire undisturbed—I may say insolently, after the
most unheard-of offences—is our sworn enemy, whether
owing to her alliances or to the members of her
Government. The distance that separates the two States
is the one cause which prevents their reciprocal hostility
from bursting into flame.'[6]

By the treaty of 1756, France secured the neutrality of
Austria on the Continent, in the event of a maritime war
with England. It was something gained, no doubt, but
it was not enough, and this was already apparent. In
every other sphere, in Germany, in Italy, in the Low
Countries, in Poland, in the East—that is to say, in the
most important matters of Continental politics—the treaty
placed France in a subordinate position, and obliged her
to fit her policy into conformity with Austria's interests,
which were almost everywhere in opposition to her own.
The treaty was, on the other hand, entirely to the
advantage of Austria. That Court ceased to support
the colonial ambitions of England as against France.
Louis XV. was left to struggle unaided at his own risk

[5] Memoir upon foreign politics, addressed to the King in 1773
by the Comte de Broglie, and edited by Favier : Boutaric, *Correspondence Secrète de Louis XV.*, vol. ii., p. 183.

[6] Choiseul to Kaunitz, July 18, 1766 : Arneth, vol. viii., p. 539.

and peril on two oceans, and for this concession, which
was a mere irony, Austria gained entire freedom of action
in the rest of Europe.   France promised never to side
against her, and pledged herself to give her armed
assistance should she be attacked.   Guaranteed in the
possession of its territories, secure that no serious opposition to its enterprises would be offered by French
diplomacy, the Court of Vienna saw in the treaty of
1756 a means of re-embarking in perfect security and
with the best prospects of success upon the achievement
of the plan of domination which it had long been
pursuing.

Prussia had emerged from the Seven Years' War victorious
and intact.   The only result of the coalition, which was
to have destroyed her, had been to sanction and secure
her right of citizenship in Europe.   If she was still only a
secondary State in the extent and resources of her territory,
she had raised herself to the first rank of Powers by the
prestige of her arms and the success of her policy.   But,
lofty as was the appearance of the Prussian edifice, it had
as yet only an exterior.   The interior, as yet hardly marked
out, was ravaged as by fire.   'The only adequate image of
this State,' said Frederick, 'is that of a man riddled with
wounds, weak from loss of blood, and almost failing under
the weight of his sufferings.   A systematic diet is needed
to restore him, tonics to give him back his strength, balms
to heal his wounds.'   Frederick's only thought was to repair
the breaches made by the war, to reform his legal system,
to re-establish the system of government, and, above all,
to re-create the army, which had lost solidity and discipline.
'If once the army were neglected, it would be the destruction of this country,' he wrote to his brother.   He had
conquered, but he stood alone.   He was resolved never
again to mix himself up with the colonial quarrels of the
French and the English.   'The only thing to do is to

avoid all alliances with these peoples, and to let them go
their way ; what have we to do with codfish and Cape
Breton ?"[7] It was wise language, no doubt ; but, in the
then agitated condition of Europe, Frederick could not
stand without a friend. At that moment Russia held out
her hand, and he grasped it.[8] This alliance—the alliance
most needed, and the only alliance possible—enabled that
great statesman to complete his work of restoration in
peace, and at the same time to carry the Prussian State
to a height of power till then beyond the dreams of her
most ambitious Sovereigns.

Russia had dealt the decisive blows in the Seven Years'
War.[9] Old Europe, from the beginning of the century,
had observed the progress of this empire with a somewhat
contemptuous notice. Henceforth it was necessary to take
account of this young Sovereign, for whom events had
prepared a part worthy of her singular genius. With
Europe disconcerted, disturbed, and at the end of its
resources, Russia could choose her ally. It was reserved
for a woman of thirty-three—a German of very ancient
race, it is true, but the daughter of a princelet who had
not even a whole vote in the College of Imperial Princes—
to make Europe resound with her name, and to propound
some of the weightiest problems that have troubled the
history of modern times. It was Catharine's aim to rule
Russia, and to make her one of the leading Powers of the
Continent. It turned out that the same methods were
needed to win the Russians, and to place Russia in the
place Catharine intended her to take among the great
Powers. There were no parties at the Russian Court ;
there were scarcely even factions. It was a Court still in

---

[7] Letter to Prince Henry, February 24, 1763 : *Œuvres*, vol. xxvi.
[8] Martens, vol. vi., p. 213.
[9] *Cf. L'Europe et la Révolution*, vol. i., book iii., chap. viii. ;
Russia, Sweden, Poland, and the Eastern Question.

a state of barbarity, and there personal rivalries filled the
place that was in other places held by parties or factions.
The Empress was beautiful, witty, and pleasure-loving ;
her views upon matters of private morality were most free,
but she kept unbroken control over her heart and reason,
if not over her senses. It was thus easy for her to beguile
men, to play them against each other, to lower them while
she appeared to raise them to her own level, and to subjugate them by the very magnificence of the favours which
she showered upon them. She remained grave and im-
perturbable in the midst of her irregularities ; but her
irregularities were excessive, and were notorious even in a
century which, if it prided itself on its license, had at least
preserved the notion of taste and of moderation. As it
has been ingeniously remarked, ' There was in her too
much of Cleopatra, and for too long.' It was all the
scandal of the Court of Louis XV., but with less refine-
ment, without the veneer, without the politeness, and
without the graces, of that Court. But if the degradation
at St. Petersburg was more cynical, it at least escaped
ridicule. While Versailles presented the piteous spectacle
of an effeminate Prince handing his State over to his
mistresses, Russia presented that of a virile-minded woman
ruling her favourites, and subordinating her excesses to
reasons of State.

It was very easy for Catharine to subdue the nobles, but
the people were not to be won so readily. She perceived
this. She felt that, in this half-formed and rough-hewn
people, religious passions absorbed and dominated all
others. Patriotism was confounded with orthodoxy ; the
people were unable to dissociate the two ideas of the
propagation of the faith and the expansion of Russian
power. Catharine, pure Voltairian as she was at heart,
posed as the orthodox Sovereign *par excellence*. It was
with the Greek cross in hand that she summoned her

people to the two great enterprises which her predecessors had prepared, the achievement of which constituted in her eyes the historic mission of the Czars—namely, the conquest of Poland, which should open the road towards European civilization, and the conquest of the harbours of the Black Sea, which should open the road to that Byzantine Empire whose greatness Holy Russia was summoned to renew, both by popular superstition and by political speculation.

Catharine found the ground prepared and the idea matured. There was a widespread idea among the peoples of the Greek religion who were under the Ottoman domination ' that the Turkish Empire should be destroyed by a fair-haired nation.' From the time when these peoples knew the Muscovites, they looked to them for salvation. From the moment when Russia emerged, they turned to her. The Christian religion and the first rudiments of a civilization had been brought into Russia by monks from Byzantium, and by emigrants from the Byzantine Empire. The links which bound Russia to the Eastern Greeks were thus formed in her infancy. They were strengthened as she grew, and when she felt her strength, it seemed to her a work of piety to gather together the scattered heritage of her godparents. The Byzantines, in giving her baptism, had set a destiny before her. In the reign of Catharine I., Greek priests from Turkey had already been found imploring protection and alms from Russia. Russia received them, and sent them back full-handed. Soon Russian emissaries had penetrated as far even as the valleys of Montenegro, carrying presents from the White Czar to the churches, and fomenting hatred of the Turk. The Montenegrins, entrenched in their mountains, and protected by the Venetian Republic, had managed to preserve their independence. They entered into established relations with Russia. Their priests studied in St. Petersburg; their Bishop had himself consecrated by Russian Bishops.

They bore greetings to their orthodox brothers, and spread the name of Russia among them, clothed in the mysterious glamour of popular superstitions and national legends.

When war broke out between Russia and Turkey, in 1735, the idea occurred to Marshal Munnich of profiting by the hopes which the Greeks had formed, and he called these nations to arms. He was planning the conquest of the Crimea and of Moldavia, and he saw, in a revolt of the nations of the Greek religion, a means of creating a potent diversion against the Turks. He propounded to the Empress Anne ' that all the Greeks regarded the Czarina as their legitimate Sovereign ; that the mood of those nations attached them to that early condition of renown to which the Russian power had then attained ; that it was desirable to seize this first moment of their hope and enthusiasm, and to march to Constantinople ; and that such a frame of mind might never again be found.' The Czarina approved. In the spring of 1739 Munnich conquered Moldavia, which welcomed him as a deliverer. He was preparing to cross the Danube, and to push forward the war into the heart of Turkey, when the Peace of Belgrade (September 18, 1739) checked his course.[10] A few years later, the revolution which brought Elizabeth to the throne conveyed him to Siberia. The new Empress contented herself with sending presents to the churches. Her emissaries penetrated as far as Mount Athos, and a Russian priest appeared in the mountains of the Peloponnese. In this manner it was that the Greek traditions took shape, and that relations were established between the Russians and the Eastern Christians.

The accession of Peter III. recalled Munnich from exile. That General supported the Czar against Catharine. Catharine pardoned him, confided great military works to

[10] *Vide* Albert Vaudal, *La Mission du Marquis de Villeneuve à Constantinople*, 1728-1741. Paris, 1887.

his charge, and used his experience. He propounded to her his scheme of raising a revolt among the Eastern Greeks, and of driving the Turks out of Europe. While Catharine's councillor was making these proposals, an agent appeared to carry them into effect. A Greek of Larissa in Thessaly, named Gregory Papaz-Ogli, who had come to Russia to seek his fortune, was, at the time of the *coup d'état* of 1762, a Captain in the artillery regiment in which Gregory Orlof was serving. Papaz-Ogli was restless and ambitious, and was trying to make his fortune. Being, no doubt, informed of Catharine's inclinations, and of the favour with which she regarded Munnich's plans, he revealed to Orlof the means by which he designed to raise rebellion in Greece. Orlof eagerly seized upon a scheme calculated at once to flatter the pride of his Sovereign, to secure his own advancement, and to make the Russian Empire the greatest in the world. The Minister Panin considered all these schemes premature and chimerical; but Orlof, promoted to the command of the artillery, and secretly encouraged by Catharine, permitted Papaz-Ogli, who was under his orders, to travel for three years in Greece for pretended reasons of health and private business. The Greek was to convince himself at first hand of the possibility of carrying out his schemes.[11]

Catharine, 'impatient for greatness and renown,' as she already was, did not feel herself as yet sufficiently firm upon her throne, or sufficiently sure of Europe, to embark upon such vast undertakings. She confined herself to thinking over the plan, and to allowing obscure servants to prepare darkly for its execution. 'So you think,' she said to the French Envoy, 'that the eyes of Europe are now fixed on me? And truly I think Russia deserves attention. They will not be able to judge of me for some

[11] Rulhière, *Histoire de l'Anarchie de Pologne*, books iii., ix., and xi.

years.' She added : ' In the meanwhile, I appear before all these Sovereigns in the light of a clever coquette.'

Above all, she needed a substantial and respected friend, alliance with whom should give some solidity to her diplomacy. There was no need for her to hesitate. It was enough to consider the dispositions of the different Courts, and to know their tendencies, in order to judge in what quarter she should seek and find such an alliance. It was not in England. Catharine professed ' a peculiar respect for the English nation,' but she feared the ' inconsistency ' of the British Government ; and, moreover, the interests of the two States, which were sufficiently in agreement to secure a good understanding between the two Cabinets, drew them towards objects too divergent for a permanent alliance ever to result from them.

France had abandoned Poland to the greed of Russia and Austria at the time of the Triple Alliance between Louis XV. and the two Empresses. At that time she saw in the preservation of that republic merely the ' prejudice of an ancient custom.' From the time when Russia began to draw towards Prussia, France began to regain her interest in her former ally. She continued also—at least, in theory and in despatches—to oppose enterprises directed against the Ottoman Empire.[12] Catharine could only regard Louis XV. as an adversary, and she never disguised the aversion, mingled with contempt, with which that Prince, his mistresses, and his Ministers inspired her.

The policy of Austria, unlike that of France, was not in direct opposition to the policy of Russia. But Catharine knew that her schemes would meet with open opposition at Vienna. If Austria, like Prussia, wished to maintain the state of anarchy which was sapping the power of

[12] Farges, *Instructions de Pologne*, vol. i., p. lxxvi ; *Instruction du Marquis de Paulmy*, 1760, vol. ii., p. 217 ; *ibid.*, p. 231. Duc de Broglie, *Le Secret du Roi*, vol. ii., p. 222 *et seq.*

Poland, it was no part of her scheme that Poland should become a vassal of Russia; and if the diplomatists at Vienna were not diametrically opposed to a dismemberment of the Turkish Empire, it was with an eye to the best share for themselves, and not in order that the trade of the mouth of the Danube and the protectorship of the Eastern Christians might be handed to Russia.

All the considerations which separated Russia from the other Powers drew her towards Prussia. Like Russia, Prussia was a late arrival upon the world's theatre; she had her future to carve out, and Catharine discerned there great means, accompanied by great inclinations. The expansion of Russia in the East was in no sense offensive to the Cabinet of Berlin, and Prussia could not fail to regard with complacency the inconveniences which that would entail for Austria. In Poland both States were equally concerned to destroy Austrian influence, to support a King who should be under their thumb, and, on the pretext of defending the Polish constitution, to maintain a state of anarchy, which should secure their influence over the unhappy republic.

The Prussian Minister, Count Solms, who had been accredited to the Court of St. Petersburg since 1761, enjoyed the full confidence of his master. He became in Russia *persona gratissima*. Before long the two Sovereigns even established an intimate correspondence.

The death of Augustus III., which occurred on October 5, 1763, and the need of a mutual agreement in view of the election of his successor, led Frederick and Catharine to fortify their friendship by a treaty involving a defensive alliance and a mutual guarantee of each other's territories. This was signed on April 10, 1764.[13] It was to last for eight years; it stipulated for a reciprocal territorial guarantee; neither peace nor truce

[13] Martens, vol. vi., p. 11 *et seq.*

was to be made except by mutual consent, and it promised mutual assistance to the extent of 10,000 men and
2,000 horses. In case the King of Prussia should be
engaged in war on the Rhine, or the Czarina in Turkey
or in the Crimea, an annual subsidy of 400,000 roubles,
or 480,000 Prussian thalers, might be substituted for
military aid. As for Poland, it was decided to bring
about the nomination for the kingship of Stanislas
Augustus Poniatowski, 'who has long been known to the
Empress of Russia, and whose person is agreeable to her,'
as Frederick expressed it by a polite euphemism. The
fact was that Poniatowski, who had been from the death
of Peter III., if not the first, at all events the most
favoured, of Catharine's lovers, seemed to combine all the
qualities required for the subordinate part for which he
was designated. But it was not enough to saddle Poland
with a King incapable of raising her; it was necessary to
prevent the Poles themselves, if patriotism should one day
open their eyes, from putting an end to their dissensions,
and to retain a pretext for interfering in their concerns.
Prussia and Russia agreed not to tolerate either the
abolition of the *liberum veto*, or the transformation of
the elective royalty into a hereditary monarchy. They
promised to suppress, if necessary by force of arms,
'principles so unjust and so dangerous to neighbouring
Powers.' As for the pretext for interference, it was
already there; and it lent itself marvellously well to the
mask of religion, which Catharine, with a profound instinct of the people whom she governed, thought it
necessary to put upon her schemes of empire and conquest. There were in Poland a body of 'separated'
Greeks and some Lutherans, who were confounded together
under the name of *Dissidents*. They had been admitted
in 1563 to the enjoyment of the same privileges as the
rest of the Polish nation. The preponderance of the

Catholics, who were from that time onwards under the influence of the Jesuits, deprived them of this. In 1736 they were excluded from almost all public employments. The Greeks had addressed complaints to Russia, the Lutherans to Prussia; Catharine and Frederick agreed to unite their efforts to restore the Dissidents to their privileges, rights, and prerogatives.[14] The Empress had attained her end, and this treaty gave her all the securities she needed. She lost no time in taking advantage of it. Russian troops were massed on the Polish frontier, ready to give forcible weight to the advice which the allies might give to the Poles, assembled for the election of their King, and to the representations which they might make in the interests of the Dissidents. At the same time, the Russian and Prussian Ministers at Constantinople received orders to use their influence with the Divan, to dissuade it from supporting the Polish patriots who were opposing the election of Poniatowski, and were demanding the suppression of the *liberum veto* by the Diet. This common action at Constantinople was the natural consequence of the treaty which had just been signed, and was necessarily imposed upon the allies. From the death of Augustus III., it was also towards the Porte that those who desired to withdraw Poland from Russian supremacy, and to rescue her from anarchy, directed their efforts.

[14] Angeberg, *Traités de la Pologne*, Paris, 1862; treaties of June 8th, 1762, and April 11th, 1764.—Frederick's Memoirs.—Beer, vol. i., pp. 100, 101.—Declaration of July 22nd, 1764: Martens, vol. vi., p. 33.

CHAPTER II.

(1764—1768.)

THE Polish patriots and their friends dreaded not only the enslavement of the republic, but also the ruin and dismemberment of Poland.

It was no new idea, thus to get rid of a turbulent neighbour, and to settle, at the expense of a third party, conflicting ambitions which could not be appeased by other means, whether of war or of negotiation. The partition of a State appeared the legitimate consequence of war, since conquest was its object.[1] The system of the balance of power, on which at that time international law was based, led by a rigid logic to the carving up of heritages, **and** to the expropriation of their owners, in order to establish peace and tranquillity in the world by a nice balance of forces.

Poland, which had no frontiers, and which lay spread over vast plains between Austria, Prussia, and Russia, seemed a field prepared by Nature for these political manœuvres. The vices of her constitution, the factions which divided her, all favoured these experiments ; and long before the balance of power had been erected into a

---

[1] *Vide L'Europe et la Révolution,* vol. i., book i., chap. i. ; *The System of the Balance of Power—Partitions,* p. 30 *et seq.*

formal doctrine, the idea had existed of applying its principles to this republic.

When the question had arisen of placing Henry of Valois upon the Polish throne, the Emperor, Maximilian II., and the Czar of Moscow, who had no liking for this candidature, had united to prevent it. The Emperor opined that the best and surest means of putting an end to vexatious competitions would be to confiscate the bone of contention, and, this cause of rivalry removed, to unite to hunt the Turks out of Europe. 'The Emperor,' said a protocol of 1573, 'expressed a wish that the kingdom [*i.e.*, Poland] might be partitioned ; the crown of Poland to go to the Emperor, and the great principality of Lithuania to the Czar of Moscow, and that the two might combine against the Sovereign of Turkey and the Tartar rulers.'[2] In 1657, Charles X. of Sweden revived this idea on his own account, but without result. Lionne wrote to the envoy of Louis XIV.: 'The good Poles who really love their country are not without apprehension, and that with much reason, that there is a secret agreement, perhaps already an express treaty, between the Emperor, the Elector of Brandenburg, and the Czar, to divide Poland amongst them after the death of the King, and for each to appropriate such parts of that kingdom and of the Grand-Duchy as may be most convenient in view of the proximity of their States.'[3] Charles XI. returned to the charge in 1667, and caused a proposal to be made to the Emperor and to the Margrave of Brandenburg for dividing the Polish territories amongst themselves as it might be convenient.

In 1710, a plan of partition, attributed by some to the Prussian Minister Ugen, by others to a Russian statesman, was discussed by Peter the Great and Frederick I. of Prussia (Margrave of Brandenburg). In the eighteenth century it

[2] Martens, vol. i., chap. xii.
[3] Instructions to Bonsy, December, 1664 : *Pologne*, vol. i., p. 81.

was almost the common ground of political speculation. The last of the Jaghellons[4] had prophesied partition in 1661; Stanislas Leczinski renewed the prophecy. 'We shall be the prey of some notable conqueror,' he said in 1749; 'perhaps even the neighbouring Powers may agree together to divide our territories.' The fact was that the Poles had not only to dread the conquest of their country by ambitious enemies; they had also to fear the trafficking of their leaders and of their own Sovereigns.

In 1733 Augustus II. meditated making the crown hereditary in the House of Saxony. 'For the attainment of this end,' said Frederick the Great, 'he had conceived the idea of partitioning that monarchy, as the means by which, as he thought, the jealousies of the neighbouring Powers might be appeased.' He addressed himself to the King of Prussia, Frederick William I., and made overtures to him. The death of Augustus II. stopped the negotiations. Frederick, who was at that time only Crown Prince, pressed his father strongly to seize Polish Prussia, which, separating as it did the kingdom of Prussia proper from Brandenburg, seemed to him a prey as easy to seize as it would be convenient to keep. It was one of his first political ideas. As early as the year 1731 he had composed a treatise 'On the Present Policy of Prussia,' addressed in the form of a letter to M. de Natzmer.[5] In it were found these lines, in which the real objective of the historic mission of the Hohenzollern was set forth with remarkable precision: 'Having already said that the Prussian territories are so cut up and separated, I conceive that the most necessary of the objects which are to be attained is to draw together or to *sew up the detached pieces* which belong to the parts which we possess, such as *Polish Prussia*.' This

---

[4] More properly 'of the Vasa Kings.' The last male Jaghellon died in 1573.—TRANSLATOR.

[5] *Œuvres*, vol. xvi.

country, which would give the Lower Vistula to Prussia, would enable her to dictate laws to Poland by means of trade. As a matter of history, Frederick recalled the fact that these territories had formerly belonged to Prussia ; but the question of principle was in his eyes a very secondary matter. 'I argue upon grounds of pure policy,' he added, 'and without alleging any reasons of right, that I may not make too many digressions.' Such juridical digressions Frederick, when he had become King, continued to regard as otiose and pedantic.

As for his views upon Polish Prussia, he disguised them very scantily, and when he concluded his treaties with Russia, in 1762 and 1764, everyone believed that the two Sovereigns had arranged the terms of a dismemberment of Poland. Catharine repudiated this in a circular couched in no humble language : ' We have never had the intention, nor are we under any necessity, of seeking to extend the limits of our empire, which, without this, forms, by its extent, a considerable part of the terrestrial globe.'[6] ' I am sure,' said Frederick to the Austrian Envoy, in May, 1764—' I am sure that your Court is alarmed at this treaty, and that people at Vienna already believe that we have partitioned Poland. But you will find that the reverse is the case.'[7]

In France, no doubt was felt upon the subject. The Marquis de Paulmy, Louis XV.'s Minister at Warsaw, wrote, on May 4, 1763 : ' The day will come, and it is astonishing that it has not come already, when some foreign Power will profit by some intestine division, by the weakness and anarchy of the Polish Government, and will find in them a plausible pretext for the dismemberment of this republic.' M. de Praslin, at that time Foreign Minister, saw in this a danger for ' the Northern equilibrium,' and

[6] November 11, 1763 : Martens, vol. vi., p. 9.
[7] Report of Ried, May 25, 1754 : Arneth, vol. viii., p. 545.

tried to revive the patriotic party in Poland ; Louis XV.,
on his side, laboured to the same end by his secret diplomacy. The two diplomacies agreed in working against
the election of Stanislas Augustus ; but this was the only
point upon which they were agreed, and on every other
point they only acted in opposition to each other. France
in those times had more agents than ideas, more representatives than influence. There were as many as three
Envoys at Warsaw, two of whom were in the King's confidence, which made five cabals. They stirred the whole
world into confusion, and disarrayed all parties ; they only
succeeded in 'throwing the minds of all men into disorder,'
and in destroying the small amount of respect which France
still commanded. After the election of Stanislas Augustus,
the Government expelled all these agents. France had no
Minister left in the republic. For the future, all that
she could do for the preservation of Poland was to stir up
the Turks. This could not be done without some difficulty,
for at Constantinople, as at Warsaw, the diplomacy and
counter-diplomacy of Louis XV. had only succeeded in
counteracting each other.[8]

It was, above all, in Turkey that the treaty of 1756
had confounded French diplomacy. Before this treaty,
M. de Vergennes, who was French Ambassador at Constantinople, was instructed to use all diligence to excite
the Porte against Austria and Russia ; above all, he was
to endeavour to induce the Turks to prevent the Russians
advancing across Poland into Germany. After the treaty,
aanther kind of language had to be held. Instead of
alarming the Turks, it was necessary to reassure them, and
to convince them that it was for their advantage that the
Russian armies, the auxiliaries of Austria, should cross
Poland. The Turks, accustomed to found the whole system

---

[8] *Vide Le Secret du Roi*, vol. ii., pp. 222-259 ; *Instructions de
Pologne ;* Despatches of General de Monnet, vol. ii., p. 243 *et seq.*

of their relations with France upon the historic rivalry
between that country and the House of Austria, were
entirely disconcerted. 'Their surprise,' said M. de Vergennes, 'soon degenerated into a feeling of mere annoyance
and bitterness, when, upon the treaty being communicated
to them, they observed that France had not thought it
incumbent upon her to except them from the cases in
which she would be bound to come to the help of her
new ally.' M. de Vergennes was instructed to combat this
opinion; he succeeded partly, but to entirely dissipate
their prejudices he would have needed a written declaration from Austria, which France was not in a position to
supply.[9] 'M. de Vergennes,' says a contemporary, 'was
not let off with only one change of language.' After the
defection of Peter III., he had to return to his former
policy, and excite the Turks anew against the Russians.
These successive transformations could not fail to damage
the credit of the French Ambassador; and, moreover,
Vergennes found in the Prussian Minister an adversary as
handy as he was active.

Sultan Mustapha, who had reigned since 1757, was by
no means the grotesque individual, the *Grand Turk* of
comic opera, in which character Voltaire tried, in his
period of adulation of Catharine, to represent him. He
was economical, deliberate, and hungry for glory; he even
possessed some enlightenment, and tried to reform his
Empire. From his disposition, he was compelled to admire
the King of Prussia. After the Seven Years' War, he sent
an embassage to him with presents. The Turks' presence
in Berlin was only temporary, but from that time Frederick
kept a permanent representative at Constantinople. This
entrance of Prussia upon the stage of Eastern politics,
and the intervention of Frederick in Turkish affairs, was
not one of the least singular results of that Seven Years'

[9] Note from Vergennes to Louis XV.

War—a war whose effect, in every question and in every place, was to recoil upon the schemes of those who had looked to it for the destruction of the Prussian Power. As soon as he had gained a footing in the Divan, Frederick acted there with his wonted resolution and address. The play was played upon lines which from that time onwards have become familiar—namely, the Prussian and Russian agents concerting policies at Constantinople, which, though their exterior aspects were often opposed, and their ways often divergent, in reality tended to the same end : Prussia holding ' the language of disinterestedness, and affecting merely the part of an honest broker,' as we say nowadays ; Russia at one time insinuating, at another haughty, but throughout exploiting with consummate art those weaknesses and passions of the Oriental, which the Slavs understand all the better in that they themselves are not exempt from them.

Thus it was that Vergennes and the Austrian Ambassador, when they endeavoured to interest the Turks in the election of the King of Poland, found the Turks convinced that that election did not concern them at all. Accordingly, the Russians were free to conduct the election as it suited them. On September 7, 1764, Stanislas Augustus Poniatowski was chosen King of Poland. On November 25 the Prussian and Russian Envoys claimed religious liberty and political equality for the Dissidents, and declared themselves opposed to the suppression of the *liberum veto*. The Diet refused to listen ; the Dissidents formed ' confederations ' to support their demands by force of arms, and the Czarina upheld them. ' The Empress,' wrote Frederick to Voltaire on March 24, 1767, ' was petitioned by the Dissidents for assistance, and she put in motion arguments fortified by guns and bayonets, to convince the Polish Bishops of the rights which these Polish Dissidents claimed.' The Russian Minister Repnin caused the recalcitrant Bishops and deputies to be seized and deported. On November 19, 1767, the Diet voted what he wished, and on February 24, 1768, a treaty between Russia and Poland sanctioned the subjection of the republic. Russia bound herself 'to preserve, to defend, and secure the integrity of the republic'; the republic placed her constitution—that is to say, the *liberum veto*—under Russia's guarantee. Catharine had attained her ends. Poland had sworn to live and die in anarchy.

Europe and her philosophers applauded this victory of 'toleration.' 'Our Sovereign,' says one of Voltaire's characters, 'sets her armies in motion to bring peace, to keep men from injuring themselves, to compel them to draw towards each other, and her ensigns have been those of public concord.' It was a pure fiction. The truth appeared in the guise of Russian soldiers. The Poles were not ripe for such tolerance as these soldiers preached, and the benefit which humanity had received in their person threw them into a revolution, the most appalling that they had yet gone through, and one which precipitated the destruction of their nation. The Catholics, and especially the smaller nobles, who were fierce, unsophisticated, and fanatical, rose, and on February 28, 1768, formed a confederation at Bar in Podolia. Poland was quickly in flames.[10] 'Almost all Poland is in confederation,' wrote the Prussian agent on August 3, 1768. The peasants abandoned themselves to the most horrible rioting. The suppression was merciless. The Poles massacred in the name of Faith, the Russians in that of Toleration. All parties appealed to foreign nations; Russia and Prussia supported the Dissidents; France attempted to support the confederated Catholics with the arms of Mussulmans.

[10] *Le Secret du Roi*, vol. ii., p. 292.

Choiseul, the most heated of Catharine's opponents—
the man whom, joking with her philosophers, she named
'Mustapha's prompter'—had returned to the head of
foreign affairs in April, 1766. France was weakened,
isolated, and discredited. 'Her old allies had detached
themselves from her, and her new ones meditated abandoning her; after having lost the command of the sea by
the Treaty of Paris, she was on the point of vanishing
completely from half the Continent of Europe.' Choiseul
had followed a system of great alliances and great policies;
their result had been deception and reverses. So he
effected a complete mental revolution, and adopted
'abruptly a policy which up to that time he had
neglected,' namely, the coalition of secondary States.[11]
But it was late in the day, and Choiseul brought an
impatient and unstable mind to work out conceptions
which demanded consistency and moderation. He formed
vast designs, but could employ but scanty means. His
dream was to act, his performance was to be flurried.

His dominating idea was to avenge the Seven Years' War
upon England. For this it was necessary to secure the
neutrality of the Continent—that is to say, of Prussia and
Russia. He counted on Austria to hold Prussia in check;
dut he had to seek everywhere for enemies for Russia: in
Poland, where he sent money and officers to the Con-
feberation of Bar; in Sweden, where he took the part of
the King; and, finally, in Turkey, where he strained
every nerve to rouse the Turks.[12] 'We must leave
no stone unturned,' he wrote to Vergennes, 'in order to
break this chain, whose end is held by Russia, and to
upset this Colossus of consideration which Catharine has
gained and maintained in the midst of a thousand impossible circumstances, which might at any moment cost her

[11] *Le Secret du Roi*, vol. ii., p. 278 *et seq.*
[12] *Ibid.*, pp. 295, 296.

the throne she has usurped. The Ottoman Empire,
which is alone in a position to bring this about, is at the
same time the most concerned in the undertaking. In
good truth, the rottenness of the Turks in every depart-
ment might make this trial of strength fatal to them;
that matters little to us, provided the object of an im-
mediate explosion be attained.' To add weight to the
Ambassador's representations, and to counterbalance the
attempts at corruption which were attributed to the
agents of Russia, Choiseul gave M. de Vergennes a free
hand, and placed a sum of three millions[13] at his disposal
with which to begin his campaign.

Vergennes had no great belief in the efficacy of secret-
service money. He justly considered that though the
Turks might be 'willing to receive presents, when a course
was proposed to them which they would follow without
them of their own accord,' some more direct and cogent
arguments were needed to drag them out of the apathy in
which they sunk themselves so readily. Russia made it
her business to provide such arguments. Since 1766 her
agents had been scattered over Greece, Crete, and Montenegro. In Greece they only succeeded in weaving plots;
they made and received promises, and the whole outcome
was a series of pompous reports which they despatched to
St. Petersburg.[14] The Montenegrins took the matter
more seriously. As early as 1765 their Bishop, who wore
a portrait of the Czarina upon his breast beside his
episcopal cross, announced that the time appointed for
the deliverance of the Greeks had at length arrived. A
monk, a kind of mystic conspirator, named Stefano Piccolo,
called the people to arms, and in October, 1767, he de-
scended from the mountains at the head of a troop of

[13] Of livres.
[14] For the curious details of these negotiations *vide* Rulhière,
Hermann, and Zinkeisen.

supporters. The fermentation reached the Slav countries, and Bosnia threatened to rise.

These revolts, which broke out at the moment when Russia was dictating laws to Poland, at last roused the attention of the Turks. Vergennes was continually prodding them into fresh searchings of heart. Negotiations of a very embittered character took place between the Porte and the Russian Resident Obreskof on the subject of Montenegro. The Turks demanded the evacuation of Poland by the Russian troops. The Prussian Resident Zegelin wrote on July 26, 1768: 'Matters here are at a very critical stage. If Russia does not give the satisfaction which the Porte demands, and does not withdraw her troops from Podolia, war between Russia and the Porte is almost inevitable. It is much to have been able to gain time under the circumstances. Though the form of government is despotic, it is such that when the people is enraged, the Government is no longer master, and must yield to the torrent.' The violation of the Turkish frontier at Balta, and the taking of Cracow by the Russians, precipitated the outbreak. On October 6, 1768, after an exceedingly stormy interview with the Turkish Ministers, the Russian Resident was arrested, and conducted to the Castle of the Seven Towers. It was the solemn form of a declaration of war, according to the Turkish practice of international law. Vergennes advised the Sultan's Ministers to address a manifesto to the European Powers; so they declared that they were resorting to arms to defend the independence of Poland. 'Russia,' said this manifesto, which was issued on October 30, 1768—'Russia has dared to destroy the liberties of Poland; she has forced the Poles to recognise as their King an individual who is neither of the blood royal nor marked out by the wishes of the nation; she has massacred those who would not recognise him, and has pillaged or laid waste their goods or their lands.' The rhetoric of the chanceries, which had made the Russians the defenders of liberty of conscience, now made the Turks the champions of political freedom. 'War has been declared,' said M. de Vergennes a few months later, 'and that was the wish of the King, which I have carried out in every particular; but I am bringing back the three millions which were sent me for that purpose. I have not needed them.'

CHAPTER III.

(October, 1768—January, 1769.)

THE declaration of war surprised and disconcerted all
men—the Turks who had made it, the Russians who had
provoked it, the French who had prompted it, the Prussians
who had discouraged it, the Austrians who had lived in
perpetual dread of it, even the English who pretended to
be indifferent to it.   The fact was, that no one was ready
for the war, whether belligerents or neutrals.   The Turks,
who had been so slow to wrath, had lost their tempers six
months too soon.   It was impossible for them to fight
before the spring, and thus they gave Russia time to get
ready.   The war took Catharine by surprise ; she had not
imagined that the Turks would come to the point, but
had counted on her diplomacy to keep them in check.
The war in Poland was absorbing all her military energies,
and, preoccupied as she was with civil and social reforms,
she had neglected the army.   Her military organization
had been remodelled after the Prussian system, but the
Russian soldiers had only the external aspect of Frederick's
troops ; their discipline, instruction, and drill were inferior ;
there were neither stores nor money for war.   It was, in
appearance, the same state of weakness and disorder as
with the Turks ; but in Turkey this disorganization was

the symptom of irremediable decay ; in Russia, on the contrary, it was but the natural result of the incoherent efforts of a nation that is emerging from barbarism. Catharine realized this, and the famous allegory of the *Sick Man* was already one of her principles of government. The Englishman Elphinstone, who was an Admiral in her service, said to her one day that the rottenness and incompetence of the Turkish fleet was the only thing that could convey an idea of what was to be found at St. Petersburg. ' Ignorance with the Russians,' answered Catharine, ' is the ignorance of earliest youth ; with the Turks it is that of dotage.'

The Czarina raised a loan in Holland, ordered out levies of men, and pushed on her armaments with all vigour. The moment had arrived for raising Greece. She despatched Alexis and Theodore Orlof to Venice—Alexis, the handsomest, the bravest, and the most ardent of the five brothers, and who deserved in every respect the title which Rulhière aptly applies to him, that of the ' leader of the faction of favourites '; Theodore, better informed, more intelligent, and not less brave, his mind filled with legends of Greek history, tinged with something of an encyclopædic character, and who mixed in his romantic imagination ' the marvels of Eastern tales with the fables of ancient liberty '—two men admirably qualified to rouse Greece, and to liberate her if she was capable of liberation.

But while preparing to attack Turkey in the rear by means of Greece, Catharine had to put herself into a condition to face the Turks on her own frontier, and that without delay. The Russian fleet could not be round in the Mediterranean before a year or eighteen months, and in the meantime the Turks might be in Poland. It was necessary to apply to Frederick, and to request the fulfilment of his treaty obligations. The Czarina wrote to him, on November 14, 1768 : ' I have to prepare for war

against the Turks ; I hold myself secure that Your Majesty
will remain faithful to our alliance.'

Frederick was expecting this demand, but he did not
wish for it.   It was not that he failed to realize the vast
advantages that might one day accrue to Prussia from a
war between the Turks and the Russians.   That great
statesman had no less foresight for the future interests of
his kingdom than insight into its present needs. He it was
who formed and prepared, in all its essential elements, that
vast scheme of expansion which distillers of quintessence
have called in later times *the historic mission* of Prussia.
Though he could not complete the picture, he at least
traced the outline.   He made the surveys of all the roads
which his successors were to open up.   In his schemes, as
in his acts, scruples were no obstacle to him.   Public
welfare was his sole principle of international law ; but, if
he had laid down as a maxim that ' the conduct of the
Sovereign must be governed by the welfare of the State,'
he had taken as his motto *Festina lente*.   ' I know how to
put myself in the place which fits me,' he wrote to his
brother, Prince Henry, in July, 1769, 'and I am not vain
or foolish enough to attribute to myself a superiority over
others which I do not in fact possess. But you will always
find that those who are in the midst of great perturbations,
and who move the biggest springs of Europe, commit more
follies than those who keep quiet, because it is appointed
for all men to commit faults, and the more they act, the
more faults do they commit.'   At the moment when the
crisis occurred in the East, he was at his country-house,
Sans-Souci, where he was meditating, as his habit was,
upon the philosophy of Prussian history.   On November 7,
1768, he wrote a *Political Testament*, in which he defined
the task which his successor would have to undertake.
One of the important features of this task was to be ' the
occupation of certain places on the Vistula, which would

enable Eastern Prussia to be defended against Russia.'
This occupation of certain places meant the conquest of
Danzig and Thorn—in a word, the annexation of Polish
Prussia. Though he consigned this annexation to the
chapter of ' Chimerical Dreams and Projects,' the conception of it was none the less clear in his mind. He was
precise and positive even in his imaginations, and even
when he thought he was merely speculating, he was still
acting. ' As for Polish Prussia, it seems to me that the
chief obstacle will come from the side of Russia; it would
be perhaps better to win this country bit by bit, by negotiation, than to seize it by right of conquest. In a case in
which Russia had pressing need of our assistance, it might
be possible to obtain Thorn, Elbing, and an outlying
place, and thus to connect Pomerania with the Vistula.'[1]
But even while writing these lines, Frederick had no doubt
that the day was at hand when he could himself achieve
this conquest which he was reserving for his nephews. He
was all for peace, and only thought of preserving his
neutrality. On November 9, 1768, he ordered his Minister
Zegelin to offer mediation, and to use every effort to avert
war.

On this point his policy was in agreement with that
of Austria. Far from supporting French diplomacy at
Constantinople, Kaunitz had counteracted it as far as lay
in his power. He was afraid of Choiseul involving him in
European complications. He knew that if war broke out
between France and England, Austria's part would be to
hold Prussia in check, and he had quite decided to use
only diplomatic means for this object. Thus, Prussia and
Austria, each of whom had an ally, were each equally
afraid of being compromised in the service of that ally.
From fear of being dragged into war, one on behalf of
Russia, the other on behalf of France, they were led to

---

[1] Duncker, p. 176.

draw together, and to come to an understanding.
Frederick had made some advances in 1766, and had tried
to arrange a meeting with Joseph II., who was one of his
admirers, and who envied his renown in spite of himself.
Joseph was very much tempted, but Maria Theresa's
antipathies stopped him, and he thus lost, as he said,
' the chance of seeing and knowing a man who excited his
curiosity terribly.' The affairs of Poland and events in
the East combined to remove the Emperor's scruples.
Kaunitz thought it necessary to reassure the King of
Prussia on the subject of Austria's intentions, and to see
him somewhat closer. His advice decided Maria Theresa,
and on October 14, 1768, the Austrian Minister at Berlin,
Nugent, was ordered to go to the King, to address him
with suitable compliments, and to declare that Austria
had renounced Silesia for all time.

Nugent saw Frederick on November 15. He placed
before him the neutrality of Germany as a common object
for the two States to pursue, an interview with the
Emperor as the means of securing their agreement, and
an exchange of letters as the best and simplest form of
sanctioning it. ' I note with much pleasure,' replied the
King of Prussia, ' that their Imperial Majesties are in
agreement with me upon so important a point as the
maintenance of general tranquillity in Germany. I will
tell you candidly that my treaties with Russia only oblige
me to pay a few subsidies, and those of no very far-
reaching character. They may squabble in Poland to
their hearts' content; I shall certainly not meddle there,
except in one event—if they think of upsetting the King
of Poland. . . .' Nugent pressed the idea that the peace
of Europe, and, above all, that of Germany, depended
upon the existence of a good understanding between
Austria and Prussia, and that the two Courts should for
the future abandon all distrust of each other. Frederick

expressed warm approval of this language: 'We are
Germans,' he said ; 'what matters it to us if the English
and the French fight for Canada and the islands of
America ? or if Paoli is keeping the Frenchmen's hands
full in Corsica ? or if the Turks and the Russians are
pulling each other's hair ? The Empress and myself have
long maintained ruinous wars, and what have we got by
it, after all ?' Nugent might have answered that he had
got Silesia, but he thought it more politic to keep silence.
'It would be the wisest thing we could do,' continued the
King, 'to agree upon a neutrality for Germany.' He
made no pronouncement upon the subject of an exchange
of letters, saying that he could not be the first to write ;
but he accepted with eagerness the idea of an interview in
the summer. He spoke of the advantages which such an
interview would have ; he spoke 'with much wisdom,' says
Nugent, remarking that there could be no question of
future aggrandizement whether on the side of France or
elsewhere. That was the chapter upon which Austria and
Prussia were most ready to agree; they were equally de-
sirous that their respective alliances should not turn too
much to the advantage of their allies. Nugent took the
hint, and understood that by 'elsewhere' the King was
alluding to Russia. 'Upon that side,' he said, 'Your
Majesty is somewhat more exposed than we are.' 'That
is so,' answered the King. 'Our friends the Russians
may expand as much as they like in the direction of the
Black Sea, and in the neighbourhood of their famous
deserts ; but in the direction of Europe——' He stopped
at these words, and began to speak of the Emperor and
of his character. Nugent knew what he had wished to
know, and wanted no more.[2]

Frederick was by no means so sure of the scope of his

[2] Nugent's Report of November 26, 1768.   Arneth, vol. viii.,
p. 562.

treaties with Russia as he had given Nugent to understand. He was much afraid that Catharine, whom he believed to be unprepared, might ask him for soldiers instead of money. He wrote to his brother Henry on December 3, 1768 : 'We are at a great crisis, and shall need luck to issue from it prosperously. The news of the war has surprised and dismayed the Russians, since they had not expected it in the least; they have never used more polite language than at present. At the same time, they ask a good deal, and I am very resolved not to embark upon a war which does not concern us, and the fruits of which would go to another.' But all the same, an answer had to be given to the Czarina. While he was endeavouring to restore peace or to localize the war, Frederick strove to secure some compensations in the event of Prussia being obliged to intervene. He wrote to Catharine on December 15, 1768, that she was right in counting upon his fidelity to the performance of his engagements, that he would even be disposed to prolong the treaty, which would expire in 1772, and to bring it into conformity with the circumstances of the time. This gave Catharine to understand that he would by no means allow himself to be embarked in war without finding something to be gained from it, and invited her to explain her intentions with regard to Prussia.

This question of 'advantages' troubled men's minds at Vienna no less than at Berlin. In face of the war which was threatening Eastern Europe, the first thought at these two Courts had been, how to keep out of it ; the second, to gain something by it. Vergennes showed great insight when he said to Louis XV., summing up his impressions of the Turkish War: 'Who knows even if the dismemberment of Poland might not be the seal of the reconciliation of the two belligerents?' Frederick considered the acquisition of Polish Prussia a necessity for Prussia ; Kaunitz was continually regretting the loss of Silesia, and brooding over means of recovering it. These were the dominating ideas of the two, and the crisis in the East brought them up by a natural sequence. But Frederick, who was less of a dreamer than any man, placed his scheme in his 'chapter of chimæras.' Kaunitz, who was as infatuated with his own ideas as it is possible for a diplomatist to be, composed a great official memorandum which he submitted to his Sovereigns on December 3, 1768. 'It was known as early as the time of Peter the Great that the Russians were determined on a Greek Empire, and the enterprises of the present Empress prove that she carries in her very vast designs.[3] Little has been wanting that she should make Poland a Russian province, as has been done in the case of Courland. This proximity would be the more fraught with danger for the Imperial House in that that House numbers among its subjects a large number of the Greek religion.[4] It would seem that our interest, like that of Prussia, were to intervene and to induce the belligerent parties to make a suitable peace. These are weighty considerations, but the most important of all is, that by that means Your Majesties might be able to compass the recovery of Silesia, if not in its entirety, at all events the great part of it, and that at no expense, and with the aid of the Porte. The idea of recovering Silesia by means of the Turks, and in agreement with the King of Prussia, is in itself so extraordinary and chimerical, that I have debated with myself whether I should submit it to Your Majesties, and incur the risk of ridicule.' And yet, according to Kaunitz, the scheme was neither impossible nor improbable. As early as the month of June, the Turks had made spontaneous overtures

[3] Literally, 'she is pregnant with'—*schwanger gehe.*

[4] They would be called nowadays 'Slav subjects,' nationality having taken in these matters the place that was occupied by religion in the eighteenth century.

to this effect. As for the King of Prussia, he would receive Courland and the greater part of Polish Prussia. It would be for him to come to an agreement with Russia on the subject of Courland; but there was reason to believe that he was much concerned at the progress of Russia, and, besides, 20,000,000 piastres, which the Turks would supply, would facilitate the transaction. Poland would be made to understand that it was to her interest to secure her repose and her independence by giving satisfaction to the King of Prussia. Kaunitz concluded that it would be necessary secretly to charge the Porte to make the required overtures to the King of Prussia, as though on its own account. Joseph examined the scheme and made weighty objections to it; the Empress refused to entertain it, doubting with justice whether Frederick would ever agree to abandon Silesia. This remarkable proposal is, however, not without interest, for it proves that, as early as December, 1768, the Austrian Chancellor felt no repugnance to the idea of a partition of Poland.

Kaunitz put his scheme away in his portfolio, and contented himself with negotiating for the interview between the two Sovereigns. On January 8, 1769, it was agreed that it should take place in August. Frederick protested that his heart was all for peace; he would do, he said to Nugent, everything that in him lay for its restoration, only insisting that no one should oppose his efforts. It was an allusion to France, and he was, in fact, complaining of Choiseul, dubbing him 'the dandified minister,'[5] accusing him, which was perfectly true, of having egged the Turks on to war, and also asserting, which was not true, that the French had expended several millions on persuading the Divan.

[5] *Vide*, in vol. xiv. of Frederick's works, the 'Choiseullade,' a short poem of very little wit, and filled with abuse and calumnies directed against Choiseul.

'M. de Choiseul is taking the bit between his teeth,' said the Comte de Broglie, who had no affection for that Minister. He saw with irritation Choiseul adopting his policy, and was convinced that he would spoil it. Choiseul, by his system of great alliances, had contributed largely to France's isolation; he was sensible of that isolation, and floundered about in it with more passion than system. In April, 1768, he had sent the Chevalier de Taulès to the Polish confederates with a certain amount of money, and with a wealth of promises. Taulès had seen the confederates, had judged of their weakness, had considered that his words would be fruitless, and had brought back the money. In January, 1769, Choiseul sent the Chevalier de Châteaufort to execute what Taulès had been unable to achieve. 'Perhaps,' he instructed him, 'certain fanatics may evince a distaste' for an alliance with the Porte. Châteaufort is to do all he can to dispel these prejudices; ' when the very existence of liberty and of their country is at stake, it is no time to consult religious differences; the Catholic religion has nothing to fear from the Turks in any case, and has everything to fear from Russia.' The Turkish War, in fact, was the whole bottom of Choiseul's combinations. He had just heard that this war had been declared, and, with the inconsistency which characterized him, had just recalled Vergennes, who had caused its declaration. That Ambassador was replaced by the Comte de Saint-Priest. At the same time Choiseul was attempting to play a game of infinite subtilty and risk; he gave Frederick the Great a direct lead.[6]

On the pretext of negotiating a commercial treaty,

[6] *Instructions de Pologne:* Instructions of the Chevalier de Taulès, April 17, 1769; of the Chevalier de Châteaufort, January 18, 1769, vol. ii., pp. 271, 283. *Le Secret du Roi*, vol. ii., pp. 295-299. Saint-Priest, *Le Partage de la Pologne*, chap. iii. Flassan, *Histoire de la Diplomatie*, vol. vi., chap. v.

Choiseul had endeavoured to resume connections with
Prussia. He had fancied that he might separate her from
Russia, and at the same time deliver a side-shot at the
Court of Vienna, with which he was dissatisfied. Frederick
lent himself readily to these approaches, which he wished
for, and which he had long been leading up to through
his friends the philosophers and the men of letters. He
was seeking the same advantage as Choiseul ; he, too, wished
to pique his ally Russia. He calculated that Austria would
feel some uneasiness over it, and that if she were still hesi-
tating to come to an agreement with Prussia, the fear of
being forestalled by France would overcome her scruples.
His calculations were correct, and it was he who won the
game of finesse in which he had engaged. 'I let the
French come on unmoved,' he said to Finckenstein ; 'it
is in order that I might find out all their plans and all
the pother which Choiseul is revolving in his head. We
can get some advantage for our trade out of it, which will
be so much to the good ; and if not, nothing could be
easier than to cut this trafficking short.' The Comte de
Guines, who was appointed French Minister at Berlin,
arrived there in January, 1769 ; that is to say, at the
moment when Frederick was in the midst of negotiating
with Russia for the renewal of his treaty, and of preparing
for his interview with the Emperor Joseph. The *dilatory
negotiations* in which he engaged with the French Minister
contributed greatly to the success of those which he was
pursuing with Vienna and St. Petersburg, which were
perfectly in earnest.[7]

The idea of renewing the alliance, and of fitting it to
present circumstances, had been received by the Czarina
with much cordiality. She replied that she was in favour

[7] *Vide Revue Historique,* vol. xxv., p. 69, and vol. xxvii., p. 322 ;
the essays of Robert Hammond, *La Mission de Guines à Berlin ;
La France et la Prusse en* 1763-69.

of it, provided that the King would make common cause with her in Turkey and Sweden. Frederick agreed on condition that the Czarina would guarantee the succession of the Margraviates of Ansbach and Bayreuth to the House of Brandenburg. At the same time (January, 1769), and to add weight to his arguments, he gave orders ' that frequent patrols should be made, and that a strong and close cordon of troops ' should be drawn along the Polish frontier, on the pretext of protecting his states against the incursions of the Confederates.[8]

As a matter of fact, these military measures had a much more important object ; and they were connected with a plan which Frederick devised at that time, and the execution of which he pursued under the cloak of official negotiations.

[8] Nugent's Report, January 14, 1769.   Arneth, vol. viii., p. 160.

CHAPTER IV.

THE PLANS OF FREDERICK THE GREAT AND THE PROJECTS OF A TRIPLE ALLIANCE.

(February—May, 1769.)

FREDERICK thought it impossible to prevent a Russo-Turkish war. From thenceforth he only thought how he could turn it to his advantage. ' This war,' he says in his Memoirs, ' changed the entire political system of Europe. As a new career was being opened out, a man must needs be without skill, or sunk in a stupid torpor, not to profit by so prosperous an opportunity.' Russia and Austria both turned to him, and made him in reality the arbiter of European politics. But arbitration was not easy ; and if there were gains to be won, there were also great risks to be incurred. Frederick's attention was peculiarly absorbed by the progress of Russian power. ' It is a terrible Power, which in half a century will make all Europe tremble,' he wrote to his brother Henry on March 8, 1769. ' Sprung from those Huns and Gepids who overthrew the Eastern Empire, they might soon encroach upon the Western Empire also, and make the Austrians weep and repent having, by their false policy, called this barbarous nation into Germany, and having taught them the art of war. The only remedy I can see is the formation, in course of time, of a league of the principal sovereigns to resist this dangerous torrent.' The time for this league had not yet

come; it was not even near, and as the torrent could not
be contained, the best thing to do was to turn it aside, to
dam it, and to exploit its strength for the greatest good
of the Prussian monarchy. 'There were,' says Frederick
again, 'two alternatives, either to stop the course of
Russia's gigantic conquests, or, which was the wiser plan,
to endeavour by adroitness to profit by them.' Frederick's
successors have for long thought as he thought, and it
is only fair to record that the 'dangerous torrent' has
singularly contributed to swell the waters of the Prussian
river. It is in this aspect principally that Europe has
learnt to know and to fear it.

Frederick considered that Russia would not stop. It
remained to be found out what Austria would do. Either
she would remain faithful to the French alliance—in which
case she would be led to side with the Turks and the Poles,
and Frederick, bound to Russia, might have France and
Austria again on his hands—or she would allow herself to
be seduced by Russia, who would promise her a slice of
the Eastern cake; and Prussia would find herself caught
between the masses of Austria and of Russia, who would
be able to dictate terms to her. To escape this dilemma,
and to escape to Prussia's advantage, means must be found
to indemnify Russia for the expenses of her war against
the Turks, to separate Austria from France, to satisfy the
Court of Vienna so that it might not be tempted either to
ally with Russia or to oppose her conquests—in sum, to
devise such a combination that Prussia, instead of being
obliged to side with either Russia or Austria, if they came
to blows, or of being crushed between them if they became
allied, might become the bond of union between the two
rivals, and might crown the edifice of a Triple Alliance
for the advantage of all three Powers. The problem would
have been insoluble if Poland had not been there—to its
sorrow. There was room for everyone in Poland. What

was the use of warring in such distant lands, at so large expense, when the desired enrichment was to be had close at hand, with so little trouble, merely for the stooping to gather it ? The scheme which Frederick had been sketching out a few weeks before as a dream, became a reality in his eyes. The King of Prussia was very little concerned for the question of right ; but his mind was classical, and he loved maxims and quotations. As he was unable with decency to invoke the *Anti-Machiavel*, he contented himself with *Orlando Innamorato*, and recalled to his mind lines which he deemed no less apt than full of poetic feeling. These *concetti*, which an amorous paladin addresses to his mistress, the King of Prussia addressed in his thoughts to the kindly goddess of politics, to Opportunity, 'Her Sacred Majesty Queen Chance,' as he loved to call her :

> ' Quante volte le disse : O bella donna,
> Conosci l' ora di la tua ventura,
> Da poi che un tal baron piu che se t' ama
> Che non ha il ciel piu vaga creatura.
> Forse anco avrai di questo tempo brama,
> Che 'l felice destin sempre non dura . . .
> Come dissolve 'l sol la bianca neve
> Come in un giorno la vermiglia rosa
> Perde il vago color in tempo breve
> Cosi fuggi l' étà com' un baleno
> E non si puo tener, che non ha freno.' [1]

[TRANSLATOR'S NOTE.—The stanzas of Boiardo as given in the text are incomplete, and in some trifling details inaccurate. The following is the complete text of the two stanzas quoted, together with an English version, for which I am indebted to the great kindness of a friend] :

' Quante volte le disse : O bella Dama Conosci l' ora de la tua ventura ; Da poi ch' un tel baron piu che se t' ama, Che non ha il ciel piu vaga creatura ;	' How oft I said to her : "O faire Ladie, Know thou the howre when Fortune standeth sure ; Sithens so great a Lord doth worship thee, And heaven hath no goodlier creature ;

---

[1] *Orlando Innamorato*, Bk. I., canto xii., stanzas 14 and 15.

'I had read Boiardo's fine allegory,' says Frederick in his 'Memoirs ;' 'I accordingly seized the opportunity which occurred by the forelock, and, *by dint of negotiation and intrigue*, I managed to indemnify our monarchy for her past losses by incorporating Polish Prussia with my older provinces.' The first chapter of the intrigue is not the least piquant. Frederick formed the scheme of a partition of several provinces of Poland between Austria, Prussia, and Russia. 'The serviceable object to be gained by this partition,' he says, 'consisted in Russia being enabled to continue her war with the Turks undisturbed, and without the fear of being stopped in her undertakings by a diversion which the Queen-Empress was in a position to create against her.' The suggestion could neither surprise nor shock the Czarina ; but she might consider it inopportune, and Frederick would not make himself responsible for it. So he conceived the idea of attributing his scheme to an individual who had made a name in the Seven Years'

Forse havrai di questo tempo brama,
Che 'l felice destin sempre non dura ;
Prendi diletto mentre sei su 'l verde,
Che l' havuto piacer mai non si perde.

'Questa età giovenil ch' è si gioiosa,
Tutta in diletto consumer si deve ;
Perchè quasi in un punto ci è nascosa,
Come dissolve 'l sol la bianca neve ;
Come in un giorno la vermiglia rosa
Perde il vago color' in tempo breve ;
Cosi fuggi l' età com' un baleno,
E non si può tener, che non ha freno.'

Belike this day thou yet shalt yearne to see,
Faire destinie will not for ever dure ;
Take, then, delight whylest yet thy life is greene,
For ever bydes the pleasure that hath bene.

' "Sith youth is still the time of joyous play,
'T' were meet thy daies in all delight should runne ;
For in a moment it is hid away,
As the white snow is melted with the sunne :
As fadeth the red rose within a day,
Losing his colour ere the morn be donne ;
So youthe as lightning out of hand doth flitte,
Ne canst thou holde it, for it hath no bitte." '

H. W. GREENE.

War—Count Lynar. He wrote to Solms, on February 2, 1769: ' Count Lynar has come to Berlin to marry his daughter to Count Kamecke. He is the man who concluded the Peace of Kloster-Seven. He is a great statesman, and still governs Europe from the village to which he has retired. This Count has conceived a sufficiently remarkable idea for uniting all the interest of the Powers in favour of Russia, and in a moment to put a different complexion on European affairs. He would have Russia offer the Court of Vienna the town of Leopol, with its dependencies, and Zips, in return for its help in the Turkish War ; that she should give us Polish Prussia with Warmia, and a protectorate over Danzig ; and that Russia should take possession, as an indemnification for the charges of the war, of such part of Poland as may suit her, and that then, as there would be no more jealousy between Austria and Prussia, they should rival each other in helping Russia against the Turks. This scheme is not without brilliancy ; it has a seductive appearance. I thought it well to communicate it to you ; knowing as you do Count Panin's habit of thought, you will either suppress this entirely, or you will make such use of it as you may think fitting, though it appears to me to contain more brilliancy than solidity.' It was in its general outline the partition of Poland which was carried out three years later. If Russia entertained these ideas, and if she brought Austria into them, the result which Frederick desired would be reached ; Prussia would remain at peace, she would enlarge herself without spending a single crown and without risking the life of a single man, and the alliance of Austria with France would receive an irreparable injury from this co-operation of the Court of Vienna in Russia's enterprises against the Turks and in the dismemberment of Poland.

It was with difficulty that Solms decided to communicate this remarkable conception to the Russians. He thought, with reason, that the Russians preferred dominating Poland to sharing her with their neighbours. However, an opportunity presenting itself, Solms read the 'so-called memoir of Count Lynar' to Panin, professing it to be the result of the lucubrations of a speculative German politician. 'Panin,' wrote Solms, on March 3, 1769, 'recognised that Zips would be very convenient for Austria, but not Lemberg, which was in the middle of Poland, and far from the Austrian frontier.' Then, as they were dealing only in speculations, the Russian Minister set forth his ideas in his turn, which do not at all yield in interest to those of 'Count Lynar,' especially when we consider the date of the interview.[2] 'It would not be worth while,' said Panin, 'to join together three such great Powers merely to send back the Turks beyond the Dniester ; but if this union could take place, then it ought to set before itself nothing less than driving them out of Europe, and out of a large part of Asia. It would not be difficult for this Triple Alliance to put an end to the Turkish Empire, which has preserved itself for so long solely owing to the jealousies of the Christian Powers. The alliance of the three Courts,' pursued Panin, 'is the best means of ensuring the peace of Christendom. The only obstacle is the jealousy felt by Austria of Prussia. Austria should march with Russia against the Turks. It is there that she would find the most ample compensation for Silesia. By this means Prussia would gain security ; Polish Prussia and Warmia would be annexed to her as in Lynar's scheme. Constantinople and those provinces which might be left to the Ottomans might form a republic.' 'And Russia,' Solms inquired, 'what would she take for her share ?' 'Russia,' Panin replied, 'ought

[2] Solms's Reports, February 17 and March 3, 1769 ; *Correspondance de Solms*, pp. 209, 215, *et seq.*

not to aim at sharing in the partition, seeing that she already possesses much more country than she is in a condition to govern; so, except for a few fortified places on the frontiers, she ought not to think of acquiring any provinces.'

At the very time when Panin was using this language at St. Petersburg, Count Goltz, who had just been established at Paris, informed the King of Prussia that the conclusion of a commercial treaty with France was subordinated to political conditions. Choiseul was letting his plan be seen, which was to induce the King of Prussia by commercial advantages to break with Russia in Poland. Frederick had received the communication; he listened, and gave no answer. Choiseul made another step, and instructed a confidant to hint to Goltz that, if Prussia entered into the views of France, she might by that means gain Warmia and Courland. Goltz wrote this to the King on March 3. Frederick hastened to communicate it to his Minister at St. Petersburg; he was waiting for formal overtures to be made, he told him, on March 12 and March 25, before he repelled such insane offers. They were insane in this sense, that the French were offering Frederick the same price for breaking with Russia as Frederick asked for maintaining his alliance with her. The only object he had in negotiating at Versailles was to raise his price at St. Petersburg, and to excite jealousy there. He thought that Choiseul's hints would be an argument in favour of Count Lynar's scheme. Solms's report of his interview with Panin proved that that scheme was premature; but from what had been said at St. Petersburg, and from what had been whispered at Versailles, it stood forth clearly that the partition of Poland was in the air, and that sooner or later Lynar's scheme might be taken up again. Frederick dropped it, waiting till he should resume it under another form. As

for the negotiations with Versailles, they were now object-
less. Choiseul saw clearly that he could not bring Prussia
round to his views, and that he was compromising himself
uselessly by continuing pourparlers with her, and he broke
them off accordingly.

In the meanwhile, the Czarina had let the King of
Prussia know the conditions which she imposed on the
renewal of their alliance.[3] She would not make a treaty
except for eight years ; she asked that Prussia should
make common cause with Denmark to defend the constitution of Sweden ; should oppose the Saxons if they
attempted to upset Stanislas, and should defend the
political rights of the Dissidents in Poland by force of
arms.   In return, she only promised to guarantee the
Ansbach and Bayreuth succession ' within the limits
traced by the constitution of the empire.'   Like Kaunitz,
she was afraid of seeing Prussia ' pegging out claims ' in
Southern Germany.   ' They are laughing at me at
St. Petersburg,' Frederick wrote to Solms, on May 24,
1769 ; ' every alliance is based on reciprocity. It is in
this case entirely disregarded ; they ask much, and
guarantee nothing.'   There was only one point which was
satisfactory to him : Russia contented herself with a subsidy, and did not ask for soldiers. It was the one thing
needful for the present.

The scheme propounded by Panin was not at all to the
King's taste. This Triple Alliance seemed to him easier
to conceive than to achieve. In any case, it was not
advantageous to him. ' It was not,' he said,[4] ' to the
interest of Prussia to see the Ottoman Power entirely
crushed, because in case of need it might be usefully
employed in creating diversions, whether it were in
Hungary or in Russia, according to the Power with which

[3] Martens, vol. vi., p. 50.
[4] *Mémoires : Œuvres*, vol. vi., p. 25.

she might be at war.' Eastern affairs were to supply
Prussian diplomacy with an inexhaustible reserve fund, to
be watched over with the same care as the war-chest that
slept at Spandau. Frederick was not one of those
prodigals who start off at random 'upon the great road
which Panurge followed to his ruin, borrowing money
before the time, buying dear, selling cheap, and eating his
corn in the blade.' He waited till events should make
Russia more reasonable and more accommodating. He
was convinced that Austria would keep still during the
campaign of 1769, but how far would she carry her condescension? It was that, above all, which he required to
know. Accordingly, Frederick let his negotiations with
Russia drag on, and concerned himself only with his approaching interview with Joseph. He had all the threads
of the 'intrigue' in his own hands, and all those to whom
he hinted his replies could be depended upon to work out
the issue of affairs. The negotiations with France ought to
arouse attention at Vienna, as they had done at St. Petersburg; the negotiations for the alliance with Russia ought
to impel the Austrians to hold the interview, and the news
of the interview ought to make the Russians decide for
the alliance. The Turks would undertake the task of
putting everyone in a whirl, and of providing opportunities.

CHAPTER V.

THE WAR IN THE EAST, AND THE MILITARY PRECAUTIONS OF
AUSTRIA.

(January—August, 1769.)

FREDERICK's calculation was right, and at that very moment
Austria, so far from dreaming of forming a Holy Alliance
with Russia, was rather on the way to quarrel with her.
Austria had done all she could to prevent the war; but
the Turks turned a deaf ear, and on February 21, 1769,
the Internuncio Brognard was ordered to suspend his
pacific operations.   Austria after this took her precautions to escape injury from the war.   Strong cordons of
troops were gathered on the frontiers, on the Turkish and
on the Polish sides.   In view of the fact that these frontiers
were in many places very ill-defined, the Chancery of
Vienna gave the order, in the beginning of February, 1769,
to set up the Austrian eagles on doubtful lands, and there
to mark out the limits which the belligerents should not
pass.   It would not have been at all fair that this operation should turn to Austria's detriment.   The Austrians
were careful to plant their eagles beyond the disputed
points, to prevent prescription, wherever the ownership
of the lands was doubtful.   At one of these points the
planting of the eagles was particularly risky and difficult.
By a sufficiently strange coincidence, it was the county of

Zips, of which mention was made in Lynar's scheme. Zips, a small mountainous country, which formed a sort of protuberance of Hungary in the Polish frontier, had been pledged to Vladislas Jagellon in 1412 by Sigismund of Luxemburg. The Crown of Hungary claimed to have retained the ownership. The Polish confederates took refuge there, and it appears that the King of Poland had been the first to ask the Austrians to occupy this county with their troops.

Kaunitz held that no conquests were insignificant. Obliged to subordinate his schemes of aggrandizement to the wishes of Maria Theresa, who felt, at all events in principle, some respect for established rights, and some repugnance for employing methods from which she had had only too much to bear, Kaunitz endeavoured to gain little by little, by small steps and by adroit methods of procedure, that which he could not get all at once, and by diplomacy on a grand scale. In this way he followed both his own inclinations and Austrian tradition, while at the same time calming the ambitious impatience which agitated the Emperor. 'Confidential with the mother and conciliatory with the son,'[1] Kaunitz conceived a system of peaceful invasions which should conduct Austria gently to her ends. The matter of Zips was the first step on this compromising journey. When the Court of Vienna, then, planted its eagles in the county of Zips, it had already thoroughly resolved not to quit that country as easily as it was entering it. It intended quite naturally to restore to Hungary this territory which had been detached from it. At the same time it by no means meant to use, in retaking Zips, the disloyal means which Frederick had employed in order to seize Silesia. No doubt it would invoke, as that King had done, 'ancient rights'; but it would make these prevail only by pacific means, and in

[1] A saying of M. de Saint-Priest.

agreement with Poland; it would, with due formality, invite that republic to give back its pledge; it would neither dispute nor violate Polish rights.

Strong in the purity of its intentions, the Austrian Government caused proclamation to be made in the towns of the county of Zips, and notified the foreign Ministers accredited at Vienna, as well as the King of Poland, that the occupation of Zips was to be in no way prejudicial to the rights of Poland over that county. The main object of this declaration was to avoid exciting the suspicions of the King of Prussia.[2] It was a useless precaution. If any-one was to take umbrage at the occupation of Zips, it was not Frederick the Great. In this same month of February, 1769, while the Austrians were planting their eagles in this county, the King of Prussia was including it in the share which ' Count Lynar' assigned to them in Poland. It is true that Kaunitz, who was pedantically in love with the form of legality, sheltered himself with the pretext of ' ancient rights,' and that ' Count Lynar,' exempt, as far as right went, from all charges of impertinence, merely founded his scheme upon convenience; yet both of them were essentially marching towards the same goal, and it is the fact that at the moment when Frederick was forming the scheme, Austria was beginning to carry it out. This coincidence formed the knot of the intrigue which brought on the partition of Poland.

Austria could not foresee the consequences of an act which was, after all, very much in conformity with her political habits, and she was too busy to give very serious thought to it. She claimed that the Turks should view the Peace of Belgrade in the light of a perpetual peace. The Turks showed themselves by no means disposed to this, but a very serious incident which occurred at that time imposed this concession on them. On March 27, the

[2] Arneth, vol. viii., pp. 170, 172, and 295.

Sultan unfurled the standard of the Prophet, which was
carried about the streets of Constantinople. The sight of
the sacred emblem excited the fanaticism of the population almost to frenzy. The Internuncio Brognard, with
his staff and his family, attempted to see the procession.
The populace threw themselves upon him, chased him,
pillaged the house in which he had taken refuge, and
massacred the Christians whom they found in it. Brognard
and his people only escaped death by a miracle. Two days
afterwards the Ambassador demanded his papers. The
Divan gave him presents, and yielded the perpetuity of
the Treaty of Belgrade, with which he professed himself
satisfied. Austria, irritated as she was at such an insult,
avoided making a disturbance about it. As the Turks
appeared much concerned over it, she considered that the
most prudent course was to turn their confusion to the
profit of her own policy. The affair, when spread abroad,
naturally awoke Catharine's wit. She wrote on May 12,
1769, to Mme. de Bielke, who played for her in Germany,
as Voltaire did in France, the part that is filled nowadays
by the official correspondents of the foreign press : 'The
cannon-shooting comedy at Constantinople has been played
to encourage the troops, who were not possessed by very
great keenness for marching. But God knows whether it
is better to be the Turks' friend or their enemy. This
Envoy from Vienna, who got a hundred blows with a stick
when the Grand Vizier was going out of Constantinople,
will vouch for that. We shall see how the Austrians'
pride will swallow the bastonnade, and whether M. de
Saint-Priest[3] will persuade M. Brognard to lick the hand
that beats him. It is an unheard-of affair ; they say that
the English Ambassador got off with a few fist-blows in
his sides ; but these are all mere trifles ; they are little

[3] Vergennes' successor ; he had arrived at Constantinople on
November 13, 1768. Vergennes left on January 9, 1769.

attentions which one laughs at, saying that there is no
point of honour with the Turks.   If that had not been
the practice, they would have long ceased to exist in
Europe.'

But while she twitted the Austrians in this fashion,
Catharine was unceasingly preoccupied over their attitude.
Austria had declared at St. Petersburg that she would
remain neutral so long as no direct injury was done to
her interests; but the Czarina was not satisfied with this,
fearing the influence of the 'enemies to the public peace,
whose intrigues and dark proceedings had stretched in a
measure as far as to the Court of Vienna.'   'We cannot
help,' she wrote to Prince Galytzine, her Minister in
Austria, 'being to a certain extent anxious about the
future as regards the true intentions of the Court of
Vienna, which it concerns us greatly to know at first
hand.'

Consequently, on May 11, 1769, Prince Galytzine asked
Kaunitz whether Austria would consider herself still bound
by the perpetual alliance which she had contracted in 1753
with Russia against the Porte, and whether she would
support the House of Saxony in the event of the Polish
confederates dethroning Stanislas Augustus.[4]   Kaunitz
answered on the 14th: 'The Empress considered the
treaty of 1753 annulled in 1762 by Russia's act, when
she at that time sided with Prussia; from that date the
Porte had given Austria cause for nothing but praise;
she was so fortunate as to have a treaty of perpetual peace
with Turkey, which she proposed to observe for so long as
the Turks remained faithful to it; she would not interfere in the elections in Poland; but if the King of Prussia
interfered, she reserved her freedom of thought and action,
as the King of Prussia would do if Austria were to interfere.'   It appears that the Russian Minister was satisfied

[4] *Articulus Secretissimus*, June 16, 1753 : Martens, vol. i., p. 185.

with these explanations—at least, Kaunitz thought he was—for he wrote on May 15 to the Empress: 'Prince Galytzine considered the reply which Your Majesty instructed me to give him full of dignity and unanswerable.' It was enough then for the Russians to take note of Austria's declarations, and they awaited news of the war before pushing matters further.

The Turks were not ready till the end of March. At the beginning of May they were still encamped on the right bank of the Danube, opposite Galatz. Their army, numerous but disorganized, with no officers to command it and no organization to provision it, advanced in uncertainty, uneasiness and disorder, as it were a great flock astray in the steppes. The Russians had used the slowness of their enemies to good purpose. Their army, mediocre as it was, was much more formidable than that of the Turks, in spite of its numerical inferiority. 'Catharine's generals,' said the King of Prussia, 'were ignorant of fortification and tactics; those of the Sultan had even less knowledge, so that, to form a clear idea of this war, one must imagine one-eyed men who have given blind men a thorough beating, and gained a complete ascendancy over them.' Hostilities began in earnest in July on the Dniester. The two armies contended together for a long time round Khotin. On September 16 the Turks attacked the Russian camp, were repulsed and routed. They fled as far as the Danube; the Russians were masters of Moldavia, and Wallachia was open to them.

Great was the joy at St. Petersburg. Catharine triumphed over European opinion, which still believed in the power of the Turks. Above all, she triumphed over her personal enemy, 'Mustapha's Prompter.' 'She made jests,' wrote the Prussian Minister Solms, 'about the thanks which she owed to the Duc de Choiseul for having

procured her the possession of three fortresses by his
intrigues — those of Khotin, Azof and Taganrog.'[5]
Voltaire, before the victory, had exhausted all the forms
of adulation for Catharine. After the taking of Khotin,
it vas delirium; the patriarch of Ferney set to work to
dance and sing hymns before the ark. 'Allah! Catharina!
I was right then. I out-prophesied Mahomet himself.
God and your victorious troops then had heard me when
I sang: "Te Catharinam laudamus, te dominam con-
fitemur!"'[6] He saw Catharine already in the city of
Constantine, 'the Triumpher over the Ottoman Empire,
and the Pacificator of Poland.' He called the Sovereigns
to arms; but, if he invited them to march against the
Turks, it was not like the 'fanatics' of the Middle Ages, for
the honour of the Christian name; it was for the glory of
their crowns and the profit of their States. Each century
has its own language, and, even when he preached a
crusade, Voltaire had no idea of passing for a Peter the
Hermit. 'The Crusades were so ridiculous that we
cannot return to them; but I profess that were I a
Venetian, I should vote for sending an army into Candia,
while Your Majesty should be beating the Turks towards
Yassi or elsewhere; were I Emperor of the Romans,
Bosnia and Servia would soon see me, and afterwards I
would come and beg a dinner of you at Sophia, or at
Philippopolis in Roumania; after which we would partition in friendly fashion.'[7] Voltaire reckoned without his
host and friend, Frederick the Great, who did not share
his views on the subject of the Ottoman Empire. The
Emperor of the Romans might meditate the conquest of
Bosnia and Servia in secret; Frederick did not allow him
to think it aloud, and if he was in fact preparing himself

[5] Beer, vol. i., p. 256.

[6] Voltaire to Catharine II., October 30, 1769.

[7] Voltaire to Catharine II., May 27, 1769.

'a partition in friendly fashion,' it was not at all in Turkey.

Poland was like an invested city, the siege of which is drawing to its close ; the parallels draw closer together, and from time to time a bursting mine announces the progress of the enemy and the approach of the assault. Nothing better shows the fatality that there was in the lot appointed for that republic than the readiness with which even her friends admitted the idea of her dismemberment. Choiseul had hinted to the King of Prussia that, if he abandoned the Russian alliance, France would facilitate his acquisition of Courland and Warmia. He made a direct suggestion of the same character to the Austrian Ambassador. ' He told me,' wrote Mercy, on August 4, 1769, 'that ideas of great consequence regarding the kingdom of Poland had occurred to him some time ago, and that he wished to confide them to me. They consisted, for the most part, of this : that it would, perhaps, be more advantageous to the general welfare that Poland should be no longer governed by a King, and that our Court should endeavour to take advantage of the critical situation of that kingdom to place the better part of it under our rule.' The idea which Choiseul was pursuing was not yet matured, and he reserved the right of developing it in the form of a project, when the time should come, especially if Prince Kaunitz showed himself inclined to use his influence with his Sovereign in its support. Mercy replied, as was his duty, with great reserve. Kaunitz wrote to him, on August 13, 1769 : ' The Duc de Choiseul's overtures on the subject of Poland were really very unexpected. His object, perhaps, is to endeavour indirectly to discover the ultimate object of the interview of His Majesty the Emperor with the King of Prussia, and whether it is not to be principally concerned with the affairs of Poland. What you have reported to me of the declarations of M. de Goltz concerning the views of his King regarding Polish Prussia and Dantzic has perhaps aroused the suspicion in the French Minister's mind that the King of Prussia would not be opposed to the idea of a partition of Poland, and would resolve to hint somewhat of this to His Majesty the Emperor.' Kaunitz advised Mercy to keep on the watch, and to listen without compromising himself. Before pushing things in any way further, the Austrian diplomatist wished to be sure of his ground with regard to Frederick's intentions. The time fixed for the interview had arrived; Kaunitz regarded as a triumph of his policy this combination, which had been so laboriously prepared, and which piqued Choiseul's curiosity enough to lead him to make such singular confidences.

CHAPTER VI.

THE INTERVIEW BETWEEN FREDERICK AND JOSEPH AT NEISSE.

(August, 1769.)

THE two Sovereigns were to meet on August 25 at Neisse, in Silesia. This interview, paid by the Emperor to the King of Prussia in a town of the province which had for so long been a matter of dispute between the two States, was the most striking confirmation of treaties on the part of Austria. Joseph was to be accompanied only by his Aides-de-camp; the great manœuvres of the Prussian army served as a pretext for the journey.[1] But though Kaunitz had been obliged to give up the idea of following his young Sovereign, he had taken care to prime him to the best of his ability, and had furnished him with a note

[1] This curious interview has for a long time been known only from Frederick's very succinct account (*Mémoires, Œuvres*, vol. vi., p. 25), and from second-hand accounts of a sufficiently doubtful character. We are now in possession of the most complete and most authentic documents. The chief of these, and notably Kaunitz's instructions annotated by Joseph, have been published by M. Beer in the *Archiv für Oesterreichische Geschichte*, vol. xlvii., and in his history of the First Partition of Poland. We have besides these Joseph's letters to his mother, published by M. d'Arneth, and an account by Prince Albert of Saxony (Arneth, vol. viii., p. 566). All these documents are in French.

in twenty - five articles, entitled ' Matters which it is probable that the King of Prussia may bring forward, on the occasion of the approaching visit of the Emperor to Neisse.' This document, in which the diplomat elbowed the pedagogue, was drawn up in French.   Armed and instructed on this wise, Joseph set out.   He maintained incognito, and bore the name of the Count of Falkenstein.

He alighted at the castle, where the King was awaiting him on the staircase ; the latter had with him his brother, Prince Henry, and his nephew, the Prince of Prussia, and was surrounded by numerous officers.   The two Sovereigns embraced, and then the King conducted the Emperor to his room.   He told him ' that he regarded that day as the fairest of his life, since it marked the union of two houses which had too long been at enmity, and whose mutual interest was to support rather than to destroy each other.' He was the first to speak of complete reconciliation, and of a general understanding upon all important matters.   ' After I had given him to understand,' Joseph reports, ' that that would require more mature reflection, " No," he said, " let us begin from to-day."   He pictured the mutual advantages which would accrue ; and I said that neutrality, once signed by letters between us, would pave the way for all that we might respectively wish to arrange afterwards.   I said to him, amongst other things, that I regarded Silesia as absolutely necessary to him, like Lorraine and Alsace for France, and that no friendship was possible between us unless he possessed it ; that we had entirely forgotten it, and that the mutual advantages which we might win without striking a blow were more considerable than Silesia would be for us, or a part of Bohemia for him.'   There was much in this businesslike opening to satisfy Frederick.   To complete their acquaintance he proposed that they should go to dinner.   It was a fast-day, and, says Joseph, ' The King fasted to keep me company, and assured me that he had

done the same out of curiosity for a whole Lent, to see if
he could gain salvation through his stomach.' This was,
however, the only Voltairian remark that he allowed himself.   ' He was very discreet in the matter of religion, and
of profane witticisms.' The dinner was long ; it lasted
for three hours, as was the custom at the Prussian Court.
Prince Albert of Saxony, who accompanied the Emperor,
found the fare ' more military than refined,' but the fruits
excellent, and the wine very good.   The King talked the
whole time, and the Emperor answered him.   The
Prussian Princes and Generals did not dare to ' open their
mouths.'   If their Austrian neighbours asked them a question, they replied quickly and in a low voice, wishing
neither to disturb the King's harangue nor to lose one of
his words.   ' The servile manner which his brother and his
nephew have in his presence is incredible.'   After the meal
the Princes exchanged visits.   In the evening the King
offered his guests the entertainment of Italian burlesque
actors, whose farces seemed to amuse him greatly, and
then they went to supper.   The King ate nothing, but
only talked the more.   ' We went to supper,' says the
Prince of Saxony, ' where he again alone talked, and
which lasted, like the dinner, for three hours by the clock,
during which time some of our Generals did not fail to
fall asleep, much at their ease.'   The next day they held
reviews, and had manœuvres by the troops.   Meals,
manœuvres, and conversations followed each other in this
way until the morning of August 28.

    These conversations were for Joseph the great interest
of the visit.   He was both troubled and charmed by
them.   He was afraid of being beguiled.   ' The King has
overwhelmed us with politeness and acts of friendship.
He is a genius, and a marvellous talker, but there is not a
single utterance that does not smack of roguery. . . .   I
questioned him about all sorts of things . . . it would be

impossible to tell everything, since we were talking at least sixteen hours a day; so that we reviewed many things.' 'This young Prince,' says Frederick, 'affected an ingenuousness which seemed natural to him; his amiable character showed gaiety joined to much vivacity. While he desired to learn, he had not the patience to inform himself; his greatness made him superficial; but what showed his character more than anything were traits which escaped him in spite of himself, and which disclosed the unmeasured ambition which burnt within him.' The King spoke of his connection with Voltaire, touched on literature in a few words, and, 'springing from bough to bough,' asked the Emperor what he thought of the Jesuits. 'I told him that we held them in esteem; he praised them infinitely, and said that all that was needed was to reform Busenbaum's book and its propositions.' It appears that that Father had maintained in his *Medulla Theologiæ Moralis* that the assassination of Kings was permissible in certain cases, to defend a righteous cause. However *provable* this opinion of regicide appeared in casuisty, Frederick the Great considered it seditious.

He spoke of foreign nations and States with disdainful superiority, but he so turned his mockery as to flatter Joseph's well-known antipathy to the English, the jealous dislike which he secretly nourished for France, and the German pride which was confused in him with dynastic ambitions. 'Of France,' Joseph records, ' we spoke hardly at all, except of their military system, which he regarded with supreme contempt, saying that all the talk of the French about war and tactics seemed to him, as it were, an air with military words taught to a parrot: he sings them, but without knowing why, still less knowing how to put them into practice.' On the other hand, Frederick lauded Prince Kaunitz in every way, ' whom he declares to be, in his opinion, the first intellect of Europe.'

He gave great praises to the Austrian army. He had
the right to be impartial. He made an affectation of
exalting the merit of his adversaries, being sufficiently sure
of his own superiority to taste the flavour of modesty,
and in this way extolling himself by the compliments he
paid to others. ' He praised the tactics of the late Marshal
Traun and of Daun, praised Marshal Lascy for two
marches, and Laudon for the affair of Frankfurt.' These
military conversations charmed the Austrians. ' When he
speaks of the art of war,' says Joseph, ' it enchants one,
and the whole of his discourse is nervous, solid, and very
instructive. There is no verbiage, but he proves the
axioms which he propounds by the facts with which
history, of which he has a wide knowledge, and an admirable memory supply him.' ' He displayed his erudition
in various branches of knowledge,' the Prince of Saxony
reports, ' and especially in matters of tactics, in the discussion of which he went back as far as to the times of the
Hebrews and the Philistines.

Running through these discussions, ' springing from
bough to bough,' the condition of Europe, and the direct
object of their interview were dealt with by the two
Sovereigns. Frederick affected the detached tone of the
philosopher disillusioned of the glories of the world, and
was even apostolic in his manner, ' avowing candidly that
in his youth he had been ambitious, and even had acted
ill.' ' He said twice,' Joseph reports, ' " When I was
young I was ambitious ; nowadays I am so no longer."
And, on another occasion, " You think I am full of perfidy ; I know it, and I have somewhat deserved it ; circumstances required it, but that is changed now." I made
no reply to either remark,' Joseph adds. The Emperor
declared that Austria's only desire was for peace, but he
took care to confide to the King all the preparations she
had made for waging war, if it were necessary ; and

Frederick was certainly affected by them. 'It appeared to me,' Joseph writes, 'that the essential object which we had before us in this interview was to inspire the King with as much confidence as was possible, to remove from him all suspicions which he might have of our desire for aggrandizement at his expense, and, broadly, to show our general desire for the maintenance of peace, and our complete indifference to his connections with Russia. . . . From the beginning, the King was the first to come to the subject of neutrality, and to show readiness for securing the maintenance of the tranquillity of our respective States.' Frederick did not disguise the difficulty of trusting a reconciled enemy; but with time, he said, 'the system of German patriotism could effect it.' There was much talk of German patriotism at Neisse. It was a sufficiently novel topic of conversation as between Prussians and Austrians. On this subject Joseph showed no less warmth and zeal than Frederick. 'This I extolled to him on two occasions,' he says, 'pretending to be sensible of its reasons, and greatly praising his wishes on behalf of humanity, and the German patriotism which should bring it about that we should be friends, and not that we should cut each other's throats.' Joseph hinted that Europe might be cut in two, and that a cordon might be drawn from the Adriatic to the Baltic for the maintenance of tranquillity; perhaps it would then be possible to disarm and relieve the peoples. Frederick did not regard it in that light. 'No,' he was the first to say, 'I do not advise you to do that, for one can never answer for the future.'

War between England and France might begin any day. Our relations with these two Powers are not what they were, said Joseph; England and Holland must not flatter themselves that they can keep Austria in the dependent position she occupied in the late wars. As for

the alliance with France, we wish to remain faithful to it ;
but we shall not go beyond the letter of our treaties. The
tendencies of Austrian policy, which are very different
from those of French policy at Constantinople, at Stockholm, and in Poland, show that Austria is not France's
servitor.   In the event of war breaking out between
France and England, Austria is resolved to use only
diplomatic means against Prussia, and she would prefer to
come to an understanding with Frederick beforehand.
The King of Prussia had no treaty with England ; he was
resolved not to mix himself up in these affairs, but he was
naturally very anxious to be assured that Austria would
not support the cause of France against him, if that
country ever felt a wish to take revenge for Rosbach.
That was the basis of the 'patriotic system' upon which
the two German Sovereigns so longed to be agreed, and
the clearest result of their agreement should be indirectly
to annul the treaty of 1756 in one of its essential clauses.
Instead of an ally against Prussia and the German States
which should support her, France would be confronted by
Prussia and Austria mutually resolved not to come to
blows.   It is true that this neutrality would secure
France from the danger of a new alliance between England
and Prussia, but it would not allow France to make war
on Prussia, should she judge it expedient or necessary to
do so, since in that case she would lose the support of
Austria. That was certainly not the intention of the
treaty of 1756.

Frederick regarded his alliance with Russia no less
freely than Joseph did his with France.   With respect to
Russia, Joseph assumed a confidence which he certainly
did not feel, the reason being that he wished to induce
the King of Prussia to pronounce against that Power, and
at the same time wished to avoid the appearance of placing
too high a value on the understanding between Austria

and Prussia by showing too much uneasiness. On the other hand, it suited Frederick to exaggerate the danger which Russia's ambition might cause to Germany, and to show that, on that side, the ' patriotic system ' had the same meaning and the same scope as on the side of France. Joseph praised the Czarina's talents; she had truly, he said, *un cervello di regina*. He declared that Austria had but one desire—to be at peace with everyone. ' This alliance with Russia is necessary to you, as you have not got us,' he said to the King ; ' but it costs you dear, and is often inconvenient to you.' ' That is very true,' Frederick replied. Kaunitz, in his note, had charged the Emperor to call the King's attention to the growth of Russia, and to hint to him that Austria looked to Prussia and Sweden to undertake the task of restraining her, before she should become a neighbour of Austria. ' I read him that paragraph in full,' Joseph relates, ' and he seemed struck by it ; but he answered nothing, except : " In time it will need neither you nor me, but the whole of Europe, to keep those gentry within bounds. The Turks are nothing to them. You will see," he said on another occasion, " I shall not be alive, but in twenty years it will be necessary to both of us to join in alliance against Russian despotism." ' Joseph conveyed to the King how much that alliance would lose in value if he were no longer alive. ' I agree,' Frederick rejoined ; ' but a monarchy is not so readily destroyed, and mine has risen high. Even if they [*sc.*, the Russians] wished to do so, they could hardly injure it.' He was continually returning to the subject of Russian ambitions. ' To stop that Power all Europe will be obliged to put on armour, since she will invade us everywhere.' Frederick advised Joseph to show toleration to his Orthodox subjects. ' They ought to be treated well, in order that their connection [*sc.*, with Russia] may not be strengthened, and that they

may not give more trouble.' The more uneasy the King
of Prussia appeared, the more the Emperor had to appear reassured. 'Sire, in the event of a general engagement, you are in the vanguard; consequently, we may
sleep in peace, since you on your side will do what you like
with the Russians. He denied it, and put it with much
candour,' Joseph relates, 'that he was afraid of them;
that his alliance with them was necessary to him, but that
he found it uncommonly inconvenient.'

These topics led them naturally to talk of the war in
the East. The Emperor declared that his mother and
himself had no idea of mixing themselves up with it, however favourable the conjunctures might be for retaking
Belgrade; but that the Porte had behaved so loyally to
them that they could not possibly break with it. Their
one wish was that the war might soon be ended, and might
not alter the system of Europe. 'He allowed me to per-
ceive, with some skill,' Frederick says, 'that as long as his
mother was alive he dared not flatter himself that he
would have enough ascendency over her mind to be able
to do what he wished to do; but, at the same time, he
did not at all disguise the fact that, in view of the existing
state of affairs in Europe, neither he nor his mother would
ever allow the Russians to remain in possession of Moldavia
and Wallachia.' The King of Prussia digressed at this
point to hint to Joseph that he might get the Porte to
invite him to step in as mediator. The mediation of
Austria was the keystone of Frederick's combinations;
that mediation would annoy Russia; a new crisis would
arise. Upon that 'Count Lynar' would step in, like
Jupiter at the end of the comedy *Amphitryon*, and, 'gild-
ing the pill,' would put everyone in agreement. But
Joseph was not prepared for this overture, and he listened
without discussing it. It was the same with Poland. The
two Sovereigns made only passing references to it, touch-

ing on it lightly and by the way. The reason was, that both had condemned themselves to reserve upon this point. Joseph had his affair of Zips in progress, which he did not wish to discuss with the King of Prussia; Frederick had his Lynar scheme, which had been too coolly received at St. Petersburg for him to judge it opportune to entertain the Emperor with it. Joseph tried to express the indifference with which Austria witnessed the events in Poland; Frederick listened without answering and, when Joseph persisted, said : ' Do not think that that is a trifle; I swear that people will repent it.' Another day he was speaking of the reports that were going about the town. ' I told him of one,' Joseph reports, ' which was, that people had said that he would give us Silesia to get Dantzic. " Yes," Frederick answered, laughing, " to be King of Poland." But he was embarrassed.'

Agreement being arrived at on the subject of the ' patriotic system,' it remained for them to sanction it. A treaty of neutrality between the two States would have constituted a breach of Austria's alliance with France, and of Prussia's with Russia. Neither of the two Sovereigns wished for this ; and while they agreed to paralyze their respective alliances, their intention was to maintain them, in case of emergency. Besides, Kaunitz had foreseen the difficulty. He had long ago suggested a secret exchange of letters between the two Sovereigns; the engagement thus contracted would have the same force as a treaty drawn up in form and initialed by Ministers; but the conventions of diplomacy would be respected, and that was all that was necessary. ' Fearing that he might think of making a formal stipulation on that point,' says Joseph, ' I proposed the letter method, which he accepted at once.' Joseph first drew up ' an abstract of certain significant matters on a sheet of paper.' Frederick drew up another, and, to show their confidence, they exchanged these minutes.

Joseph gave his up first. After having discussed their terms, they separated in order to write the official letters. Frederick called on the Emperor in the evening after the theatre, and asked whether his letter was ready, adding that he had his own in his pocket. Joseph, who had given up his minutes first in the morning, and who regretted that mark of eagerness, answered that he had been receiving some visits, and that his letter was not yet ready. It was Frederick's turn to give a mark of confidence ; he acquitted himself with fairly good grace, deposited his letter, and departed. ' The next morning at the review,' Joseph relates, ' I handed him my letter, not, however, before I had kept him languishing for some minutes, during which time I very clearly saw the uneasiness which was upon him, but which he did not dare make apparent, at having let go of his letter before he had got mine. He insisted that I should give him the letter with every appearance of the greatest mystery. He even pretended to take snuff and to blow his nose, that no one might see him slip it into his pocket. . . . He took it quite away from every- one in order to read it, and assured me that he was very pleased with it.' Frederick strongly urged that the matter should be kept secret, and that they should say nothing of it to their respective allies. ' I told him it should be so or not, as he liked,' Joseph writes ; ' that we were not in such dependence and tutelage, that we could not make stipulations which did not affect them (the allies) at all, but were private to ourselves, without being obliged to communicate with them. On that he begged me to promise not to say anything about it, assuring me and promising that he would not speak about it to his friends, and men- tioned the Russians by name.'

Frederick's letter is dated August 27, 1769,[2] Joseph's

[2] Arneth, *Joseph II. und Maria Theresa*, vol. i., p. 313.

the 28th.[3]   They begin and end with ingeniously balanced
compliments.   'I feel it impossible in my heart to be the
enemy of a great man,' says Frederick.   'I have been
enabled,' Joseph replies, 'to make the personal acquaintance of one who very amply belies the proverb, ancient as
it is, that great objects lose by being seen from too near
at hand.'   Frederick is unwilling to speak of the impression which the Emperor makes upon him.   'I respect his
modesty.'   Joseph thinks that 'the pure and simple truth
would appear flattery to the modesty' of Frederick.   The
King of Prussia notes the 'perfect reconciliation between
the two houses'; the Emperor declares that, 'as they are
completely reconciled,' there is nothing to prevent the
establishment of confidence and friendship between them.
Among these official effusions, both insert in identical terms
'the significant matters' which constitute the engagement.
Frederick in his own name, Joseph in that of his mother
and himself, promise 'on the faith of a king, and on the
word of an honourable man, that if ever the torch of war
is re-lit between England and the House of Bourbon, they
will maintain the peace fortunately restored between them,
and even that in the event of some other war occurring,
whose causes it is impossible presently to foresee, they will
observe the most scrupulous neutrality as regards their
present possessions.'

It was no very notable result, but it was reconciliation,
a beginning of an understanding, and the opening of a
way towards a common policy.   Both sides were fairly
satisfied.   'The thing is innocent and perfectly fair, leaving
the hands of each free to interfere in any foreign war to
which he may feel inclined,' said Joseph.   It was much,
merely in the interests of this freedom, that neither had
anything more to fear from the other; and, besides, the

[3] Ranke, *Die Deutschen Maechte und der Fürstenbund*, vol. ii.,
p. 327.

reciprocal neutrality of Austria and Prussia singularly limited the number of foreign wars in which they could take part. The Austrians thought that Frederick was infinitely less afraid of the Russians than he pretended to be, and that his true object was to keep the Courts of Vienna and St. Petersburg in the state of mutual suspicion in which they then were. After all, and in spite of all the civilities which had been showered upon them, the Austrians were only half reassured. 'Everyone,' says the Prince of Saxony, 'privately reflected that these demonstrations would not stop us from being liable one day or other, perhaps at no distant time, to catch each other anew by the throat, and it was with these thoughts in our minds that we filed down the road from Neisse to Glatz.' Joseph, no doubt to flatter his mother's sentiments, and to counteract the expressions of admiration which he had not refused to the King of Prussia, wrote on the morning of August 28, at the time of leaving: 'We may count upon it that the old distrust is still in his mind, or, rather, in his nature. It is an interesting object to see once, but Heaven preserve us from a second time! . . .' In his heart, the Emperor had been both beguiled and frightened; he felt a sort of fascination in spite of himself, and from that time onwards he was divided in his mind between his prudence, which advised him to avoid temptations, and his pride, which tempted him to measure himself once more against the King of Prussia. At first prudence won the day, and two lines of his notes sum up his impressions well: 'I think that he wishes for peace sincerely, but that he would like us to embark upon some bad business.' This judgment was more penetrating than the Emperor could have believed it to be. Joseph felt no doubt but that, by his occupation of Zips, he was himself in a fair way to prepare all the elements of that 'bad business' for the King of Prussia, on which he suspected that the latter wished to embark Austria.

Frederick's judgment was much more definite.   On September 2 he wrote to his Minister Finckenstein : ' The Emperor is quick-minded ; personally he is attractive and made to win men.   He has a serious notion of military matters.   He assured me that he had forgotten Silesia, but I take that assurance for what it is worth.   He then proposed a reduction of our respective armies, which I declined with as much politeness as was possible.   He is consumed with ambition.   I cannot at present say whether his eyes are turned towards Venice, Bavaria, or Lorraine ; but one thing is certain, which is that Europe will be ablaze as soon as he is master.'   And a few days afterwards, on the 7th, sending Finckenstein Joseph's letter : ' This is so much the better as I have no treaty with England, and as the Russians at the worst can only compromise me with Sweden or Poland.   Besides, the Emperor is frank and full of candour, and I am almost morally convinced that he wishes me no harm—on the contrary, a good deal of personal good.   For the rest, however, policy often draws princes into engagements and measures which force them to act against their inclinations, so that I will not guarantee anything for the future.   All these documents must be religiously kept in the secret archives. . . .'

CHAPTER VII.

FREDERICK THE GREAT'S DIPLOMACY AND HIS HISTORICAL
PHILOSOPHY.

(October, 1769—January, 1770.)

THE reason why the King of Prussia so greatly wished secrecy to be observed on the subject of his interview with the Emperor was that he hoped to make good use of it. The interview at Neisse had naturally aroused some uneasiness in the Czarina's mind. While her victorious armies were occupying Moldavia, she saw Austria and Prussia drawing together, and making arrangements in secret. She had everything to fear for her conquests. If she had known what the letters were which had been exchanged at Neisse, she would have been much reassured; but the mystery with which the King and the Emperor surrounded themselves gave her matter for thought. Then it was that Frederick resumed the negotiations with her which he had allowed to drag on since May. Russia showed an accommodating disposition quite different from that which she had displayed in the spring. She agreed to prolong the treaty of alliance till 1780, and to guarantee the succession to the Ansbach and Bayreuth margraviates, omitting the restriction relating to Germanic Law; she only stipulated that the King of Prussia should guarantee the constitution of Sweden.

Frederick agreed to this, and even promised to create a diversion in that quarter; but he added that it was to take place in Swedish Pomerania, which might make Prussia's stay in that province a permanent one.[1] The Czarina made no opposition to the clause, and the treaty was renewed on October 12, 1769. On the 4th, Catharine wrote to Mme. de Bielke : ' May God give the new Princess of Prussia a fine boy as soon as may be, and at the end of the first one's year a second, *and then there will be a line of friends for me, at which I shall rejoice.*'

The Russians, who had been at Jassy since September 26, pushed forward their march. On November 16 they occupied Bucharest. This obliteration of the Turks and rapid progress of the Russians struck Europe with astonishment. Frederick, who had seen the Russians close, and knew them well, was neither surprised nor disconcerted. He twitted Voltaire with the zeal with which he was inspired against the Crescent, and appealed wittily from the Prophet-in-Ordinary to Catharine the Great, to the author of the *Essai sur les Mœurs :* ' Had I not read the history of the Crusades in your works, I might perhaps have abandoned myself to the folly of conquering Palestine, of delivering Zion, and of gathering the palms of Idumæa; but the follies of so many kings and paladins who have fought in those distant lands have prevented me from imitating their example, being assured that the Empress of Russia would give a good account of the matter. . . . I would have Europe at peace, and all the world satisfied. I think I must have inherited these sentiments from the late Abbé de Saint-Pierre, and maybe I shall remain, like him, the only one of my sect.'[2] With his brother Henry, Frederick the Great was more serious. Prince Henry was fruitful in vast conceptions ;

---

[1] Martens, vol. vi., p. 48 *et seq.*

[2] To Voltaire, November 25, 1769.

he anticipated the Holy Alliance, and talked as the
Prussian diplomatists talked half a century later at the
Congress of Vienna. ' The agreement with Austria will
be a fact,' he wrote, on November 22, 1769, ' only upon
the day when you divide the empire with the Emperor,
after the fashion of Octavius and Antony.' To Frederick's
taste these seemed ideas not at all fitted for an old man to
entertain. ' I shall not be the man, my dear brother, who
will bring the agreement with the House of Austria to
maturity.' He reserved this task for his nephews, and in
fact a hundred years were to pass before the agreement
could be sealed at Gastein, before the House of Hohenzollern could give an Octavius to Germany, and Prussia
could have her battle of Actium. Frederick constantly
came back to the two principles of his historical philosophy : the destiny which is unknown, and the opportunity
which is seized. ' There is a sort of fatality, or, if not a
fatality, secondary causes equally unknown, which often
shape events in a manner which we can neither imagine nor
foresee. We are blind men who advance groping in the
dark. When favourable circumstances present themselves,
there is a kind of sudden lightening by which adroit men
profit. Everything else is the sport of uncertainty.'[3]

[3] This letter, which is published by M. Duncker, and translated
by him from the original, which is in the Prussian Archives, is
not in Frederick's *Works*. Frederick often expressed the same
thoughts. He wrote to Voltaire, on May 1, 1771 : ' What often
appears the most probable thing in politics is the least so. We
are like blind men, we go groping our way, and we are not so clever
as the Fifteen Score* who know the streets and crossways of Paris
without a mistake. What is called the art of conjecture is no art ;
it is a game of chance, in which the most skilful man may lose like
the most ignorant.' And on December 6, 1772 : ' All this depends
on a number of secondary causes, obscure and impenetrable . . .

* An allusion to the hospital for the blind, called Quinze
Vingts.—TRANSLATOR.

The King of Prussia well knew that it was his alliance
with Russia that made Austria so conciliatory. He rightly
judged that a closer and closer approach to Austria would
produce an equally favourable effect on Russia. Accordingly, he urged the Court of Vienna to offer mediation,
prepared for a fresh interview with the Emperor in the
following summer, and instructed his Minister at Constantinople to proceed in agreement with Austria. He wrote to
his brother Henry in these months of the winter of 1769-
1770 : ' I have found means of suggesting to the Queen-
Empress, without compromising myself, that if she could
take in hand the mediation for peace with the consent of
the Porte, I would use all my influence at St. Petersburg
to secure the acceptance of that mediation. The Empress
desires it, but she is prevented by the French at Constantinople, so that we find ourselves really hampered. Nevertheless, there has been some progress made. We shall see
what more we can do at the time of our journey to Moravia.
It must never be forgotten that in politics distrust is the
mother of security. I confine myself to preparing what is
needful, to collecting means, to sharpening the knife well,
so that my nephews may have no complaints to make of
my negligence.'[4]

Austria hesitated to commit herself. The French were
to a certain extent responsible for this behaviour, but
their influence was much less than it suited Kaunitz to
make the King of Prussia believe. The Austrians entrenched themselves behind their pretended deference for
France, when they wanted a pretext for declining the
King of Prussia's proposals, in the same way that Frederick

---

and so the world goes. It is governed only by handiness and trickery.
Sometimes, when we have sufficient premises, we may guess the
future ; often we mistake it.'

[4] Unpublished letters of the King of Prussia, December 3, 1769,
and February 1, 1771 : Duncker, pp. 189-191.

confronted them with Catharine's exactions, when he did not want to defer to their wishes. In reality, at Vienna, as at Berlin, they only acted as it suited themselves, they attended solely to their own interests, and troubled themselves very little about their allies. In December, 1769, the Austrian Ambassador in France, Count Mercy, had come to Vienna, where they were very busy over the approaching marriage of the Archduchess Marie Antoinette with the French Dauphin. Choiseul had given him, when leaving Paris, a memorandum which was to enlighten Prince Kaunitz upon the political views of France.[5] In it there manifestly appeared the distrust which the Neisse interview had inspired, and the fear lest Austria might draw towards Prussia to the detriment of the French alliance. ' The King of Prussia,' Choiseul wrote, ' who certainly wishes for war, that he may fish in troubled waters, will not dare to move if the Court of Vienna will hold him in check. . . . The best thing for our alliance, according to the views of France, would be for the Turkish war to continue for a few years with equal successes to the two parties, so that they may reciprocally weaken each other, and, if we have the advantage of time, all the chances are for us. It is not known in France what the views of the Court of Vienna are regarding Poland and the Turkish war, but we confide to it [*sc.*, to the Court of Vienna], with the utmost frankness and simplicity, what the opinion of the King is, to whom, moreover, it matters very little who is King of Poland, provided Poland is kept in motion, and Russia be kept occupied with her and with the Porte for a few more years.'

That was not at all Kaunitz's view. He had just asked the new Austrian Envoy at Constantinople, Thugut, to hint to the Turks that, if they showed a desire for it,

<hr>

[5] This memorandum, together with Kaunitz's reply, has been published by M. Beer : *Documents*, pp. 5 and 7.

Austria would offer her mediation.[6] The divergence in
the interests and policies of the two allies betrayed itself
openly in the reply which he addressed to Choiseul. ' It
seems,' he says, ' that there is, at the very least, the greatest
possible risk in having recourse to a prolongation of the
war.' His view was that they should strive to secure a
peace on the basis of the *status quo ante*. In this way
Russia would emerge weakened from a useless war. She
would be for long unable to return to her ambitious schemes
in the North; ' whereas,' he continued, ' we should no
longer be able to hope for such a peace if it should happen,
as happen it will, that fresh success should increase her
inflexibility. As for us, it is certain that the prolongation
of this war does not suit us, seeing what risks are attached
to its continuance ; we must consequently endeavour to
bring it to an end sooner rather than later.' Deaf to the
advice of her ally at Versailles, who reminded her both of
her treaty obligations and of her true interests, Austria
allowed herself to be drawn little by little towards the
perilous adventures to which the King of Prussia lured her.
She began to disclose her secret thoughts, which were less
how to keep Russia in check, and to preserve the Turkish
Empire, than to seek an opportunity for profit, and a
pretext for conquests in the Eastern crisis. In reality, her
mediation had no other meaning.

6 Despatch of February 20, 1770 : Arneth, vol. viii., pp. 189-
206.

CHAPTER VIII.

ENGLAND AND THE EASTERN QUESTION.

(1769—1770.)

ENGLAND had taken no part in the troubles which had followed the election of Stanislas Augustus in Poland, and she played only a very subordinate part in the Eastern crisis which was its result. After having kept Europe in a blaze for seven years, she seemed to withdraw within herself, and to disconnect herself from Continental politics. Statesmen on the Continent paid very little attention to her, and even pretended that she no longer entered into their calculations. This reciprocal indifference deserves explanation. In 1770 the Eastern Question had already been propounded by the Russians in the terms in which they claim to solve it in this century. With the English it was otherwise. Pitt's oft-quoted sentence, 'They say to us, Let Russia keep all her conquests ; let her carry on to the end, and drive the Turks out of Europe—that has nothing to do with us! With those who lay down this principle, I refuse to argue,' had not yet been laid down as the fundamental article of the Magna Charta of English diplomacy. England's ideas on this point were not yet very settled, because her interests in the East were still somewhat vaguely defined. It was scarcely seven years since she had conquered the French colonies in the East

Indies, and the authority of the Company had been established there for only four years.   Russia was not threatening to take the English Empire in the Indies in the rear.
The Russians, who did not dominate the navigation of the
Black Sea, did not disturb that of the Mediterranean, and
as their fleets could only reach the latter sea by the Channel,
and enter it by Gibraltar, England troubled herself little
over the Russian navy, which, moreover, she regarded with
much scepticism.   The enemy that threatened the Indian
Empire was France, who might re-establish her forces
there, and once more contend with Clive's successors for
the establishments which Dupleix founded.   That was
what the English especially dreaded, and, as Russia was at
open enmity with France, a partiality for Russia was the
inevitable result in England.   There a Russian alliance
seemed necessary, as Austria was bound to France and
Spain, and Prussia refused to meddle any more in colonial
wars.

These political considerations were fortified by motives
of commercial interest.   A publicist of the time, Favier,
indicates them very well in the memoranda which he drew
up for the Comte de Broglie, and which that diplomatist
handed to Louis XV.[1]   England shared the trade of the
Levant with France, but she had the Northern trade entirely
in her hands.   This trade was of capital importance to
England ; it made Russia economically her client.   The
English exported into Russia the commodities and produce
of Europe and of the two Indies, and imported thence the
raw materials required for their shipbuilding yards.   They
attached too much importance to this Northern traffic to
wish to inconvenience Russia in the East, and, moreover,
their Eastern trade had nothing to fear from the advances

[1] 'Article V., On Russia.   Second memorandum, separated to
serve as supplement to the article " Russia, 1773 " ' : Boutaric,
vol. ii., pp. 16-70.

of Russia towards the shore of the Black Sea. England
even saw in the opening of that sea to the Czarina's ships
an opportunity for advantages to herself; the English flag
would profit by the advantages which would be accorded
to the Russian flag. 'We may even,' said Favier, speaking
of the opening of the Black Sea, 'deduce a melancholy
consequence from it: which is, that France alone would
lose by it, and lose heavily, but that England might gain
by it considerably. Under the name of Russia, or even
under her own flag, she would open a new and cheaper
outlet for her cloth, her hardware, the produce of her
colonies, and all that she draws, through Cadiz, from
Spanish America.' Hence the existence of a very powerful
and active Russian party in the City of London—a party
which at that time counselled peace, and which later on,
when England was more enlightened and wished to check
Russia, had a remarkably paralyzing influence upon the
action of her policy. Relying upon these facts, Favier
arrived at this conclusion, which explains the whole conduct
of England from 1763 to 1775 in the affairs of Poland
and in the Eastern crisis: 'In view of these principles,
and of England's interests as a maritime and commercial
Power—in view of the wishes of the nation and the popular
clamour—it is impossible to suppose that Russia has anything to fear from the Court of London for the accomplishment of her designs in the war against the Turks.
Nor does she need any guarantee of her influence in the
negotiations for peace. The English Ambassador at Constantinople is, so to speak, the *chargé d'affaires* for Russia.'
'Your lordship knows that I am quite a Russ,' wrote
Lord Chatham to Shelburne in 1773.[2]

In the autumn of 1769, when the Russian ships—one of
which was commanded by Elphinstone, a former officer of
the British Navy—appeared in the harbours of England

[2] Stanhope, *William Pitt and his Times*, vol. ii., chap. xiv.

to put in and complete their armament, they had a great reception. They were received all the more warmly, in that their appearance was not so formidable as it might have been. 'One can hardly describe the amusement,' says Rulhière, 'with which the English viewed these ships of pine-wood, their enormous heaviness in manœuvring, their poops loaded with relics, the unhandiness of the sailors, the incredible dirtiness of their equipments, which was the veritable cause of a contagion that consumed them. Sometimes five or six English sailors would amuse themselves by working, in a moment and with extreme quickness, a ship of the same size as a Russian ship, which was hardly got under way by two or three hundred sailors of that nation.' Choiseul wished to stop this Russian fleet on its way. The French and the Spaniards could have sent it to the bottom in a moment. This energetic action would have changed the face of affairs in the East as well as in Poland ; the Turks would have recovered confidence, and Austria would have been obliged to depend more upon her ally. The French nation, which was, as Voltaire put it, 'a trifle *Mustapha'd*,'[3] might have regarded the enterprise with favour, and the prestige of the Government would have been raised by it. Choiseul presented a memorandum to the Council in which this scheme was developed, but it was thrown out. England, moreover, declared that any warlike measure directed against the Russian fleet would be considered as an act of hostility to herself.[4] France withdrew, but it was much more owing to her own weakness, and to the line of *in*-action she had taken up, than from fear of England.

England, indeed, had lost the greater part of the prestige which her naval victories in the Seven Years' War had given her. After that great effort of foreign

---

[3] To Catharine, May 18, 1770. [*Un peu Mustapha* in original.]
[4] Boutaric, vol. ii., p. 176 ; Zinkeisen, vol. v., book vi., chap. iii.

policy, she had become absorbed in her internal affairs,
the critical state of which demanded all her attention. It
was the Heroic Age of Parliamentary government, and
England then learned the cost of free government. Conflicts between King and Parliament, between the House of
Lords and the House of Commons, strife between parties
in Parliament, between Liberals and demagogues—the
letters of Junius give a striking picture of that troublous
time. Parliament had been dissolved in 1756;[5] the
elections provoked such an abuse of corruption as up to
that time had not been seen. The county of Middlesex
elected as its member a demagogue named John Wilkes,
who was at that time undergoing a term of imprison-
ment. While the Commons were discussing his election,
the populace set him free. Meetings followed each other,
and soon degenerated into riots. The Commons encroached
upon the Executive Government and commanded arrests.
In 1771 the people threatened to invade the precincts of
the Legislature. Parties contended for power with passion
and violence. At every other moment the impeachment
of Ministers was talked of. It was a century since the
Rebellion had ended, but it had left behind it traditions
of violence and habits of suspicion which still moved men's
minds. Ministries crumbled one after another; in 1771,
the Cabinet was the seventh in ten years. At the same
time the American colonies rose ; blood flowed in the
streets of Boston. An appalling famine devastated the
Indies, and public opinion accused the Administration of
responsibility for this disaster that was threatening the
conquest for which England had sacrificed so much both
in money and men. 'A nation torn by factions,' says
Macaulay, 'a throne assailed by the most violent invec-
tives, a House of Commons hated and despised by the
nation, England inflamed against Scotland, Great Britain

---

[5] *Sic* in original. The date should be 1768.

struggling with America'—such was England at the
moment when the Eastern crisis was holding all the attention of the Continent.[6]

Old Europe witnessed this spectacle with astonishment
mingled with disdain. These popular tumults, these con-
tinual convulsions of the State, confounded and frightened
the ' dandified Ministers' at Versailles, the ' pedagogues of
Vienna,' and the 'favourites' of St. Petersburg. They
quite failed to understand the intermissions which are,
as it were, a law of history in England, and saw in them
a symptom of old age and decadence. The most clear-
sighted among them regarded her with contempt. At
Neisse, Frederick and Joseph had spoken of England.
Joseph considered ' that she was in a state of decadence,
that the Parliament was behaving with excess, and that
the colonies might be her ruin.' Frederick agreed and
' abused the Parliament.'[7] ' He spoke of England,' Joseph
relates, ' with much disdain, for the troubles and present
insolences of the opposition party against the Court, and
said that however small a German Prince he was, he would
not change places with the King of England.'[8] It was to
Catharine's interest to load the English with flatteries and
caresses. She needed them, and so paid them compliments.[9] At bottom, she had small esteem for their

---

[6] M. Sorel is inaccurate in one or two particulars, such as the
liberation of Wilkes and the threatened invasion of the Legislature.—TRANSLATOR.

[7] Joseph II.'s notes to Kaunitz's Instructions : Beer, *Archiv*,
l. xlvii.

[8] Joseph II.'s Journal at Neisse : Arneth, *Joseph II. und Maria
Theresa.*

[9] She wrote to Mme. de Bielke, on January 4, 1772 : 'The
letter of the English Minister, who calls me " his dear Empress,"
has given me pleasure. I am so accustomed to the friendship of
the English that I am wont to regard every Englishman as a well-
wisher, and I act accordingly, as far as it depends on me.'

political system, and held Parliamentary government to
be incompatible with durable alliances. 'I naturally like
the English,' she wrote to Mme de Bielke, 'but I am
sorry to see them with so little nerve at so critical a time
as this ; one would say that they are quite pleased when
they have had a good squabble in that Lower House of
theirs, which as often as not has its majority in its pocket
and nothing else besides.' In 1770, on December 13, at
the time when the English were harbouring her fleets, she
was already applying to them that trite reproach with
which the jealousy of poor and despotic States consoles
itself as against States which manage to be at once free
and prosperous. 'The complaint of England,' she wrote
to Voltaire, 'can only be cured by a war. *They are too
rich* and disunited; 'a war would impoverish them and
would unite men's minds. For that reason the nation
wishes for it.' Catharine II. saw through the passing
weaknesses of the State ; she saw the latent strength of
the nation.

At Versailles men abandoned themselves to the empty
pleasure of decrying the government of an implacable
enemy, of a conqueror who was hated and always feared.
Choiseul wrote to Kaunitz in December, 1769 : 'England
is in a state of trouble and divisions which cannot be
calculated, for it is very possible that that Power may
engage in war, prompted merely by the weakness of her
Administration. . . . As the greatest resolves of the Court
of London depend on the particular interests of the different
factions, and as those interests are changing every month,
according to the fears and sometimes the fancies of those
who govern, one can answer for nothing.' It would have
been only too easy, against the internal troubles and
Ministerial crises of England, to set the closet revolutions
and the political inconsistency of a Court where systems
and Ministers changed at the will of favourites. Kaunitz

added to the scantily disguised contempt of Choiseul the bewilderment of an old diplomat brought up in the classical pedantry of the Austrian Chancery. ' As regards England,' he wrote to Choiseul, ' it is true that the present state of troubles and divisions which reign there may give us hope for the continuation of peace on that side ; but I cannot disguise the fact that I regard it as still more true, as M. le Duc very well observes, that with regard to a nation and a constitution in which the most extreme and contradictory parties often depend upon a momentary circumstance, and ·sometimes even upon the slightest change among those in office, nothing can be really counted upon, and that therefore, in fact and *a priori*, it would seem that it behoves us constantly to be no less attentive than circumspect in face of so singular a government.'[10]

Evidently, in the eyes of these statesmen, England was only a kind of island-Poland, a rich, deliberate and compact Poland, which owed her apparent. solidity merely to the lucky chance which had deprived her of neighbours, but was made by her ' singular government' no less incapable of continuity in her designs than of energy in her actions. And yet Montesquieu had warned his contemporaries ; he had shown them that ' the friendship of England was more to be sought, her hatred more to be feared, than the instability of her government and her internal commotion would seem to warrant ; that it would thus be the destiny of the executive power in that nation to be almost always troubled within and respected without ;' finally, that ' if some foreign Power threatened the State and imperilled her fortune or her glory, lesser interests yielding to greater, all would unite in support of the executive power.'[11] It was indeed what happened a few years later, when Europe tried to contend with a France raised by the most terrible

[10] Beer, *Documents.*
[11] *Esprit de Lois*, book xix., chap. xxvii.

revolution and led by the greatest man of war of modern
times.   But, pending the time when they were to give
Europe that great spectacle and that great lesson, the
English were preparing to learn to their cost that they
can never dissociate themselves from Eastern affairs, even
when they believe it to be the adroit course, or judge it to
be necessary.

CHAPTER IX.

THE VICTORIES OF RUSSIA AND THE DEMAND FOR MEDIATION.

(February—August, 1770.)

THE end of the campaign of 1769 had been highly favour-able to the Russians. Their victories had given them Moldavia and Wallachia, and the Orthodox population of those principalities welcomed them as deliverers. Catharine's generals received the homage of the Bogars at Jassy and Bucharest, and set up a Russian administra-tion. In the meantime two fleets, one commanded by Spiritof, the other by the Englishman Elphinstone, were entering the Mediterranean and preparing to liberate Greece. 'I cannot resist saying once more to Your Majesty,' Voltaire wrote on January 2, 1770, 'that Your Majesty's project is the greatest and the most astounding that ever was formed ; Hannibal's did not come near it.' Spiritof's fleet took up the two Orlofs on its way, and reached the Greek coasts at the end of February. The Russian contingent was far from equalling the Greeks' illusions, and the contingents which the Greeks supplied deceived all the hopes of the Russians. The Turks and the Albanians advanced ; at their approach these bands took to flight. The insurrection collapsed. Alexis Orlof, who on May 2 had called the Greeks to freedom, was obliged at the end of the month to re-embark upon his

ships ; and the Russian Admirals had barely time to collect
their forces, to advance to the encounter with the Turkish
fleet. Catharine the Great was a philosopher ; she concluded from this fiasco that the Greeks were not ripe for
freedom. ' The Greeks, the Spartans,' she wrote to Voltaire,
' have much degenerated ; they love rapine more than
liberty. They are forever lost unless they profit by the
dispositions and the counsels of the hero whom I have sent
to them.'

The Greek enterprise had failed ; but it was only an
episode in the great war which the Russians were preparing
for 1770, and which was soon to provide them with an
opportunity for a striking revenge. The Turks hoped for
the same ; they expected it, and war was the breath of
their nostrils. ' Mustapha will hear no word of peace,'
the Czarina wrote ;[1] ' so much the worse for him. The
poor man is pitiably deceived.' Kaunitz had acted prudently
in instructing the Austrian Resident, Thugut, not to offer
his good offices before the Turks asked for them. The
Turks were looking, not for counsellors and conciliators,
but for allies ; and, as it was written that Poland was to
pay the charges of the war, it was to Poland that they
looked to provide the bait which was to secure them the
help they needed. - They had declared war to defend the
liberties of Poland ; war once declared, they had no scruple,
in order to secure its successful issue, in trafficking with the
independence of that republic. ' Is it better that the people
should perish or that the Prince should break his treaty ?
Who is the fool who would balance these to solve this
question ?' said the King of Prussia. In the matter of the
public weal, the Divan was of the same opinion as Frederick
the Great ; the political morality of the Turks was no less
accommodating than that of the Christians. On March 24,
1770, Thugut wrote that he had had a secret interview

[1] To Mme. de Bielke, March 31, 1770.

with the Reis-Effendi, and that the latter had offered to
conclude a close alliance; the humiliation of Russia was
to be its object, and Poland was to provide the price.
Austria declined the offer, and on April 21 Kaunitz wrote
to Thugut that the Turks must look to a friendly intervention for the solution of their difficulties.

The King of Prussia gave the same advice; Zegelin
pressed the Turks to ask for his master's good offices. The
fact was that Frederick, who had everything to gain from
the restoration of peace, saw with uneasiness symptoms of
war declaring themselves on every side. Voltaire wrote to
him : ' I should like you to amuse yourself by beating
Mustapha too, and to share with the Empress of Russia.'
Frederick answered jestingly, as was his wont : ' What, my
dear saint! you are astonished that there is a war in Europe
in which I am not engaged! That is not very sanctified.
Know, then, that the philosophers have made me peaceable,
by their perpetual denunciations against those whom they
call mercenary brigands. The Empress of Russia may
fight away at her ease; she has got a dispensation from
Diderot, for good cash down, for making the Russians
fight the Turks. . . .'[2]   At bottom, it was not exactly
' encyclopædic excommunication ' that Frederick feared,
but expense without profit, and complications without an
outlet. ' It seems,' he wrote to his Minister in Russia,
' that the Empress is gaily labouring to involve all Europe
in the whirlpool of war.' But the dark ambitions of
Joseph II. disturbed him no less than the open ambitions
of Catharine. He imagined, quite wrongly, that France
was urging Austria to throw herself into the struggle.
Choiseul was working with this object; but it was distasteful to Louis XV., and at the very moment when the
King of Prussia was so much occupied with the warlike

[2] Catharine had just bought Diderot's library.   **Voltaire to
Frederick, May 4 ; Frederick to Voltaire, May 24, 1770.**

plots of the Court of Versailles, the King of France was writing to the Comte de Broglie, on March 21, 1770: 'With regard to the Porte, a treaty with that Power is very risky. Assistance (to the Poles) might bring on war, which I do not desire.' Frederick was none the less impatient to know what the Austrians thought, and to give them a skilful hint of his own plans; it was important to him to know how Count Lynar's scheme would be received at Vienna, should the case arise.

Austria had decided to change her Minister at Berlin. Nugent, who was accredited there, came to take leave of the King, and was received in private audience at Potsdam on May 6, 1770. The conversation, which Nugent relates with a good-humour slightly tinged with scepticism, as the Austrian manner is, shows the King of Prussia in his game of diplomacy to the life.[3] Never was there a player more interesting to observe, for never was there one at once more alert, bolder, and more circumspect, more fruitful in feints and expedients, and, above all, more adroit in discovering and deceiving the designs of his opponent. He began by covering the Austrians with praises in the light tone in which he excelled, admiring Joseph II. for his 'filial love,' for his 'respectful attachment to his august mother,' his 'fund of noble ambition, which excites to great enterprises, and all the qualities fitted to make a great man.' 'He is still holding himself in hand,' said Frederick, 'but let a little time pass, and you will see how the Emperor will flash out.' What would be the direction of the flashes? That was what the King of Prussia so strongly desired to know. He unfolded the kingdoms of the Continent before Nugent's eyes. After observing 'how inconvenient it is to have one's provinces cut up and separated from each other,' he put his finger on the points

[3] ' The last interview with the King, at his farewell audience at Potsdam, May 10, 1770': Arneth, vol. viii., p. 573.

where he knew the eyes of the Emperor and of his Minister preferred to rest, the latter being 'the greatest statesman whom we have had in Europe for a long time, and whose policy was simple but very profound.' These points, marked out beforehand for the planting of the Austrian eagles one day or another, were Bavaria, half of which Joseph wanted to take in 1778 ; Venice, whose dismemberment he planned in 1782 ;[4] Parma, where he had had a sister since 1768 ; Modena, where he placed his brother in 1771 ; in fact, that Italy the domination of which was always the passion and the bane of the House of Austria. He did not stop at the possessions of the King of France, the ally and brother-in-law of the Emperor, to which, however, he did not think he could attract the covetousness of Austria, as he was certain afterwards to denounce it to the French.   'He came,' says Nugent, 'to the provinces which have belonged to the House of Austria, and, speaking of Lorraine and of Alsace, he provided a plan of military operations for the conquest of both, saying that it would be a matter of two campaigns.'[5]   Here

---

[4] 'From Belgrade, the straightest and shortest possible line which the land would allow would be drawn towards the Adriatic, up to and including *il golfo della Drina ;* and, finally, the possessions on the dry land, such as Venetian Istria and Dalmatia, would furnish the only means of giving value to the products of my States ' : Joseph to Catharine II., November 13, 1782.

[5] This plan was not a mere conversational argument.   Frederick had thought seriously about it, and a few years later he wrote it down, as a distraction from the gout, which was troubling him.   It is to be found in his military works, at article iv., 'Reflections on Plans of Campaign,' with this note, ' *Scriptum in dolore,* December 1, 1775.'   It was a question of attacking France with two armies—one in Alsace, to hold the French in check ; the other, in greater force, to march on Paris.   A single trait will suffice to show how the King entered into the circumstantial details of his plan.   He says : ' Suppose Paris taken, it would be very necessary to avoid putting in troops, as they would be softened, and would

Frederick pressed his point too far, and showed his hand ; the proposition was too bold, and Nugent did not attempt to make any reply. It was a question reserved at any rate till the time when there should be an idea of making war on France, as it came to pass in 1791. 'Some objections which I made to his plan,' Nugent reports, 'caused him to enter with warmth into circumstantial details of the arrangements which would have to be made in connection with his scheme, and he ended by saying : "I clearly see that you do not approve of my plan ; but what do you think of Italy ? You already have Mantua, the Milanese and Tuscany ; the States of the Duke of Modena come to you. If you added to these Parma and Piacenza, with something of the State of Venice, you would have a very convenient rounding-off."' Nugent agreed that nothing would be so comfortable as rounding one's self off, pro- vided everyone had a good will to the operation. Frederick had carefully avoided speaking of Poland ; it suited him to have advances made to him on that subject, and to be tempted in his turn. This time Nugent did not see the trap, and, tired, no doubt, of the King's banter, he tried to adopt the same tone to him. 'But, sire,' he said, 'I could easily make a rounding-off for Your Majesty (saving the pleasure of Your Majesty's neighbours), which would not be so difficult to carry out. If one drew a line from the frontiers of Prussia by Graudenz, Thorn, and Posen up to Gross-Glogan, the country which would lie between that line and the sea would be very convenient to Your Majesty, and the communication between a large part of Your Majesty's States would be established. Taking with that the bishopric of Warmia, which is enclosed in the kingdom of Prussia, the rounding-off would be complete.'

---

lose their discipline ; it would have to suffice to draw large contri- butions from the town' (*Œuvres*, vol. xxix., p. 75).

Count Lynar himself could not have spoken better.
Thenceforth Frederick knew that the Court of Vienna
would consider his pretensions in no way exaggerated
whenever he should be in a position to prosecute them.
The thing was to reach that position; and the means
was for Austria to offer her mediation.   Frederick went
straight to it.   He answered Nugent nothing, remained
for a time in thought, then rejoined, with a smile: 'All
that is very well to talk about, but I will tell you one
thing which you must keep secret. . . .   I have sure
advices from Constantinople that the Turks are sighing
for peace, and that the Porte would readily accept the
mediation of your Court. . . .   In case they should wish
to use me for the correspondence with the Court of Russia,
I would undertake it with pleasure ; but much economy of
terms will have to be used with that Princess, for there is
a strong dose of vanity at the bottom of her character.'

This discourse could only increase the Emperor's inclination to the interview which was to take place in the summer.
As regards the mediation of Austria, which was the pivot of
all his combinations, Frederick justly thought that Austria
would not decide on it until the pretensions of Russia made
it imperative.   Accordingly, he devoted himself to discovering those pretensions, and, at the same time, to preparing
the Czarina for mediation.   On May 21 he wrote to Solms
that the Turks had begged him to inquire at St. Petersburg what Russia's conditions of peace would be.   Panin
answered on June 15 that there was one preliminary condition, which was the release of Obreskof ; that the Czarina
had not entered on the war out of ambition, that she
claimed to make no conquests, but that her honour
demanded that she should obtain some guarantees for
her co-religionists.   The answer was evasive, and Frederick
insisted.   The Austrian armaments provided him with an
argument.   He could only make Russia and Austria decide

to negotiate together by persuading them that they had
both of them decided on war. ' The Austrians are forming
magazines on their Hungarian frontiers,' he wrote to Prince
Henry on June 17 ; ' to tell you the truth, I do not think
they are very considerable, but I use them at St. Petersburg
for all they are worth.'

The Czarina was waiting for the results of the campaign
before making a pronouncement. Those results crowned
all her hopes. On July 5, 1770, the Russian fleet destroyed
the Turkish fleet at Cheshmeh. On August 1 Roumanzow's
small army gained the victory of Kagoul over the masses
of the Turks commanded by the Grand Vizier. Terror
reigned at Constantinople. The Turks could no longer
think of disputing the possession of the Danubian principalities against the Russians. Justly proud as she was
of these successes, the Czarina did not allow herself to be
dazzled by them. She knew that it is hard to obtain forgiveness for great conquests, and that in such cases friends
show least indulgence. She was disturbed by the behaviour
of the King of Prussia, by his activity at Constantinople,
and by his new intimacy with Joseph, whom he was to
meet again in a few weeks. Sweden disturbed her also ;
Frederick had pledged himself to work in agreement with
her in that quarter, and had just sent his brother Henry
to Stockholm.[6] It was important to the Czarina that she
should have exact information regarding Prussian policy
in Sweden ; it was also of importance to her that a Prussian
Prince should make his appearance at her Court at the
time when Frederick and the Emperor were to excite the
curiosity of diplomatists, and inflame the imagination of
newsmongers by a fresh interview. On July 19, 1770, the
Czarina wrote to the King of Prussia, and asked that
Prince Henry might visit St. Petersburg on his return

    [6] On the affairs of Sweden, *vide* Geffroy, *Gustave III. et la Cour
de France.* Paris, 1867.

from Stockholm. The invitation was not one to be declined. The Princess of Prussia had just given birth to a son; it was the eldest of that ' line of friends' for which the Czarina was looking from the marriage of the heir-presumptive; Frederick made her the godmother, and then wrote to Prince Henry, on August 12 : 'You understand, my dear brother, what skilful handling that woman will need. . . . You will there get to know many people of whom we have need. You will, please, make the Empress the most flattering compliments from me, and you will say everything you can of the admiration with which she inspires everyone—in fact, all that is necessary.' While the King of Prussia was writing these lines, events were transpiring which were to transform the visit of courtesy into a diplomatic mission of the highest importance. Some of these events Frederick had himself prepared ; others arose unknown to him, and he took advantage of them. ' The older one gets,' he often used to say, ' the more convinced one becomes that His Majesty King Chance does three-quarters of the business of this miserable universe.'

The Russian victories had thrown all the diplomatic world into commotion. The Eastern Question, in fact, was from that time propounded. The thing to be known was, whether the Turkish Empire was to be dismembered, and whether the Russians were to be allowed to establish themselves on the Danube. There arose a desire for action in France. The Sultan proposed an alliance to Louis XV.; we know that the King did not wish for it, but it was a question of supplying the Turks with twelve or fifteen ships of war in return for a subsidy. At the same time, Choiseul sent money and officers to the Confederation of Bar, among them an adventurer who by himself was worth a whole headquarter staff, Dumouriez.[7] The English

[7] The Duc de Broglie, *Le Secret du Roi*, vol. ii., pp. 305-310 ; Farges, *Instructions de Pologne*, Dumouriez's Instruction, June 30, 1770, vol. ii., p. 294.

themselves were disturbed. As has often happened, their Ambassador at Constantinople, Murray, was infinitely more Turkish than his Government. More enlightened upon English interests in the East because he saw things from closer at hand, he strove to get the Turks to ask for the mediation of England. The Turks replied with much good sense : 'It is so extraordinary for England to offer her mediation to the Porte while she has ships in the Russian fleet, that there is every reason to fear that this apparent solicitude may be only a mask disguising hostile projects ; let England, then, explain herself straight-forwardly, that the Porte may clearly know what cause she has embraced.' England had earned this distrust and disdain. She perceived that she had carried her com-plaisance to Russia too far ; she recalled the officers who were serving on the Russian fleet, and suspended enlist-ments for the service of the Czarina. But it was too late, and when the effect of these prudential measures could make itself felt, mediation had been asked of others. But how did the Turks, who looked askance at the intentions of England, a mere busybody in Russia's service, come to show so much confidence in Prussia, the ally of their enemy? Frederick the Great's art, and the skill of his Minister Zegelin, certainly went for something. And, moreover, the Turks showed their perspicacity in preferring an ally of Russia who would not fight for her to a so-called friend of the Turks who had supplied Russia with the true victor of Cheshmeh. However, it was not for himself alone that Frederick desired the task of mediation ; he desired it, and desired it mainly, for Austria. Zegelin, 'by dint of reiterating the same representations,' managed to convince the Turks ' of the decisive weight which so great a Power as that of the House of Austria might lend to the negotia-tions,' and on August 12, 1770, the Divan resolved to address an official demand to the Sovereigns of Prussia and Austria.

The Austrians, alarmed for their interests, their self-esteem pricked by the Russian successes, were awaiting this demand with much impatience. The Court of Vienna was continuing its precautions, completing its armaments, and extending the cordon which covered its frontiers on the side of Poland. The Zips affair had run its course. After discovering that it had ancient rights to make good over that county, the Chancery of Vienna, which professed the cult of forms and a taste for procedure, hunted up the titles upon which these ancient rights rested. The study of the titles naturally furnished a proof that the rights were infinitely more extended than had at first been imagined. By a lucky coincidence, it was found that the famous salt-mines of Weliczka and Bokhnia were contained in the territory to which it was thought a legal claim might justly be made. The right being established, Austria did not hesitate to take the object of the dispute in pledge, pending the issue of the suit which she proposed to institute on this matter against the Polish Government. On July 19 the order was given to take up the eagles which had previously been planted, and to carry them as far as the ancient rights demanded. Thus, at the moment when Prince Henry received his orders to go to St. Petersburg, the King of Prussia was starting for Moravia ; Joseph was coming to await his arrival there, and two very different but equally important events—the demand for mediation by the Turks, and the occupation of districts of Poland by the Austrians—combined to make each interview the starting-point of unexpected negotiations.

CHAPTER X.

THE INTERVIEW AT NEUSTADT.

(September, 1770.)

THE Emperor and the King of Prussia met at Neustadt on September 3, 1770, but this time the Emperor was accompanied by Kaunitz. The old Chancellor held the front of the stage alone, keeping all matters of business for himself, leaving to Joseph only the reviews, the parades, and the table-talk—in fact, treating him, says Frederick, ' with much haughtiness, and more as a subaltern than a master.' Frederick and Kaunitz talked for a moment after dinner on the first day, ' in each other's pockets, as the saying is, near the embrasure of a window in the dining-room.' These conversations by fits and starts, just skimming each subject, suited the King of Prussia's nimble intellect, suited his incisive manner, and the effects of surprise which he loved to produce; but they were disconcerting to Kaunitz's pedantry. ' He talked for a good while about the present war and the future pacification,' he wrote to Maria Theresa; ' but with little enough of order and sequence in the arrangement of his ideas.' Frederick said that it was above all on Austria's account that he wished for peace. ' If Russia were to cross the Danube,' he added, ' Austria would not be able to allow it, and a general war might ensue. It would be well to be beforehand, and to

make peace during the winter.   It was to be believed that
the Russians would be satisfied with the Crimea and Azof,
and with the independence of Moldavia and Wallachia.
The Turks, in the present dilapidated state of their affairs,
would probably accept those conditions ; Austria should
support them with all her weight.'   Kaunitz deemed this
policy of the King of Prussia very lacking in enlightenment, ' very petty and very inconsequent.'   He asked for
a meeting on the morrow, promising himself that he would
show him how to link fine ideas together, and teach him
how to treat great matters learnedly.   ' It was necessary
before all,' he wrote to Maria Theresa, ' to make him take
a larger and better view in matters of policy, to give him
some opinion of our enlightenment, and an entire confidence
in our intentions.'

In the night two couriers arrived, one for the Emperor,
the other for the King of Prussia.   They brought the
demand for mediation from the Turks.   Kaunitz was
determined to lay down his principles and to propound
his argument, so the couriers caused no change in his
plans.

On September 4 he betook himself at the appointed
time to the King, who begged him to be seated.   Scarcely
had he sat down, when, without giving Frederick time to
begin the conversation, he begged him to listen quietly
and without interruption to the exposition which he had
to give him.   It was a discourse in eight headings, and its
object was to show that the policy of Austria was at once
the wisest, the most able, the most loyal, and the most
pacific that could possibly be imagined.   Following this
system, the Court of Vienna had avoided taking any part
in the troubles of Poland, had refused to join with Russia
for the destruction and partition of the Ottoman Empire,
' which in that case would not perhaps have been very
difficult to effect,' and had sought to live sincerely at

peace and with a good understanding with Prussia. She looked for the same sentiments from the King of Prussia. His alliance with Russia was the corollary of the alliance of Austria with France; it gave Prussia 'the advantage of having her back free for the future; the alliance with France rendered Austria the same service.' An alliance with Russia was contrary to the pacific system of Austria, 'since she had renounced all idea of reconquering Silesia, unless Prussia should make a fresh war upon her. By coquetting with Russia, Austria would only succeed in strengthening that Power as against Prussia, and in making her more exacting; the case would be similar if the King thought of coquetting with France. It would be better, then, for each to practise abstention, and for each to behave with honour and honesty towards the other's ally, but nothing more.' There was no obstacle to a good agreement between Prussia and Austria; for its sanction, there was no need to have recourse to treaties, which, moreover, could only be made with the participation of their allies. It was enough to agree upon principles. These principles Kaunitz had 'minuted' in the form of a *Political Catechism*; they would promise to conform to them, 'and that,' he said, 'would be infinitely more service-able than all the treaties in the world.' The *Catechism* summed up Kaunitz's declarations, was the object of a reciprocal undertaking, and laid down that the two Courts would in all things behave the one towards the other with the most entire confidence and with the largest loyalty.

Frederick allowed Kaunitz to talk his fill. When the old Chancellor had finished, the King rose, embraced him, and declared that it was impossible to speak better language; that the *Catechism* was a masterpiece, and that he would be fortunate in having it always before his eyes. Then he came to business—that is to say, to the mediation. 'This accursed Turkish war alarms and disturbs me,' he said; 'I

should be distressed to find myself drawn against my will
into a fresh war against you; and I am sensible that if the
Russians cross the Danube, as you would be quite unable
to remain passive spectators of that event and of their
further advances, that misfortune might come upon me,
if, among the different courses that are open to you, you
were to choose that of going to war in Poland. . . .'
Kaunitz answered that everything depended upon Russia;
that Austria would certainly be obliged to go to war if
Russia attempted to keep any considerable conquests, or
to stipulate that matters in Poland should remain on such
a footing as should make that kingdom a Russian province.
'Things in Poland will easily be arranged if there is agreement upon the rest,' Frederick rejoined. He added that
he considered Kaunitz's observations most luminous; 'but
the Czarina is a woman and is vain; she will need careful
handling. Provide me with some weapons, I beg of you,
which I can use to frighten her.' And, after appearing to
reflect for a moment, he resumed: 'Could you not, for
instance, let Roumanzow know that you count on his not
resolving to cross the Danube? Or else, could you not
persuade France to make a declaration to you that if, on
the Russians crossing the Danube, you were to determine
to break with her (Russia) and to go to war with her, she
(France) would send you a hundred thousand men to help
you? You would confide the news to me, I would make
use of it, and no doubt it would have its effect. Pray be
so good as to tell me what you think of it.' Kaunitz, for
all his experience, was too infatuated with his system and
ideas to fathom the deep design which lurked under this
suggestion casually thrown out. He had no suspicion of
the way in which the King of Prussia meditated 'arranging
matters in Poland,' and how much Frederick wished that
the Czarina might feel herself compelled to seek elsewhere
than on the Danube for an indemnification for her ex-

penses, and for the reward of her victories. ' I was much astonished,' Kaunitz reports, ' to hear such puerile ideas issue from the lips of the Prince, who is, moreover, possessed of considerable intellect.' He refrained, nevertheless, from showing any signs of this, and out of ' consideration for a great Prince like him,' he confined himself to saying that the means were not good, and that he advised the King to write to the Czarina. He was even so obliging as to give the substance of the letter. Frederick listened, and complimented him greatly ' upon the depth and form of all that he had just heard ; he added that he would make notes upon the subject as soon as he reached his room, so that he might forget nothing.'

Before leaving the King, Kaunitz thought fit to tell him frankly what Austria meant to write to France on the subject of the interview. This confidence is interesting, as it shows clearly the light in which the chief author of the alliance of 1756 regarded its execution. ' I told him,' Kaunitz reports, ' that we would certainly leave nothing to be desired by our ally France as to the scrupulousness with which we discharged our obligations to her, nor even in our manner of so doing ; but that, as we had not accustomed her to venture to demand from us accommodations out of conformity with our system of peace, or any sort of dependent attitude, we would confine ourselves to informing her ;' that the interview between the two Sovereigns, agreed upon a year ago, had passed off very well ; that ' as affairs of State had not been its object, probably there would have been no question of dealing with them, had it not happened that precisely while the King was at Neustadt, despatches from Constantinople had reached him at the same time as they reached us '; that the Porte had asked for mediation ; that they had spoken of the matter ; that it had been decided to consent if Russia agreed to it ; and that, if the Czarina wished to bring England into it, Austria would stipulate that France should also take part. Frederick, of course, thought it admirable. Austria, he said, had been accommodating to France ; she had allowed her to take Corsica ; from the same motives Prussia ought to be accommodating to Russia. ' It is not,' he went on, ' that I am not sensible of its inconvenience ; but what can I do ? As long as one is the ally of another State one cannot do otherwise. I understand very well that some day this Russia may make it necessary for us to unite against her, to check the course of this torrent which may engulf us, and for that reason I confess I was ·not sorry when France made her miss her blow at the last diet in Sweden ; but the time for that has not yet come, and in the meanwhile we must have patience.'

This interview had exhausted all the great matters of State. It was agreed that Frederick should write ' to his Empress,' that Austria should use her influence with the Divan, and that, if the answer from St. Petersburg was favourable, the two Courts should take in hand the arrangement of a peace. The Austrians left on September 7. At the moment of parting from Kaunitz, Frederick said again : ' Will you not give me your little *Catechism*, then ? It seems to me so full of sense, and I should much like to have it always under my eyes, because I sincerely wish to conform to it.' Kaunitz answered that he would refer the matter to the Empress. He was under the spell. The impression which he carried away from Neustadt was that he had fathomed the King of Prussia, that he had subjugated him, and that from thenceforth he could guide him any way he chose. The letter which he wrote to Maria Theresa on September 7, the day of his departure from Neustadt, is a monument of fatuity. ' I am convinced,' he said, ' that my conversation has made a very lively impression on the King of Prussia, and has modified his

sentiments.' The King would address himself to Russia
in his own name, and so as not to compromise Austria,
should Russia refuse mediation. There was every reason
to believe, he added, that the King of Prussia 'has adopted
with much deference the direction which I suggested to
him, and which he was to give to this step ; that, moreover, he has undertaken with much docility to try to carry
out, with regard to Russia, a method which I suggested to
him to make it possible to settle the troubles and distractions of Poland ; that for the future he will trust us as
much as it is possible for him to trust anyone, and that
we shall be able to trust him much more than it would
have been reasonable to do up to now.' As for the *Political
Catechism*, Kaunitz opined that copies should be exchanged
with a promise to conform to it.[1] It was not at all the
opinion of the Sovereigns, and all that was effected was
an exchange of autographs without signatures and without
promises.

Maria Theresa was far from sharing the passions of her
son or the illusions of her Minister. She had an infinitely
greater store of common-sense than Joseph, and of rectitude
than Kaunitz. She feared adventures, and understood
nothing of all the subtleties of her Chancery's new system.
Joseph's hatred against France made her uneasy ; she was
attached to the alliance, and more than ever since Marie
Antoinette's marriage. 'This anti-French leaven breaks
out on every opportunity, and at the present time more
than ever,' she wrote to Mercy on September 1. 'I have
the annoyance of being unable for the most part to per-

---

[1] For the story of the interview at Neustadt, *vide* Kaunitz's
reports to Maria Theresa of September 3, 7, and 18, published by
Beer, *Archiv für Oesterreichische Geschichte*, vol. xlvii. ; Beer, *Erste
Theilung Polens*, vol. i., chap. viii. ; Duncker, pp. 198-205 ; Arneth,
vol. viii., pp. 210-225 ; Ranke, vol. i., pp. 9-12 ; Frederick, *Œuvres*,
vol. vi., p. 29.

suade the Emperor to share my views; his are very often
different; this injures our affairs greatly, and makes my
life unbearable. I sigh only for peace. Try to make men
think the same where you are ; the good Mussulmans are
sacrificed to the excitability of your gentry; plague, famine,
and everything else is coming, and none will suffer from
them more than we shall.' On September 16, after receiving
Kaunitz's reports on the interview, she replied to him : ' I
recommend you, still in preference to the Prussian, to
preserve the French alliance, which is your first and only
work ; we should support and flatter them occasionally.'
They were flattered, and it suited them to be satisfied with
flattery;[2] but that was all the Empress could obtain. The
instinctive fears which she expressed to Mercy were only
too well founded, and Frederick the Great was soon to
give the Austrians, in his own way, a lesson of prudence
and of loyalty.

[2] *Vide* Mercy's report to Maria Theresa of October 20, 1770.

CHAPTER XI.

THE MEDIATION.

(September, 1770—January, 1771.)

FREDERICK returned from Neustadt perfectly satisfied ; but the instructions which he addressed to his brother Henry were far from being as formidable as Kaunitz would have wished. The Austrian diplomatist soothed himself with an empty hope when he imagined that he had led Frederick into a blunder. That King wrote on September 9 : 'I am about to send a courier to Russia to learn whether the Empress approves of this mediation, or whether she refuses it. I believe that the Court of Vienna will allow Russia to have Azof without jealousy, provided that Wallachia and Moldavia are given back, and that the despot of those provinces remains under Turkish sovereignty.' He hinted that if the Czarina showed no moderation either in the East or in Poland, there might result ' such considerable troubles that they would engage all Europe in this quarrel.' It was an allusion to France, and Frederick counted greatly on this argument to move the Czarina. A few days afterwards, on October 1, he returned to the same subject, and in a more urgent tone: 'The Porte has asked for my mediation, and for that of the Court of Vienna. We are awaiting the answer of the Empress ; will she accept this mediation—yes or no ?'

Frederick had his reasons for putting this pressure on the Czarina. The offer of mediation could not be received with much eagerness at St. Petersburg. There they were victors, and they preferred to negotiate directly with the Sultan. The Turks had no army remaining on the left bank of the Danube; the places which they still held were falling one after another into the hands of the Russians. Roumanzow was pushing on the sieges with vigour; he had grounds for hoping that within six weeks the Turks would be dislodged from all their fortresses, and that the left bank of the Danube, which had been really won since August, would be wholly subjected to Russia. Count Panin, on his side, was labouring to establish his Sovereign's supremacy over the Tartars. On August 17 he had treated with the delegates from the Tartars of Bessarabia; he had promised them independence, and they had pledged themselves to endeavour to induce the Tartars of the Crimea also to throw off the Ottoman yoke.

The Czarina did not wish to be stopped in so fine a career. Warned by England of the demand for mediation addressed to Prussia and Austria, she wanted to be beforehand with it, and to confront the mediation with an accomplished fact. On September 26 she instructed General Roumanzow to write to the Grand Vizier that she would be inclined to open *pourparlers* for peace as soon as her Minister Obreskof should be set at liberty. This direct step was the best pledge of her pacific intentions, and she did not fail to call the attention of the Prussian Minister, Solms, to it, when he asked her, on Frederick's behalf, whether she was disposed to accept mediation. She charged Panin to set forth the inconveniences attaching to the proposal.[1] That Minister turned aside Frederick's arguments with great skill. The King of Prussia proposed his mediation in order to avoid French intervention in the

[1] Note to Solms, September 29, 1770 : Beer, *Documents*, p. 104.

war ; Panin replied that, if mediation were to take place, France would move heaven and earth to mix herself up in it—that nothing was so decidedly distasteful to the Czarina ; that, moreover, if there were mediation, the Czarina would be obliged to invite England to take part in it, as that country had behaved very handsomely to Russia. To avoid all these complications, wrote the Czarina to Frederick on October 9, ' the name and form of mediation must be avoided. I am ready to accept the good offices of the Court of Vienna. I claim those of Your Majesty.'

The counter-stroke was clever, and was not at all to the King of Prussia's taste. Fond as he was of bantering others, he did not at all like being repaid in the same coin. ' I am firmly resolved not to mix myself up in the affairs of Poland, but to be a mere spectator of events,' he wrote to his brother on October 26 ; ' those people may accept or refuse us as mediators, but they must not be allowed to laugh at us openly.' It was only a passing fit of temper; if he readily abandoned the procedure of mediation, he by no means abandoned his thoughts in the direction of peace. On October 30 he urged the danger of a conquest or subjugation of Wallachia; he demanded that Russia should make ' a tolerable plan of pacification for Poland,' and that she should communicate it to Prussia and Austria. At the same time he took precautions against every eventuality. Russia appeared to wish to order the affairs of Poland by herself; Austria had just occupied Zips. The plague was raging in Poland, and the war in the East had aggravated the scourge; the number of Russians and Poles who had succumbed was estimated at 16,000. Berlin and Vienna both trembled at the approach of the contagion.[2] Frederick drew a preventive

[2] Mercy to Maria Theresa, September 19 ; Maria Theresa to Mercy, October 30, 1770. ' Thiébault relates that Berlin thought

cordon along the Polish frontiers,[3] with the possibility in view of transforming it into a corps of observation, and of extending it, if necessary, if Russia became too arrogant, and if Austria pushed the assertion of her claims too far. The measure served two objects: it protected the health of the Prussian people and ministered to the King's policy.

In the meanwhile Prince Henry had reached St. Petersburg on October 12. There he was fêted and flattered in every way. The Czarina meant that all Germany should hear of the esteem she had for the Prince, and of the brilliant reception which she was giving him. She wrote to Mme. de Bielke: 'He has asked to be at his ease; that is what we like, too. He is fond of conversation; I enjoy a talk. I think he is not altogether without enjoyment here. That is as I wish it to be. We must do him justice; this hero does not belie his great reputation; putting aside his birth, it is a man of the first merit.' Prince Henry had a high-flying mind, he was a great lover of speculations in politics and philosophy, and was always ready to improvise vast systems. At St. Petersburg he found accommodating listeners and interlocutors ready to discuss with him. In truth, there was a great deal of chatter. Panin had formerly replied to the Lynar scheme by a plan for a Triple Alliance. It was an idea for the future to realize, and Europe has known something of it. The Partition League of 1772, the coalitions of 1792 to 1814, the Holy Alliance of 1815, the alliance of the three Emperors in 1872, Poland erased from the list of States, Napoleon I. exiled to St. Helena, Napoleon III. a

---

itself seized with the Plague; the entire town armed itself with aromatic vinegar': Saint-Priest, *Le Partage de la Pologne*, chap. iv.

[3] Letter to Prince Henry, October 15, 1770: Duncker, pp. 210 and 226.

prisoner at Sedan, France invaded thrice and dismembered, Germany unified in the hands of Prussia, the Turkish Empire encroached upon on every side—so many and so great revolutions in the European system, carried out within the space of a century, have shown all the scope of Panin's idea, and placed Prince Henry of Prussia's journey into Russia among the events of history. That Prince, in his very precise and lucid diplomatic letters, composed in his own style his *Soirées de Saint-Petersbourg*. It is a remarkable book, of which some pages are known and deserve study.

On October 31 the Prince wrote to his brother the King: 'Saldern called on me yesterday, and asked me whether Panin had spoken to me of the advantages which Austria might have obtained. I answered, " Yes," and added: " If we are to deal in political dreams, we might think of forming a Triple Alliance between Prussia, Russia, and Austria, in the event of its proving impossible to make the Turks decide for peace, which would secure advantages for the three Courts respectively, when the Turks were reduced to peace." ' Saldern reported the remark to Panin, and the same evening, at the Court, the Russian Minister showed a strong disposition to take up the conversation on his own account at the point where Prince Henry had left it with Saldern. So the Triple Alliance was again spoken of, and also the particular arrangements which Prussia and Russia would have to make in the event of Austria refusing to adhere to that system. 'On this last point,' wrote the Prince on November 27, 'I was unwilling to make any further advance, not yet knowing your answer on the subject of the Triple Alliance. I see that it is thought very desirable here, if it is possible. Solms, to whom I have never spoken of it, came and told me that I might rest assured that, if a Triple Alliance could be formed, it would be preferred here to all the advantages that could be gained. I replied that I had no answer to give, as I had received no orders from you. If this alliance were formed, it could only be on the condition that a good account should be kept on your behalf of the advantages which Austria might gain over the Turks, as you could not admit any modification of the balance of power between yourself and Austria. . . . If you think this alliance possible, I am of opinion that an understanding should first be arrived at with Austria. If you succeed, I can almost guarantee the consent of this Court. In the contrary case, it would still be easy to attain the end here, if it were only a question of acquisitions in Germany. If your share had to be taken in Poland, I have grounds for believing that considerable obstacles would be presented here. Austria can obtain all that she has lost, and more besides, all that she wants, at the expense of the Porte, even if she will go to the gates of Constantinople.'[4] Scheme-makers have been in all times very generous with their neighbours' goods. The law of nations as practised by the inventors of the Triple Alliance for themselves, and as taught to their successors, rests upon an adage which has become proverbial in the Chanceries : ' No one may enrich himself save at the expense of a third party.' This maxim is as old as statecraft, and, though we would not wrong the Greeks and Romans, Plutarch informs us that, as early as the times of Numa, ' violence, and the desire for forcible usurpation from others, were praised among the Barbarians.'

But while pursuing these speculations, the Russians were at no pains to formulate the conditions which they

---

[4] For this exchange of views on Poland, *vide* Martens, vol. vi., p. 67 ; Solms's Correspondence, Reports of October 16 and November 3, 1770, pp. 318, 320 ; Précis of Count Panin's Views, November 2, *ibid.*, p. 323 ; Count Solms's scheme regarding Poland, November 2, *ibid.*, p. 329.

claimed to impose upon the Turks ; they spoke of them
merely cursorily and in very vague terms, always postponing their reply to Prince Henry's questions upon this
point.   The fact was that the reply to Roumanzow's
overtures had not yet been received, and that there were
still some places to be taken to establish the Russian
power in the principalities of the Danube, and to prepare
for the independence of the Crimean Tartars.

Frederick had a very good notion of this, and he was
just as impatient to anticipate the accomplished fact as
the Czarina was to confront the mediators with it.   So
much as had transpired of the Russians' intentions seemed
fairly moderate ; Frederick enjoyed exaggerating the scope
of these half-confidences ; he hoped, by praising the
Czarina's moderation, to strengthen her inclinations, and
to induce her to give official confirmation to her Ministers'
hints.   ' Forgiveness to our enemies is an admirable
quality, and it is still more so not to overwhelm them
when it is in our power to crush them,' he wrote to
Prince Henry ; ' clemency, humanity, generosity—these
issue from the heart of the Sovereign ; this glory is a
personal glory, and none may dispute its possession.   The
attributes that made Cæsar the first of the Romans were
his vast genius and his clemency ; and I am rejoiced to
find the same great qualities in the Empress, whose faithful ally I am.   I could go on for ever on this subject, my
dear brother ; the matter is inexhaustible. . . .'   He thus
celebrated and glorified the Czarina's virtues, in the hope
that there would be something to show for it ; at heart
he was waiting uneasily for Panin to translate the fine
sentiments of his Sovereign into the style of the Chancery.
Zegelin and Thugut had persuaded the Turks to talk of
peace, and even of an armistice.   Frederick hastened to
notify his brother of this.   ' I hope,' he wrote on November 11, ' that the Rubicon (i.e., the Danube) will not be

crossed. The Turks are asking for peace with might and main. . . . They will let Obreskof go as soon as they know for certain that Russia wishes for peace. . . . If the Russians cross the Rubicon, it will no longer be possible to check the Austrians, and you may depend upon it that a general war would inevitably result.' That was what he feared beyond everything.

The Triple Alliance appeared to him by no means a sufficient compensation for the dangers of a fresh war. ' This work, so expedient for humanity,' as Panin described it, seemed to Frederick to be inexpedient for Prussia, and he did not wish for it. Before speculating upon the future, he aimed at ordering the affairs of the present, without allowing himself to be lured away by pompous promises. ' We shall see spring upon us,' he wrote, on December 5, ' and then it will be said that to continue the war is indispensable. I am very much afraid that that is what it will come to, and then I shall be treated as a milch-cow, for subsidies which are merely money thrown into the sea. I hope, my dear brother, that my guess is wrong, but I fear that those gentry have not got their system quite arranged, and that they will try to keep you hanging on as long as they can.'

While Frederick, to soften the Czarina, and to persuade her to take the Court of Vienna into account, was threatening her with a general war, in which France should intervene, the Chancery of Vienna was using all the resources of its diplomacy to divert the French from mixing in Eastern affairs. At Berlin, as at Vienna, they waged what may be called in military language a war of make-believe, and the pretended warlike wishes of France served for a pretext to cover the true designs which they pursued. The promptness with which the Czarina had repudiated the idea of any accession whatever of France to the mediation occupied Kaunitz's thoughts

continually. He calculated that the French Government,
inconsistent and weak though it had become, would be
profoundly offended at seeing its ally, Austria, taking
part in a negotiation from which it was itself excluded,
especially if the Czarina brought England into it. The
Empress Maria Theresa would with difficulty be persuaded to give Louis XV. so good a ground for complaint.
Kaunitz, who was much attached to the idea of mediation,
saw but one way out of the difficulty. This way was as
bold as it was subtle; it was to throw the solution of the
difficulty upon France. Accordingly he wrote to Mercy
on October 25, 1770, instructing him to lay the state of
affairs before M. de Choiseul, to show how inconvenient
it would be for Austria to refuse the mediation, to add
that the inconvenience would be all the greater for France,
inasmuch as she herself would be excluded from the
negotiations, while England would be admitted to them;
that the Court of Vienna, nevertheless, wishing to do
nothing displeasing to the Court of Versailles, placed in
the hands of King Louis XV. the care of deciding what
line of conduct it should adopt, if the Czarina persisted in
inviting England and in excluding France.[5]

These refinements of diplomacy alarmed Maria Theresa
and pricked her conscience. She was sincerely attached to
the French alliance, and preferred giving up the mediation.
' I confess,' she wrote to Mercy, on October 30, 'that I
should wish to be out of it, and that the Russians might
come to a straightforward understanding with these
wretched people.' But Kaunitz, who possessed the art of
soothing his Sovereign's scruples, had not allowed himself
to be stopped. Without shutting his eyes to all the equivo-
cations and dangers that were involved in the step he had
ordered Mercy to take, he hoped for its success.

It was presuming too much on Choiseul's agreeableness.

[5] Arneth, vol. viii., p. 238.

His affection for the Austrian alliance did not go to the
extent of blindness, and he was not in the least deceived
as to the true intentions of Maria Theresa's Minister. He
wrote to Mercy on November 12, 1770: 'Your Excel-
lency's Court fills up the measure of its courtesy by
referring to the King the acceptance of the mediation concurrently with England and with His Majesty of Prussia,
or the refusal of the mediation without the admission of
France. We are sensible that the interests of France
would be in jeopardy in the hands of the Courts of Berlin
and London, if their partiality were not enlightened and
restrained by an Austrian mediation; but this essential
opposition itself, which has attracted the attention of the
King, appears to him another reason for thinking that, the
Imperial Court being, so to speak, disinterested in the
mediation, the interests of the King and those of the
alliance itself demand of us that Their Imperial Majesties
shall not accept the mediation concurrently with England, and to the exclusion of France.' According to
Choiseul, there were only two alternatives: to reject the
mediation if Russia persisted in her refusal, or, if it were
accepted, to give France 'formal and positive assurance
that no stipulation should be made which could be prejudicial to France, concerning the two essential points of
the commerce of the Black Sea and of the establishment
of the English in those quarters.'

Mercy, who had tried 'every means that prudence would
allow' to convince Choiseul, considered this reply 'most
extraordinary'; 'it was dictated,' he said, 'by a spirit of
distrust and jealousy;' it proved how the courtesy and
complaisance that Her Majesty had been pleased to show
to the most Christian King were abused at Versailles. . . .'[6]
Kaunitz regarded it as 'hardly serious,' and he was quite
right.   The resentment it aroused in him naturally

[6] Mercy to Maria Theresa, November 16, 1770.

strengthened his wish to come to an understanding with
the King of Prussia.   Frederick had known how to flatter
him; he had been skilful enough to admire his subtleties;
he thus brought him gently into his game, and little by
little he attached Austria to his own policy, and dominated
her while appearing to be beguiled by her.

Prince Henry exerted himself to convince the Russians.
He tried in vain; the Czarina resolved to disclose her
conditions of peace only at the end of December.   The
reason was that the campaign was then over; Bender had
been taken after a two months' siege; Ackermann soon
followed suit; Braïla surrendered on November 22.   The
little fortress of Giurgevo alone on the left bank of the
Danube remained in possession of the Turks.   In the
East General Tottleben, after having subdued Georgia,
had advanced up to the Black Sea.   Roumanzow did not
think it wise to cross the Danube and to pursue the Turks
on the right bank.   The Russian army went into winter-
quarters; it had made great conquests, but the time of
year condemned it to rest.   The Czarina thought there
was now no obstacle to negotiation.   She wrote to the
King of Prussia on December 20, that the last events of
the war enabled her to secure an equitable, honourable,
and safe peace for her subjects; that the object which she
had in view harmonized with the interests of all the Christian Powers which judged these matters impartially; that
the release of Obreskof remained the condition preliminary
to all *pourparlers* for peace; that those *pourparlers* might
be opened in a town of Moldavia or of Poland.   As for
the conditions, the Czarina thought it premature to communicate them to the Turks; before informing the Court
of Vienna of them, it was necessary to wait for a better
knowledge of that Government's intentions.   'I confess,
however,' she continued, 'that I should be very unwilling
to lessen the advantages which a closer intimacy with

Austria would give to our alliance by any excess of reserve, or by any signs of estrangement. For if it were possible to tear Austria away from the insensate system which she has adopted, and to induce her to share our views, Germany would be brought back to its natural condition, and Austria, drawn towards other objects, would cease from directing glances prompted by her present connections against the possessions of Your Majesty.'[7] A memorandum attached to the letter gave the conditions of peace, which the Czarina confided to the King of Prussia : they were, the cession of Azof, and of Great and Little Kabarda in Circassia; the independence of Moldavia and Wallachia, or the retention of those principalities under Russian rule for twenty-five years by way of an indemnity ; the independence of the Tartars of Bessarabia and of the Crimea, the free navigation of the Black Sea, an island in the Archipelago to serve as a centre for Russian trade, and a general amnesty for the Greeks who had taken the side of the Russians.

The independence of the principalities, and of the country of the Tartars, really meant the subjection of those countries to Russia. 'Convincing as were,' according to a Russian historian, 'the arguments which the Empress Catharine brought to bear, to show the need for indemnifying Russia for the sacrifices she had made, and, once for all, to make the Turks harmless as against the Christian populations of Europe,'[8] Frederick failed to be touched by them. The letter of December 20 was very far from confirming the confidence which had formerly inspired him with such fair meditations on the clemency and moderation of Kings. 'Conditions of such enormity,' he says in his *Memoirs*, 'would have been the last straw for the Court of Vienna.' He was the more stirred by them in that,

[7] Duncker, p. 219 ; Frederick, *Œuvres*, vol. vi., p. 33.
[8] Martens, vol. ii., p. 10.

during one night between December 2 and 4, the Reis-
Effendi had declared to the Austrian and Prussian
Ministers that 'the existing Constitution of the Ottoman Empire allowed its ruler to enter upon no private
negotiation with a State with which it was at war'; that
he had informed General Roumanzow of this; and that he
persisted in his unwillingness to negotiate for peace, save
through the mediation of Prussia and Austria.[9]   Frederick
had communicated the first Russian note on the subject of
the mediation to Vienna; the Austrians had replied ' that
they were being laughed at,' and the King of Prussia had
deemed the answer not 'edifying' enough to be sent to
St. Petersburg.[10]   Thus, the Turks persisted in their
demand for mediation, and the arrangements of Russia
made that mediation impossible.   Frederick wrote to
Prince Henry on January 3, 1771: 'I was dumfounded,
my dear brother, when I received the proposals for peace
which the Russians put forward.   I can never undertake
to propose them to the Turks, nor to the Austrians, for
in good truth they are quite unacceptable.   That which
concerns Wallachia could not possibly be fitted in with
the Austrian system; in the first place, the Empress will
never abandon the French alliance; and, in the second,
she will never tolerate the Russians in her neighbourhood.
You may regard that document as a declaration of war.
They are laughing at us when they give us a lure of that
sort; for my part, as I can in no way compromise myself
to oblige the Russians, I shall make some remarks to them
on the consequences of their proposals, and, if they do not
change them, I shall beg them to charge some other Power
with them, and I shall withdraw from the game; for you
may depend upon it that the Austrians will go to war
with them; that is too much, and is insupportable for all

[9] Hammer, vol. xvi., p. 477 : *Pièces*.
[10] Frederick to Prince Henry, December 19, 1770.

the Powers of Europe. States are guided by their own interests; one may do something to oblige one's ally, but there are limits to everything; thus, whatever may be the result, I cannot possibly dissemble at this moment, and must speak out.' Consequently, Frederick instructed his brother to declare to the Russians, and he himself wrote to the Czarina, on January 5, 1771, that if she wished to avoid war with Austria, those articles would have to be struck out which concerned Moldavia, Wallachia, the independence of the Tartars and the island in the Archipelago; if she would be contented with Azof, the two Kabardas and the navigation of the Black Sea, mediation was possible, and Frederick undertook to secure the adhesion of Austria.

CHAPTER XII.

THE PRELIMINARIES OF THE PARTITION OF POLAND.

(November, 1770—January, 1771.)

THE line of conduct which was to be held with regard to the King of Prussia was at that time the problem that mainly absorbed the Court of Vienna. That Court debated it at length in the last days of November and at the beginning of December, 1770. The great thing, it seems, was to persuade Frederick to support the cause of mediation by force of arms, and, as a result of that, to detach him from Russia. Kaunitz proposed to promise him, in case of success, the provinces of Courland and Semigallia; as a compensation for this, Austria would keep Zips and the Moldavian territories, which she had occupied on the frontier of Transylvania. Poland would willingly pay that price for her liberation. It would be a partition, but a moderate partition, since Courland was only a fief of the Polish crown, and Zips a pledge over which Austria had 'ancient rights.' Maria Theresa did not approve at all. 'The plan of partition is finely conceived, but it is out of my reach,' she replied to Kaunitz. The divergences of opinion between her and the Emperor gave rise to discussions on every occasion, which affected her profoundly. And there was, besides, one point on which she appeared to be immovable: she would not have war at any price.

'I have too much affection for my people, for my own tranquillity, and at the least for securing it out of doors, as I do not enjoy it in my family,' she wrote to Marshal Lascy on November 27, 1770. '. . . Continue your advice to my son, but do not egg him on to war, and never, *never* against my Mussulmans.' Austria ended by deciding on a middle course, which was neither peace nor war. She armed herself, but less that she might be in a condition for fighting, than to intimidate Russia and to influence the resolutions of the King of Prussia. Van Swieten was sent to Berlin to find out Frederick's views.

Van Swieten's instructions are dated December 8, 1770. Kaunitz had 'thought it fitting to express them in French, since it is in that language that it is customary to speak to the King of Prussia.' They prescribed that Van Swieten should inform himself what were the intentions of the King, in the event of the Czarina insisting on her conditions of peace; to inform him of the secret designs on the East which Russia was pursuing, and in which she had proposed that Austria should join; to represent to Frederick the dangers attached to an increase in the Russian power, and to offer to oppose it. Joseph II., in a letter addressed to his brother, Leopold of Tuscany, summed up the ideas which were guiding Austrian policy, in spite of the opposition of the Empress. He indicated the circumstances in which Austria would be in a position to take action, and to indemnify herself at the expense of Turkey. 'The eventuality,' he said, 'may be twofold: 1. If the Russians cross the Danube in force and march towards Adrianople, it would be the time to move with an army corps on to the Danube, to cut them off in the rear, and consequently to compel them to execute a precipitate retreat; in this their army might be destroyed, and the Turks, saved from their destruction, would lend themselves more readily to a compensation for our real expenses. This would consist of the part of Wallachia which was ceded at the Peace of Belgrade, and which lies between the Banat, Transylvania, the Danube, and the Aluta. 2. If by sea, by the forcing of the Dardanelles, Constantinople, and consequently the whole empire, could be threatened with ruin, whether by a revolution or otherwise ; for we should necessarily have to occupy such provinces as would suit us, instead of leaving them to the Russians. For these two eventualities alone, Her Majesty has resolved to prepare the collection of a corps of 50,000 men. . . . So there we are, my dear brother, and, nevertheless, I believe it is all to no purpose, because the Russians will never cross the Danube, but will only trouble themselves to keep the Danube, and there to cover their operations against Otchakof and against the Crimea, which will be the real objects of their next campaign.'

The resolutions which Austria had just taken, and the military measures which were their result, precipitated the dénouement of the Zips affair. Under the impetus imparted by the Emperor, which was endured with much equanimity by Kaunitz, that affair had been roundly carried on, even too roundly, since the Government of Poland showed itself neither convinced of the 'ancient rights' of Austria, nor satisfied with the precautionary measures which she had taken. The more or less voluntary consent of Poland was the chief point in the method adopted by Kaunitz. If Poland showed herself recalcitrant, that would at once transform the assertion of rights into a brutal occupation, and nothing was more repugnant to the diplomatic delicacy of the Court of Vienna. The Chancery strove to save appearances by the aid of subtle distinctions. 'It is not,' said a report of October 18, 1770, ' *ad lucrum captandum,* but merely *ad damnum evitandum* that the eagles of Your Majesty have been advanced.' But none the less the Poles persisted in their protests ; all the first principles the schools could produce had nothing to do with the matter, and the High Chancellor of Poland needed to be no great jurist to ascertain that the territory of the republic had been invaded, a deed which has in all times passed for a violation of International Law. He said so in so many words, and Kaunitz was distressed. 'To my great regret,' he wrote to the Empress on October 30, 1770, 'from what reaches me from all sides as to the validity of our titles, I very much fear that this man is only too right in calling that which we have thought ourselves able to undertake a conquest.' 'I have a very poor opinion of our titles,' Maria Theresa answered. But though they had a taste for scrupulousness at Vienna, reasons of State always carried the day against conscience. When that Court decided, at the end of December, to take up a more threatening attitude with regard to Russia, and began to discuss the compensations which it might demand if an agreement was arrived at with the King of Prussia, it was deemed prudent to take possession of part of those territories in Poland to which it had laid claim. On December 9, 1770, the Crown of Hungary definitely took possession of Zips, and the Governor adopted the very significant title of Administrator Provinciæ Reincorporatæ.

The Cabinet of Versailles might be justly offended by the incorporation of the county of Zips, and by Swieten's mission to Berlin; but this consideration, it appeared, had not stopped the Court of Vienna. The Emperor, whose will always prevailed in the end, took no thought for the interests of France, because he had no opinion of her strength. He wrote to Leopold on December 18: 'The troubles between Spain and England, far from being ended, appear to be more serious than ever, and a rupture seems almost inevitable. People will quarrel about very little; in the meanwhile, our neutrality with the King of Prussia, not to allow war in Germany, is secure, and that removes all uneasiness. In France they are in great difficulties, seeing in what a pitiable state they are, and people have even talked of breaking the Family Compact and of leaving Spain to get out of her difficulties alone. Time will enlighten us.' What time did show, and that much too quickly and much too clearly, was the ruin of France's political credit. A fortnight after he had written this letter, Joseph learnt that Choiseul had fallen. That Minister, who had some greatness of imagination, had neither system in his wishes, firmness in his ideas, nor consistency in his character. He had had a finger in every affair, had made enemies everywhere, and had made sure of a line of retreat nowhere. All his allies were failing him. The Court of Vienna, to which he had sacrificed everything, entangled his whole policy. The Poles brought him nothing but deceptions. He had no longer any hope from the Turks. He had affronted England, and Prussia and Russia were his declared enemies. At home he was at open strife with the Parlements. He sought to lean upon the party of the Philosophers; but that party was from its nature entirely Russian and Prussian, reproving the fanaticism of the Poles and condemning that of the Turks. The 'Faction of Mistresses' regarded Choiseul as a venturesome man whose policy disturbed the leisure of Versailles. The devout faction could not forgive him either for the expulsion of the Jesuits or for the alliance with the Crescent. Choiseul was left alone to struggle in 'an inextricable strait'; to issue from it, he would have had to have been a great diplomatist and a great reformer— in a word, a great statesman. For this Choiseul had only the requisite ambition and the pose. A Court dispute, which he had nevertheless in a measure provoked, arose opportunely to throw him out of a maze of affairs, from which he could scarcely by himself have found an issue.[1]

---

[1] *Vide Le Secret du Roi*, vol. ii., p. 318 *et seq.*

There was a seraglio revolution, as people liked to call it then, at Versailles; the harem had long been warring with the divan, and it ended by gaining the day. Madame du Barry triumphed over Choiseul. The quarrel between England and Spain furnished the pretext. Choiseul's enemies alleged that he had fomented their differences in order to draw France into the war, to make himself indispensable, and to keep himself in power. Louis XV. wanted at any price to avoid war; the detestable coterie which governed him would have sacrificed the Family Compact to avoid that extremity. The King contented himself with sacrificing Choiseul. On December 24, 1770, the Minister was banished to his estates. France disappeared from the Eastern, and became insignificant upon the European, theatre. For six months she was without a Foreign Minister. Official diplomacy ceased to exist. What remained of the King's secret diplomacy was, in spite of the efforts, the zeal, and the invention which the Comte de Broglie displayed, a mere phantasm by means of which Louis XV. sought distraction from his incurable ennui, and strove to shut his eyes to the humiliating impotence to which he had condemned himself.[2]

Choiseul was the only man who still inspired the allies of France with some respect and her enemies with some fear. His disgrace was a relief to all the adversaries of French policy. Kaunitz ceased to take any heed of what was thought at Versailles. The Austrian Ambassador in France was even no longer informed of the negotiations. Mercy wrote two months afterwards, on February 25, 1771, in one of the direct and secret letters which he was wont to address to the Empress : 'Prince Stahremberg writes me that Your Majesty has deigned to authorize him

[2] *Vide Le Secret du Roi*, vol. ii., chap. viii. *Cf. Essais de Critique et d'Histoire*, the study entitled *La Diplomatie Secrète de Louis XV.*

to inform me of the resolutions that have been arrived at
with regard to the peace and the war between the Porte
and Russia ; he has, consequently, informed me of the
point which has been arrived at in view of this important
object, and has given me some light, *by some details*, on
the matter which the State Chancery *briefly notified to me*.'
Perhaps Maria Theresa was the only person who sincerely
regretted the Duc de Choiseul. ' I confess,' she wrote to
Mercy, on January 4, 1771, ' that I am very sensible of
the loss of Choiseul, and I fear that its effects will be felt
by us only too much. . . .' ' I am very grieved,' she
wrote to her daughter, two days later ; ' I have seen in
their behaviour [*sc.*, of the French] nothing but what is
honourable and humane, and betokening a sincere attachment to the alliance. . . .' The Empress's regrets were
but too well founded. She felt a presentiment that for
the future there would be nothing to check Austria in the
perilous course towards which she was being drawn by
Joseph's chimerical ambition, aided by the blind fatuity
of Kaunitz, and the machiavelic skill with which the King
of Prussia was able to exploit the passions and the weaknesses of men.

The fall of Choiseul and the effacement of French
policy completed the triumph of Catharine II. For
Louis XV.'s Minister she evinced a commiseration marked
rather by contempt than by magnanimity. ' I have so
little rancour against M. de Choiseul,' she wrote to Mme.
de Bielke,[3] ' that I pity him for his banishment. That
man, who thought to do me the greatest injury, has always
been mistaken, because his flatterers have never said anything to him save what was agreeable, and have left him
in perpetual ignorance of the truth. That has cast him
into a labyrinth of mistakes, from which there has resulted,
on the contrary, nothing but glory for me. I feel no ill will

[3] January 31, 1771.

against him; he had a perpetual "bee in his bonnet."[4] . . .'
Choiseul was the chief obstacle to an agreement between Russia and Austria upon Polish and Eastern
affairs. This agreement was desired by the Czarina;
before she knew of the disgrace of the French Minister,
she was endeavouring to prepare an adjustment, and,
when we know what the plan was which she was forming
at that time, we may understand with what joy she saw
herself freed from an adversary who, without being very
redoubtable in reality, might become very troublesome.
Panin had many times talked to Prince Henry of the
advantages which might accrue to Austria from an agreement with Russia, and from a Triple Alliance. Frederick
made one principal objection to this, which was Austria's
alliance with France, and the influence which he very
gratuitously attributed to Choiseul over the Court of
Vienna.

The Czarina had gone to Moscow towards the end of
December; she came back on January 6, 1771. Prince
Henry had accompanied her. On her arrival she heard
of the military preparations of Austria and of the incorporation of Zips. These measures were directed against
Russia. If the least doubt had been felt on this subject,
the King of Prussia's letters to his brother would have
removed it. The Czarina, however, did not appear at all
disturbed by the circumstances, and so far from finding
them a reason for abandoning her scheme of conquests,
she discovered in them a means of assuring its success.
The King of Prussia counselled moderation, because otherwise Austria would go to war, and because he had no wish
to be involved in such war. To adjust everything, an
expedient had to be devised of such a character that it
should satisfy at once the King of Prussia and the Court

[4] The original expression in French, ' Il était étourdi comme un
hanneton,' has no very exact equivalent in English.—TRANSLATOR.

of Vienna. It was necessary at the same time to reassure
Frederick, to attach him more closely than ever to Russia,
and to bring it about that, instead of his holding aloof
from fear of Austria, his interest should be to persuade
that Court to subscribe to Russia's conditions. The Czarina
found herself placed in circumstances analogous to those
in which Frederick was standing when he sketched out Count
Lynar's scheme; the same difficulties led Catharine II. to
propose the same solution.

Prince Henry wrote to the King on January 8, 1771,
that if the Court of Vienna were not so solidly attached
to France, Prussia might gain some profitable arrangements from the present conjunctures; that General Bibikof,
a friend of Panin and a man in high favour with the
Czarina, had talked to him of the gains which the Cabinet
of Vienna might get at the Peace. Bibikof had added
that in that case it would be just that Prussia, too, should
have her gain ; that they were ill-informed at Vienna of
the intentions of the Russian Court ; that Russia was
disposed to lend herself to everything, provided it was
only a question of spoiling the Turks, and that she would
content herself with the smallest share of the booty.[5]
Having written this letter, the Prince betook himself to
the Court, and on his return he added the following
postscript to his despatch :[6] ' I have been at the Empress's
this evening, and she said to me, joking, that the Austrians
had seized the two starosties,[7] and that they had set up
the Imperial arms on their frontiers. She added : " But
why should not everyone take something too ?" I answered
that although you, my dear brother, had drawn a cordon
in Poland, yet you had not occupied any starosties. " But,"
said the Empress, laughing, " why not occupy some ?" A
moment later Count Czernichef came up to me, and spoke

---

[5] Duncker, p. 229.   [6] Frederick, *Œuvres*, vol. xxvi., p. 345.
[7] Zips and Sandecz.

on the same subject, adding : " But why not take the bishopric of Warmia ? For, after all, each must have something." Although these remarks were only spoken in jest, it is very certain that they were not made idly, and I am convinced that it will be very possible that you may profit by this opportunity.' On the same day Solms wrote to the King of Prussia : ' The taking possession of the starosty of Sandecz has made a great impression at St. Petersburg. It is said that Prussia should take Warmia, as an indemnification for the subsidies which she has paid, and that the Russians, to recoup themselves for the charges of the war, should annex Polish Livonia and Lithuania up to the Dwina and the Dnieper. These circumstances are very favourable for the three Courts,' the Prussian Minister added.

Prince Henry resumed the conversation with Panin. That Minister was but moderately pleased with the Austrian invasions in Poland. ' He said nothing to me about the bishopric of Warmia,' Prince Henry wrote on January 11, 1771. ' That all comes of divided counsels ; all those who are drawn towards aggrandizement would have everyone take something, so that Russia might gain also, while Count Panin is inclined for tranquillity and peace. However, I will get some light upon this business ; and I am still of opinion that you risk nothing by seizing that bishopric on some plausible pretext, if the news is true that the Austrians have, in fact, taken those two starosties, over which it is said that they claim some rights which they have looked up in the archives in Hungary.'

While this talk was going on at St. Petersburg, Frederick was losing patience at Berlin, and, thinking it sound policy to make Russia uneasy, he did not disguise his ill-humour. He wrote to Prince Henry on January 11 : ' If I were to undertake the negotiations on the bases proposed by the Empress, war would be declared in the spring between

Austria and Russia.   Do you not see that the Russians wish to have their back free, so that they may dispose of Poland as they please on the first opportunity ?   I should commit the unpardonable fault of myself riveting my own chains, and all the profit I should enjoy would be that of Polyphemus—to be devoured at the end of it all. They wish for war; otherwise they would not insist on Wallachia, nor on the independence of the Tartars, nor on the island in the Archipelago.   I will not slave for their aggrandizement without some stipulation in my favour.   I stand by what I have written to the Empress, and if that produces no effect, I retire from the game. You will do well to think about returning.'   This letter made an impression at St. Petersburg, even too much impression.   'I did not expect,' said the Czarina, 'to hear the King of Prussia plead the cause of the Turks.'   However, she showed a more accommodating disposition, and gave it to be understood that in the course of the negotiations she would abandon part of her claims.   She wrote to the King of Prussia on January 20, 1771.   She would never negotiate, she said, at Constantinople, and never before Obreskof was at liberty.   Azof and the two Kabardas had formerly belonged to Russia, and they were necessary for the security of her frontiers.   As for the sequestration of Moldavia and Wallachia, she abandoned it entirely, and was in no way opposed to those countries being made independent.   That was the interest of the Court of Vienna, and the Court of Vienna was wrong not to see that it was so.   The equilibrium in the East would not be changed because the frontier of Turkey was carried back from the Dniester to the Danube.   As for the independence of the Tartars of the Crimea, the interests of humanity demanded it ; the power of the Porte would be in no way diminished by it, and, moreover, the Crimea did not touch the frontiers of Austria.   'I shall never

obtain a good peace,' the Czarina concluded, 'unless I
stiffen myself against the pride of the Turks, and against
the partiality which supports them.'

On the day on which Catharine II. wrote this letter,
Prince Henry left St. Petersburg. 'Know that with this
Prince nothing is lost,' the Czarina had said.[8] Europe
was soon to testify to the exactness of this judgment.
The march of events had been hastened in the last weeks
of 1770, and singular connections had been established
between events which were very diverse in appearance.
While the Russians were completing the conquest of
Moldavia and Wallachia, Austria was taking possession
of Zips and Sandecz, was planting her eagles in Poland,
and was including 500 villages within the line, which
was pushed forward up to ten leagues from Cracow. The
King of Prussia had considerably enlarged the cordon
which he had drawn in Poland for purposes of public
health; his troops had entered Prussian Poland; they
had spread over the bishopric of Warmia, and over a part
of the palatinate of Kulm and of Pomerelia; they had
even extended along the Silesian frontier into several
districts of the palatinates of Kalisch and Posen.[9] Vienna
was arming; Berlin was losing patience; the Polish confederates were in extremities. On December 24 Choiseul
fell; France no longer counted for anything. At Vienna,
at Berlin, at St. Petersburg, the wish was to take much,
and at the same time to fight as little as might be. The
events that had taken place, the interests that were at
stake, the passions that were excited, seemed to be conflicting, but in reality were marching to the same goal.
The King of Prussia had seen it as early as January, 1769;
he had considered that there was but one pacific solution

[8] Letter to Mme. de Bielke, December 11, 1770.

[9] Reports of the Saxon Agent at Warsaw, November 19, 28, and
December 25, 1770 : Herrmann, p. 483.

of the conflict, and that that solution was an advantageous
one for the Prussian monarchy ; Count Lynar's scheme had
been two years in advance of the march of events. But so
piercing was the King of Prussia's glance, so penetrating
his knowledge of men and things, that that State which
seemed to have the least inclination and the least interest
in justifying his conjectures, was yet the first to do so.

Frederick had formed the plan, Austria had given the
impulse, the Eastern war provided the means. All that
remained was to lay hold on the secret agreement which
bound together the diverse causes. The Czarina did this
on January 8, when she said, joking with Prince Henry :
' Why should not everyone take something, too ?' Wars
and revolutions are but the spectacle of history ; criticism
applies itself less to describing these great tragedies than
to seeking the reason of their being in the characters of
the men who are the actors in the drama, and in the
nature of the events which provide its plot. The historical
hour is not that in which the play unfolds itself before the
eyes of the spectators, it is that in which the author, master
of his subjects, allots the parts, and pushes forward the
action towards a catastrophe which the very force of things
shall seem to make inevitable. That hour had struck for
Poland, and it is in the month of January, 1771, that the
famous words may fitly be inscribed in history : *Finis
Poloniæ*.

CHAPTER XIII.

THE OFFICIAL OVERTURES FOR PEACE AND FOR PARTITION.

(January—June, 1771.)

ON January 22, 1771, the King of Prussia received the letter in which Prince Henry gave him an account of his conversation of the 8th with the Czarina.   The idea of solving the Eastern Question by partitioning Poland was not one calculated to surprise Frederick the Great, still less to shock him.   'This overture came opportunely,' he says in his *Memoirs*; 'for, everything considered, it was the only means that remained of avoiding fresh troubles and of satisfying everyone.'   But he had no intention of doing things by halves; if a partition was to be made, the operation must be serious and effective.   By means of it war between Austria and Russia must be prevented, and therefore Russia must renounce all claims to Moldavia and Wallachia to choose a province of Poland at her convenience.   The King of Prussia cared little for the injustice of the partition, provided it were profitable, and that 'by this political levelling the balance of power between the three Powers should remain approximately the same.'[1]   By her occupation of Zips and Sandecz, Austria had set a precedent of which it was expedient to take note, but her uncertain, timid conduct was not an

---

[1] Frederick, *Œuvres*, vol. iii., p. 36.

example to be followed. The bishopric of Warmia, of which the Russians had spoken to Prince Henry, would, indeed, be a compensation for what Austria would gain by keeping the two starosties ; but the two starosties would not be enough to remove Austria's interest in Eastern affairs, and would not compensate her for the conquest of the left bank of the Danube by the Russians. The main object, which was peace, would not be attained, and it would all end in the committal of an act of useless violence. This had not been Count Lynar's intention.

At heart Frederick had very few scruples on the score of the ' law of nature and of nations,' but he knew the strength of ideas, and could measure the force of prejudices. While he thought that reasons of State might occasionally compel Sovereigns to shock their contemporaries by startling actions, he yet thought it imprudent to goad the consciences of mankind with gratuitous prickings. In his eyes, the conscience of a Prince should show itself not less accommodating to great than scrupulous towards little injustices. Venial sins, he thought, are those which history least pardons in her heroes ; a mischievous skirmish in which a village is burnt is called a massacre ; the battle which kills thousands of men and ruins an empire is a glorious deed ; it is all a question of proportion and of distinctions. A man who gains glory by taking a province is called a knave for taking a district. Such was the great King's morality ; if it had no other merit, it had at least that of being clear, and of conforming to the practice of the century.

Frederick wrote to his brother on January 24 : ' The Austrians will never allow the Porte to be crushed. . . . What they show you in perspective, Ermeland (Warmia), is not worth the trouble of spending six sous to acquire it. If the Austrians go to war with the Russians, which I very much fear they will do, there will be many other

things to be settled between them besides this cordon in
Poland, which country they have invaded ; so I shall not
be in a hurry, but shall wait and see whether circumstances are favourable for making some acquisition, or else
I shall stay as I am. . . .   I should think myself guilty
of an unpardonable blunder in policy,' he added, ' were I
to labour for the aggrandizement of a Power which may
become a formidable neighbour for the whole of Europe.'
What he wanted to get he very well knew, and on
January 31, after receiving Prince Henry's report of his
conversation of the 11th with Panin, he wrote to him :
' I see that there is not so much union as there might be
in the Council of St. Petersburg ; but I venture to say
that it is manifestly impossible to carry out Count Panin's
idea with regard to Austria.   The secret hatred of the
Russians which exists in those countries passes imagination. . . .   And as for the item of taking possession of
the duchy of Warmia, I have refrained because the game
is not worth the candle.   That portion is so slender that
it would not repay me for the clamour that would be
aroused ; Polish Prussia, however, would be worth while,
even'if Danzig were not included, since we should have
the Vistula and free communication with the kingdom
(Prussia proper), which would be an important item.   If
it were a question of spending money, that would be
worth it, and even worth a large expenditure.   But when
one takes trifles with eagerness, it gives an impression of
avidity and insatiability, which I would not have people
attribute to us more than they already do in Europe.'
Frederick's chief concern was to know exactly what were
the intentions of the Court of Vienna.   He even hinted
to Prince Henry that it would be well if Russia undertook
to feel the way in Austria.   The wished-for information
came four days later, directly, and it fell to Van Swieten
to give it.

STATE COLLEGE
LIBRARY

FRAMINGHAM. MASS

Van Swieten had reached Berlin on December 26, 1770 ;
he had had his audience with the King on December 30,
and on January 4, 1771, Frederick had spoken to him in
vague and disquieting terms of Russia's conditions of
peace : they were ' so excessive that he dared not communicate them,' he said.[2]   This naturally caused great
perturbation at Vienna, and that Court spent the last
fortnight of January in deliberating what line of conduct
should be held.   The disagreements between the Emperor
and the Empress were aggravated and inflamed during
these thorny discussions, which the pedantic ways of the
Court of Vienna prolonged beyond all bounds.   ' I shall
always be of opinion that one must either do everything,
and act with lively vigour, or else do nothing,' Joseph
wrote on January 10.   On the 14th he addressed a long
memorandum to his mother,[3] expounding his policy.   He
repudiated the idea of Austria going to war with the
Russians alone and without an ally.   Such a war would
make the King of Prussia the arbiter of peace in the East
and in Germany ; all the advantages would be for him ;
he would economize his forces, look on at the spectacle,
and dictate its outcome.   Joseph suspected him, moreover, of making an agreement with Russia to divide the
spoils.   His conduct ' reeked of partitioning.'[4]   Russia
must have done everything, she would still do everything,
to preserve the alliance.   ' Would she not readily sacrifice
to him, in this hour of distress, Danzig, Polish Prussia,
everything, indeed, that he could even wish for, to induce
him to take action ?   Can his integrity, his promises, his
policy, be relied on ?   The first has never been a part of

[2] Joseph to Leopold, January 10, 1771.

[3] Beer, *Documents*, pp. 16-23.

[4] Letter to Leopold, January 31, 1771 : ' He would almost give
reason for suspecting that they had agreed together to divide the
spoils ' (*partager le gâteau*).

his character ; the other two he has always governed
according to his wishes and to the convenience of the
moment.   For his policy, what reliance can be placed
upon a man whose sole system is to take advantage of
circumstances from day to day ?' . . .   He must be compromised and unmasked.   By what means ?   By telling
the Turks that Austria was ready to go to war for them,
if they could persuade Frederick to take part.   The
Turks, whom the King of Prussia had soothed with the
fairest promises, would not fail to appeal to his friendship.
' In short,' said Joseph, ' my idea is to force the King of
Prussia, by means of the Turks, to measures which we
cannot get him to take, or entirely to ruin his credit and
influence, which would, in my opinion, be well worth a
good battle, which we should win against the Russians.
The Turks would be obliged to throw themselves entirely
into our arms. . . .'   In any case, Austria must be ready
to act promptly on any side, whether to take advantage
of Russia's moments of weakness, if such should occur, or
to ' hang on to them,' if necessary, to get a share of what
might be going, and ' to find means of exchanging all our
mutual jealousy of aggrandizement for the common advantages and *roundings-off* which we may secure.'   The
King of Prussia, though deceived by this decisive stroke,
would certainly be forced to submit to it, in order to get
his share.   ' What can he do that we could not turn to
our advantage ?'. the Emperor concluded ; ' the overthrow
of the Ottoman Power must necessarily enrich us with
some fine provinces ; not, it is true, so considerable as
those which the Russians will have, but less devastated.'

To ask the King of Prussia to break with Russia ; to
propose alliance to the Turks, while still retaining the
means of treating with Russia directly, at the expense of
Turkey in any case, and, if possible, to the detriment of
Prussia—was not this an imitation, point for point, of the

conduct which was justly blamed in Frederick II. ? Would it not expose Austria to the same charges of lack of good faith and political inconstancy which were made against him ? Maria Theresa felt this, and her letters show that she was cruelly distressed at finding such unscrupulousness and such blindness in her son. She wrote her answer to the Emperor. ' It is not well done,' she said to Kaunitz, when communicating the note to him ; ' my heart is too heavy ; my gray head is no longer able to govern ; I feel my decay, but I shall hold out as long as there is no war, and as long as you support me.' ' In all my painful career,' she wrote to the Emperor, ' nothing has been harder for me than the decision which it is my duty to come to at the present time. . . . But what most influences me is that the Turks are the aggressors, that the Russians have always shown us every consideration, that they are Christians, that they are enduring an unjust war, that they have been given a free hand in Poland, have been allowed to oppress a free nation, and that at the present time help is arising for the Turks. . . . Never, *never* could I join with the Russians to pursue and destroy the Turks. . . . But what I could never agree to, any more than I could agree to go to war with Russia, is the means by which it is sought to draw the King of Prussia into the matter. . . . My maxim, which I owe to Prince Kaunitz, and which has always sufficed for me, is to practise uprightness and candour, and to use no double-dealing or decoying towards others. . . . This decision will be thought weak and timid, I confess ; but I do not feel able to decide upon a war which I deem unjust, and which is therefore against my conscience.'

Maria Theresa did Kaunitz too much honour. The elevation of her character, the uprightness of her conscience, her instincts as a Sovereign, had an infinitely greater share in these wise and good maxims than had the cunning diplomatist who had succeeded in gaining her confidence. Noble scruples, moderation and respect for right, are a religion at the Court of Vienna; Austrian diplomacy has lent them much suppleness in practice. On many occasions, after proclaiming the purity of her intentions, Austria has been found making a compromise with her principles, trying to reconcile adroitness with virtue, and allowing herself insensibly to glide down the steps of equivocation into acts of iniquity. Thus, after these painful deliberations, Kaunitz declared, both at Berlin and at Constantinople, with the Empress's approval, that Austria would lend herself to any methods, even the most violent, provided the King of Prussia supported their execution. He asked that Prince to give a secret undertaking not to defend Russia, if Austria attacked her elsewhere than in Poland. He begged him to inform the Turks that Austria would go to war with Russia rather than permit the destruction of the Ottoman Empire. He sounded the Divan to learn whether it would be inclined to buy a defensive alliance at the price of an annual subsidy of 34,000,000 florins, the abandonment of Little Wallachia and of Belgrade, and, lastly, by giving Austrian subjects the commercial advantages granted to the most favoured nation. An apparent armament of from 50,000 to 60,000 men was to lend weight to these proposals.[5]

Van Swieten saw the King of Prussia on February 10, 1771, and made him his declaration. Frederick replied, as he had often done, that his treaty with Russia only obliged him to support the Czarina in Poland; but Van Swieten could not get the promise of neutrality which he asked for. The King always evaded the question. ' The case has not yet arisen,' he said ; ' the people at St. Petersburg will put a little water into their wine, and we shall

[5] Rescripts to Van Swieten and to Thugut, January 26 and 27, 1771 ; Joseph to Leopold, January 31.

have peace.' Frederick had smelt out the trap; he was too clever to fall into it. It was not at all what had been expected at Vienna. The language held by the Russian Minister, Galytzin, completed the deception. Russia politely declined the mediation. 'She promises,' Joseph wrote,[6] 'to confide all her desires to us, which incline in no way to conquests, but only to compensations for the past and securities for the future, assuring us, in so many words, that in her proposals our interests will be kept no less before her eyes than her own.' Frederick, who knew what the Russian conditions were, described them as exorbitant; Galytzin declared that they would give nothing but a mere indemnification. The Emperor rightly judged that it was all a mere game to lull Austria to sleep. Austria was, in fact, asleep, and although her slumber was disturbed and crossed by dreams, Joseph was in despair. 'I also am becoming disgusted, and am abandoning everything to Providence; then it will go on finely!' he wrote to his brother Leopold. These were some of the irreverences which distressed the Empress. The worst was, that the whole of this policy had but one result, and it was the very result that they had wished to avoid, namely, to make the King of Prussia the arbiter of peace and war. From Constantinople, from St. Petersburg, from Vienna, all men looked to him, and recognised that without him nothing could be done.

'The more I reflect on the negotiations for peace between Russia and the Porte, the more difficulties do I discern in them,' he wrote to his Minister Finkenstein on February 7. 'The most essential thing for us is, not to allow ourselves to be dazzled either by Russia or by Austria, and to agree to nothing which does not harmonize with our plan of neutrality. . . . I tell you of this as of a principle which I shall never let go.' In the meanwhile

[6] To Leopold, February 21, 1771.

Prince Henry returned to Potsdam on February 17. His report of his visit completed the account that his letters had given. Frederick hesitated no longer ; the moment had come for action. To the laughing suggestions of the Czarina, and to the hints of her councillors, he replied by a diplomatic despatch, which at once transformed the irresponsible suggestions of the St. Petersburg soirées into formal negotiations. On January 30 he wrote to Count Solms, saying that the occupation of the starosties by Austria was no mere trial shot, that it was a perfectly premeditated action, that Austria would keep what she had taken, and that the Chancery of Vienna would formally justify and sustain its occupation of the different territories. 'Thus apprehending the true state of the question,' he pursued, 'there is no longer any question of preserving Poland in its entirety ; but there is the question of preventing this dismemberment from affecting the balance between the power of the House of Austria and that of my House, the maintenance of which is so important for me, and touches so nearly the Court of Russia itself. I see no other means of securing its preservation than that of imitating the example set me by the Court of Vienna, of prosecuting, as it has done, ancient rights, with which, moreover, my archives supply me, and of putting myself in possession of some small province of Poland, to restore it if the Austrians desist from their enterprise, or to keep it if they intend to give effect to the alleged titles which they put forward.'

He ordered his Ministers to search out the titles, and, while they were performing that task, he wrote to Solms to the effect that, if Austria insisted on keeping the occupied territories, Russia might give up the left bank of the Danube, indemnify herself in Poland, and indemnify the Poles with a piece of Moldavia and of Wallachia.[7]

[7] February 20, 27, and March 5, 1771 : Duncker, p. 235 ; Angeberg, *Traités de la Pologne*, p. 85.

The archivists of Berlin were just as expert, and much more active than those of Vienna. By March 25 the titles were in order. 'I am much obliged to you,' Frederick wrote to Finkenstein, 'for your promptitude in sending me the documents of my claims on Poland.' It appeared that the 'ancient rights supplied by the archives of Prussia' bore precisely upon those territories which, ever since 1731, Frederick had regarded as detached pieces, which it was important to sew on again to the State of Prussia. They were also those which Count Lynar, with no pretence to erudition on the subject of ancient rights, had indicated in his prophetic scheme in 1769. The King of Prussia pointed them out to Solms with great clearness on March 25. 'Everything at present depends on my luck,' he said to Finkenstein; 'we shall see how Count Solms will set about it, and whether he will be intelligent and fortunate enough to choose a good channel for the success of this important and delicate negotiation.'

The negotiation was indeed very delicate. Panin, whose aim was to make Poland a vassal of Russia, was opposed to the partition ; but the Czarina inclined to it. Her ambition was tempted by so easy a conquest. The 'faction of favourites' enlisted itself on the side of her inclinations, and the Council pronounced a favourable opinion. Before coming to a definite decision, however, Panin contrived that the King of Prussia should be invited to inform himself of Austria's real intentions regarding the starosties which she had occupied. He thought that if the Austrians were shown the consequences, which the King of Prussia and the Czarina affirmed would follow from their action, Kaunitz would be induced to draw back, and would rather give up the starosties than help to fortify the power of Prussia to so formidable an extent.

The Austrian Minister at Berlin wrote to Kaunitz on

February 26, 1771 : ' There is more and more ground for believing that this Court has come to an understanding with that of St. Petersburg, that they have agreed upon a formal treaty of partition, and that they intend to labour to obtain our adhesion to it.' The hints which he received caused him no surprise. On March 28 Finkenstein sent, asking him to call on him ; he told him that the Czarina had been informed that Austria had taken possession of the starosties, that she had viewed that action with no distrust or jealousy, and that the King of Prussia found in it an opportunity for showing his friendliness to the Court of Vienna, by giving it some good advice. ' The King thinks,' said Finkenstein, ' that all that your Court has to do is to put forward or prosecute any ancient rights or claims you may possess over these starosties, especially as the other neighbours of Poland will do likewise.' It was a proposal for the partition of the republic in so many words. And, indeed, the thing was no longer a secret. The Swedish Minister at Berlin said to the French Minister, who communicated it to his Government on April 2 : ' It is all over already ; the King of Prussia has settled everything, and peace will be signed before four months are over. Poland will be the victim of it all ; I need say no more.'

This was somewhat jumping to conclusions, and it failed to take into account the hesitations, scruples, and intentional delays of the Chancery of Vienna. Panin was right, and the confidence produced the expected effect upon Kaunitz. At that time Kaunitz was entirely absorbed in his negotiations with the Turks. He hoped to obtain more advantages from them than from Russia, and thus to avoid the necessity of helping the King of Prussia to an accession of territory. At the very time when Finkenstein was making this very ' cordial ' overture to Van Swieten (to use the King of Prussia's adjective), Joseph

was writing to his brother Leopold:[8] 'We are in daily
expectation of receiving most interesting news from Constantinople, of an interview that Thugut is to have with
the Reis and Osman Effendi, which will partly decide the
course we shall take.' In the meantime, the Court of
Vienna had nothing better to do than to preserve the
advantages of 'candour and honesty.' On March 16 the
Empress ordered the Governor of the starosties to change
his too-compromising title to that of 'Administrator dis-
trictuum . . . qui linea cæsarea includuntur,' and two
days later she wrote to the archivist, ordering him to
complete the précis of the 'ancient rights.' The occupation was transformed into a military cordon, like that of
the King of Prussia, and appearances were once more
saved. This precaution taken, on April 10 Kaunitz instructed Van Swieten to reply to the Prussian Government
that Austria had only occupied the districts by way of
taking what had been already pledged ; as for the ancient
rights, she had never thought of prosecuting them save by
the paths of peace and legality, and in agreement with
the Polish Government ; on the restoration of peace, she
would evacuate the occupied territories, if Russia and
Prussia would also withdraw the troops which they had
in Poland.

Frederick at once saw that, if this answer of Austria
were transmitted to St. Petersburg, it would notably
strengthen Panin's opposition to the scheme of partition ;
but he had an extraordinary knowledge of the people with
whom he had to deal. He knew that the Czarina was
disposed to yield to the temptation, and that it needed
only that Austria should provide her with a pretext ; he
also knew that Austria, confronted by an accomplished
fact, would eventually give in, and he acted accordingly.
On receiving the reply of the Court of Vienna on April 27,

[8] March 14, 1771.

he said to Van Swieten : ' Have another hunt in your
archives,[9] and see whether you have not some claims to
raise to something more than that you have already
taken possession of, something like a palatinate, which
might be convenient to you.   Believe me, the opportunity
should not be lost ; I, too, shall take my share, and Russia
will do the same.'   While he was thus exciting the avidity
of the Austrians, by hinting that he had already agreed
with Russia, he was striving to bring the Russians to that
agreement, by persuading them that Austria had resolved
to keep the starosties.   ' This is evident,' he wrote to
Solms on April 28, giving his own summary of Van
Swieten's declarations, ' these people set the example ;
therefore the Russians and myself are entitled to do no
less.'   It was not exactly what Panin had expected from
him, when he had begged him to sound the Court of
Vienna ; still less was it what Kaunitz could expect, after
the declaration with which he had charged Van Swieten ;
but Frederick had chosen his line.   ' In a matter of this
importance,' he says in his *Memoirs*, ' one could not allow
one's self to be discouraged by trifles.'   On May 15 he
wrote to his Minister Finkenstein : ' I confess, my dear
Count, that M. van Swieten's reply contains no matter for
satisfaction. . . . These people are afraid that their share
of the partition may be too slender, and rather than see
our gain, they will give up their own.   That is . . .
anticatechismatic behaviour ! for it is written in the Kau-
nitzian *Catechism* that the Powers will reciprocally refrain
from being envious of small advantages.   But what matter
whether the Court of Vienna gives or refuses its consent
to this acquisition ?   If we are in agreement with Russia,
Austria will certainly be obliged to consent, with the best
grace she can, to things that she cannot alter, and for

9 [' *Faites donc encore fouiller dans vos archives.*']

which she will not go to war. No doubt they will thereupon increase their own share, and choose the part of
silence. . . . One matter, which deserves some attention,'
he added, ' is to hint to M. van Swieten that the scheme
of partitioning certain districts of Poland comes directly
from the Court of Russia, and not from my shop. When
these gentry hear of this, they will think more than
once before hurling themselves against two Powers who
are at one in their plan, and it seems to me that
eventually they will do what the Russians and ourselves
project.'

Frederick saw but one obstacle to the success of this
plan ; this was France, who would doubtless be opposed
to the partition, and whose resistance might possibly stop
Austria. But since Neisse and Neustadt, the King of
Prussia knew what construction Austria put upon the
alliance ; he remembered Kaunitz's words, that Austria
had not accustomed her ally ' to venture to demand from
her accommodations out of conformity with her system of
peace, or any sort of dependent attitude.' He also knew
that Choiseul was no longer in power. As he no longer
feared him, his only thought was to ridicule before slan-
dering him. ' Your idea of a dead men's dialogue between
Alberoni and Choiseul is admirable,' he wrote to his
brother Henry ; ' their intellects were of very much the
same stamp—restless, wide-ranging, and superficial.' But
while thus indulging in the scarcely regal pleasure of
mocking a fallen adversary, he was yet forced to do him
homage. 'It is a good thing,' he said to Finkenstein,
' that this France is in her present worn-out condition ;
the Austrians will be more tractable and gentle without
her assistance.'

The Austrians at that moment were striving after
cleverness ; so far from preparing to deliver themselves
into the hands of the King of Prussia, they were flattering

themselves that they would turn his positions, and surprise
him in their turn. The Russians were astutely soliciting
them to commit themselves. Panin, who put no faith in
Frederick, was negotiating with them directly. He hinted
to Lobkowitz, their Minister at St. Petersburg, that if
Austria came to an understanding with Russia, she might
get Moldavia and Wallachia, either for herself, or for
an Arch-duke, or else for the Prince of Saxe-Teschen.[10]
He assured him that the Czarina was resolved to keep the
friendship of Austria, and that for it she would sacrifice,
if need were, that of Prussia ; that Frederick was the sole
author of the schemes for the partition of Poland, that
Russia had nothing to do with them, and that the King
of Prussia's wish was to deceive all parties. ' They consider his behaviour double-faced,' Joseph wrote to his
brother Leopold, in May, 1771 ; ' they think that he is
intent on picking up some scraps of Poland, which would
not suit them at all. So the King of Prussia stands con-
victed of lying, when he proposed the dismemberment of
Poland to us as coming from St. Petersburg.'

Kaunitz wrote to Van Swieten on May 7, 1771, to
decline officially all idea of partition, and to repeat the
declaration that the Empress was prepared to give up the
starosties which she had occupied, if everyone else would
do the same. By this declaration the Court of Vienna
thought to strip the King of Prussia of his mask. But
Frederick had fully realized that the Austrians must be
handled gently ; he let them talk, convinced that they
would be brought to serve his ends in spite of themselves.
And he was not disappointed. Alexis Orlof, who was at
Vienna on April 30, gave it to be understood that the

[10] Lobkowitz's Report, April 12, 1771 : Arneth, vol. viii., p. 310 ;
Le Secret du Roi, vol. ii., p. 366, interview between Mercy and the
Comte de Broglie.

Czarina would be satisfied with the independence of the
Tartars, and with that of the Principalities. It was a
far cry from there to Panin's seductive suggestions.
Kaunitz cried out, and declared that these conditions
were not to be reconciled with Austria's interests. This
language, the news of the Austrians' military preparations,
and the rumour of their secret negotiations with the
Turks—all these facts, magnified and adroitly grouped by
Frederick, eventually, as he says in his *Memoirs*, 'drew
the Court of St. Petersburg out of the lethargy in which
it was sunk.' On June 2, 1771, Solms wrote to the King
of Prussia that the Czarina was only waiting for a scheme
of partition before entering into conference. On the same
day Kaunitz was informed by Lobkowitz that Russia
strongly insisted on the independence of the principalities
and of the Tartars, on the cession of Azof and of an
island in the Archipelago, and on guarantees for the
Christians of Turkey.

While the Russians and Prussians were thus concerting
measures for imposing their will upon the Court of
Vienna, Kaunitz was preparing a great stroke, which was
to take them by surprise and divide them, but whose only
effect, as a matter of fact, was to tighten the links between them, and to hasten the conclusion of their agreement. He wrote to Van Swieten on June 5, telling him
to refrain for the future from speaking of the partition of
Poland, and to confine himself to transmitting what was
said to him upon the subject. Once more verifying the
King of Prussia's conjectures, the Austrians kept the most
profound silence in the direction of Versailles, upon the
subject of all these negotiations. 'I need not say how
strictly this matter must be kept secret, because it would
have a terrible effect if it were spread abroad, especially
in France,' the Emperor wrote to his brother in May,

1771.   The combination which was at that time the
pivot of Austria's whole policy was the negotiation which
Thugut was pursuing at Constantinople, and it was on
the point of coming to a head; but the Court of Versailles
had managed to get news of it, by a channel of which
Kaunitz had no suspicion.

CHAPTER XIV.

THE AUSTRO-TURKISH ALLIANCE, AND THE PROJECTS FOR THE DISMEMBERMENT OF TURKEY.

(January—October, 1771.)

The rôle of Austrian Resident at Constantinople was of the most delicate, demanding, as it did, singular dexterity and never-failing self-possession. This school it was which formed the adventurous and subtle diplomatist who eventually was to succeed Kaunitz at the head of the Chancery of Vienna, and who was notably to surpass his master in the art of reconciling contradictions, and of fitting the severest principles to the most equivocal policy that has ever been. This individual, Thugut by name, was of inferior origin, had raised himself by very tortuous ways, and, even at Constantinople, was in a more than ambiguous position. Born in 1736, the son of a petty clerk, educated by the Jesuits, admitted in 1754 to study Oriental languages at Vienna, he had become dragoman at Constantinople. Kaunitz, who had noticed him, recalled him to Vienna in 1766, and gave him a place as secretary in the State Chancery, with the title of Court Interpreter. Choiseul, who was at that time in the full strength of his Polish ardour, distrusted Kaunitz. He sent a certain Sieur Barth to Vienna, with instructions to find someone to watch Maria Theresa's Chancellor for him. Thugut was

well-placed for this employment; he was needy, greedy,
and ambitious. Sieur Barth picked him out. Thugut
allowed himself to be picked out, and, to use the
euphemism of an Ambassador who became his colleague
at Constantinople, M. de Saint-Priest, 'he entered the
King's service in the year 1767.' We must conclude that
the King was pleased with Thugut's services, for in 1768
he granted him a pension and a brevet of Lieutenant-
Colonel, in all 13,000 livres a year, with the promise of an
asylum in France in the event of the secret being discovered. Thugut continued to ' serve ' at Vienna up to
the time when Kaunitz sent him to Constantinople as
Resident. 'As he remains unshaken in his devotion,'
Sieur Barth wrote in July, 1769, he asks what conduct he
is to hold towards M. de Saint-Priest. That Ambassador
was in all the secrets, in those of Choiseul and in those
of the King. Barth was told in reply: ' Tell M. Freund
[Mr. Friend, Thugut's pseudonym] to confine himself to
establishing relations of personal confidence with our
Ambassador.' Thugut did so, and continued to write to
Paris directly. M. de Saint-Priest had no suspicion that
Thugut was ' serving ' the King, and in that he showed
his perspicacity. Thugut was not serving, and never did
serve, anyone except the House of Austria, and if he did
not scruple to receive the money of the King of France, it
was because he had a deep affection for nourishing his own
fortune without damage to the interests of his masters.
He won his way into the secrets of Louis XV., but he was
far from admitting that too-credulous libertine into the
secrets of the Court of Vienna. This also needed
dexterity, which he displayed to a considerable degree
during the months of the winter of 1770-1771.[1]

He had, at one and the same time, to deceive Saint-

[1] *Vide Revue Historique*, vol. xvii., the essay entitled *L'Autriche
et le Comité de Salut Public*, p. 37 *et seq.*

Priest, to provide Choiseul with occupation, and Louis XV.
with distractions, to encourage the Porte to resist, and to
dissuade it from accepting the support of a foreign Power.
Choiseul, who paid him, to all appearance, to induce the
Turks to seek the support of France, gave him an opportunity for exercising his skill. The Turks had solicited
the alliance of France; the offer had been declined; but
the French Minister had suggested the idea of giving the
Turks the support of a French fleet, in exchange for a
subsidy, giving it to be understood that it would be
followed by a Spanish fleet. For the Turks, the most
seductive feature of this scheme was, that they saw in it
a means of bringing Austria, as the ally of France, into
the war. Thugut, who managed to get the Ottoman
Ministers to confide the French proposals to him in
January, 1771, did not allow them to retain this hope.
He showed them that a fleet would be of no use to them
against the Russian armies; he depicted the inconsistency
and the weakness of the French Ministry; he persuaded
the Divan that that alliance, instead of shortening the
war, would, on the contrary, prolong it; that it would
exasperate Russia, and that the Porte would, in a word,
pay for the satisfaction which M. de Choiseul would have
gained of causing the Czarina a momentary embarrass-
ment. The Prussian Minister, Zegelin, supported his
Austrian colleague in this matter, and the French scheme
appeared to be given up by the Turks, when the fall of
Choiseul put an end to the negotiation.

Thugut learnt of the disgrace of his ally, whom his
Court treated as a rival, and he himself as a dupe, at the
same time as he received orders to resume, in the strictest
secrecy, negotiations for alliance between the Porte and
Austria. After having caused the failure of Choiseul's
combinations, on the pretext that Austria would not
support them, he now had to offer the Turks what it had

been his duty to refuse them a few weeks before. The fact was, that the ground was now cleared. Austria meant to retain the profits of mediation and the advantages of war; she negotiated with Russia and with the Porte simultaneously. By treating with the Turks single-handed, she remained free to support them or to abandon them, as her interests of the moment might dictate; on the other hand, intervention in common with France would have allowed the Court of Vienna neither to join hands with Russia, nor to indemnify herself, whether at the expense of Turkey or of Poland, since both of these were allies of France. Though Thugut's rôle was changed, the character was the same, and in his new negotiation he had to thwart his Prussian colleague underhand, just as he had formerly thwarted the French Ambassador. Austria behaved towards the friend of Neustadt as she did towards the ally of Versailles, and she put no less free an interpretation upon the *Political Catechism* of 1770 than upon the treaty of 1756.

Circumstances appeared to be in her favour. The campaign which opened in the spring of 1771 confirmed the overthrow of the Turks; if they did not suffer any great disasters, it was because they avoided great battles. The Russian generals realized that by crossing the Danube they would lay themselves open to an attack in the rear from an Austrian army, and would venture uselessly into a country barren of resources. They confined themselves to keeping the territory which they had won upon the left bank, and to holding the Turks in check upon the right bank of the river. They turned all their efforts in the direction of the Crimea.

On July 1 the Tartars of the Crimea submitted, and the treaty which they concluded declared them to be, like the Tartars of Bessarabia, independent under the protection of Russia. In consternation at such speedy successes, the Turks reflected that if they would save any part of the territories conquered by the Russians, the only course remaining to them was to throw themselves into the arms of Austria, and to subscribe blindly to Thugut's wishes.

They gave in, and the treaty was signed during the night of July 6-7, 1771. Austria undertook to join with Turkey ' to deliver out of the hands of Russia, by means of negotiations or by means of arms, and to cause to be restored, the fortresses, provinces, and territories which, being in the possession of the Sublime Porte, have been invaded by the Russians.' She promised to hasten the conclusion of peace, which was to be made in such a way ' that the independence and the liberties of the Re-public of Poland, the subject of the present war, shall not endure the slightest alteration,' and in a manner satisfactory to the dignity and the interests of Turkey. As the price of this alliance, Turkey promised a subsidy of 20,000 purses of 500 piastres each, or 11,250,000 florins ; 4,000 purses were to be paid at once, the rest was to be paid by quarters from month to month. A secret fund of 2,000 to 3,000 purses should be put at the disposal of Austria, if necessary. The Porte would grant the subjects of Austria commercially the treatment of the most favoured nation ; it would settle the thorny question of the frontiers of Transylvania in such a way as should satisfy the Imperial Court. Finally (and this was the chief item), it would yield to Austria the territory of Wallachia contained between Transylvania, the Banat of Temesvar, the Danube, and the Aluta. The treaty was to be kept strictly secret, especially from France. Thugut hastened to announce this great success of his diplomacy at Vienna, and to demand the ratification of the Imperial Court.

Kaunitz followed the negotiations step by step, and the hope which he held of seeing them quickly brought to a prosperous conclusion decided the whole course of his conduct. He declared at St. Petersburg, and at Berlin, that Austria would take up arms if the Russians crossed the Danube, and that she would in no case hear any word of a partition of Poland. These declarations, under which her Minister concealed so many mental reservations and secret implications, were confirmed by the Empress in absolute good faith. On the day that Kaunitz sent off these despatches, July 1, 1771, she said to the English Minister, Lord Stormont: ' For my part, I do not wish to keep a single village which does not belong to me. I wish to encroach upon no one's rights ; and I shall not allow others to do so, as far as lies in my power. No plan of partition, however advantageous, could tempt me for a moment. . . . I take no credit to myself for this, for by acting in this way I shall be following the dictates of prudence and policy, no less than the principles of law and equity.'

While Austrian diplomacy was entangling itself in the intricate net of its own combinations, the King of Prussia was pursuing his plan with the methodical audacity peculiar to himself. As soon as he had found that the Russians were well disposed towards the partition, he had hastened to send Solms the necessary powers to conclude it. He informed him, on June 14, 1771, after defining the share which he had long reserved for himself, that he would give Russia a blank cheque, to choose such a share as might suit her interests and her good pleasure. Austria had nothing to say, since they took their stand upon the example which she had set ; if she found her share too slender, she would be offered the outskirt of the State of Venice, which separated her from Trieste, to quiet her. ' And even should they make themselves unpleasant, I will answer for it with my life, that a well-established union between ourselves and Russia will make them submit to

anything that may be desired.' 'Once that is brought
to a conclusion,' he wrote two days later to Prince Henry,
' I snap my fingers at the Austrians.'

Everything conspired for the success of his plan. In
Poland the Russians, impotent to subdue the confederates,
were beginning to despair of an issue without Frederick's
help. That help Frederick was not at all inclined to
give. When he learnt, on July 9, of Austria's formal
refusal of the Russian conditions of peace, he concluded
that, in the straits in which they would soon be placed,
the Russians would assent to all that he might wish. He
was right. On July 21, 1771, he wrote to his brother :
' I have to-day received letters from Russia concerning our
convention ; my share, I believe, will consist of Pomerelia
as far as the Netze, Kulm, Marienburg, and Elbing. That
is very honourable, and is worth the subsidies I have paid,
and the other unavoidable expenses which this Turkish
war caused me. They write me from Vienna that Prince
Kaunitz continues to be in a very ill temper. As I believe
that he cannot count upon the French, it may well be that
that has something to do with it.'

Kaunitz was not taking France into account at all, and
troubled himself very little about her ; but he did all he
could to bring her into his game. His game, at that
moment, was to proclaim the most complete disinterestedness with respect to Poland ; he took great credit to
himself for this with the French Ministry. He fully
thought that the Cabinet of Versailles would inform the
Prussian Court, and he considered that it would have the
ultimate advantage of entirely reassuring France, so that,
should Austria think it expedient to accede to the plan
of partition, France would regard her with no suspicion,
and would offer no resistance to it. The French Ministry,
in which M. d'Aiguillon had replaced M. de Choiseul on
June 6, continued to display a zeal on behalf of the Poles

which was more ostentatious than effective.[2]   Up to that
time it had vainly begged the Court of Vienna to facilitate,
at all events secretly, the conveyance of the help which
was being sent to the confederates.   Suddenly Austria
appeared to change her line of conduct.   M. d'Aiguillon,
upon the reports of the French Chargé d'Affaires at Vienna,
wrote to M. de Saint-Priest at Constantinople, on August 1:
' The expectation of having recourse to arms, which exists
at Vienna, has already effected a change in Austria's attitude
towards the confederates.   She has lately caused it to be
notified to us that she is grateful to the King for the help
which he is giving them, and she promises, on her side, to
give them every assistance possible, though she will provide
them with neither troops nor money.'

Kaunitz thought to impose upon the King of Prussia
with the same ease with which he deceived the French
Ministry.   On April 5 he addressed a long despatch to
Van Swieten, intended to disturb Frederick, and to make
him suspend the execution of his plans.   The infatuation
of the Austrian diplomatist here paints itself to the life.
Read at this distance, this despatch seems the more
strange when we consider that the writer, in spite of all his
pretensions to forethought, only succeeded in paving the
way for the dissolution and humiliation of the Austrian
State, while the Prince to whom it was addressed, in spite
of his affectation of inconsequence, and his taste for expedients, founded the most solid structure that Europe has
seen for a century.   ' It is important at the present
moment,' wrote Kaunitz, ' that the King be cured of the
idea that we might perhaps even yet allow ourselves to be
induced, by the bait of a miserable momentary advantage,

[2] Farges, *Instructions de Pologne*, Vioménil's Instruction, July 9,
1771, vol. ii., p. 298 ; Duc de Broglie, *Le Secret du Roi*, vol. ii., pp.
293, 377 *et seq.*   See the fantastic and romantic episode of the
abduction of Stanislas Augustus.

to lose sight, as he does, of the sole and true political interest of great States, which consists in sacrificing every-thing, even in risking everything to secure, before every other consideration, the security and tranquillity of those who are to come after us.   I regard it as important, at the same time, to keep him in a kind of uneasiness regard-ing the possibility of an arrangement with the Porte, in case Russia should venture to insist obstinately upon con-ditions of peace which we could not allow.   Those are my views upon the information which I give you to-day officially; I shall add nothing more, because *sapienti pauca.*'

The Russians received simultaneously the news of the successful conclusion of their treaty with the Crimean Tartars, and that of the threatening declaration of Austria upon the peace conditions.   The Czarina showed great irritation at the resistance offered her by the Court of Vienna, and the official answer which she addressed to it on August 15, 1771, in no way disguised her senti-ments.   She gave Lobkowitz to understand that, if there were war, she had reason to count upon the support of the King of Prussia.   Panin showed no less annoyance than his Sovereign.   Russia, he said to Lobkowitz, cannot depart from her conditions ; but, putting that aside, if Austria is so dismayed at the thought of the Danubian principalities changing hands, why does she not take them for herself?[3]   It was no mere fanciful suggestion ; the Russian Minister was only taking part in the partition of Poland against his will and on compulsion.   The system he always preferred was to induce Austria to order Eastern affairs in agreement with Russia.   Like Frederick, he thought that if the Austrians complained so loudly, and took up such a threatening attitude, it was because they

[3] Lobkowitz's Report of July 24, 1771: Arneth, vol. viii., p. 319.

considered their share too small and their advantages too precarious. He wished to sound them, and while addressing a bellicose reply to their threatening declarations through the official channel, by an indirect route he caused a proposal to be whispered to them for a partition of Turkey. Count Massin, who had been in the service of Russia with the rank of Rear-Admiral, and who was then at Florence, was charged with the confidential communication. These proposals do not deserve study merely as curiosities of history ; they soon issued from the sphere of secret, to pass into that of official diplomacy ; the Court of Vienna discussed them with great gravity, and a few years later they received solemn sanction from the hand of Catharine herself.

Count Massin's secret proposals were concerned with six different hypotheses upon which Austria and Russia might come to an agreement, and find mutual advantages. The two first presupposed an alliance intended to drive the Turks definitely out of Europe ; in this case the partition might be effected in two ways. First, Austria would take Servia, Bosnia, Herzegovina, Albania, and Macedonia up to the Morea ; the rest, with Constantinople and the Dardanelles, would be assigned to Russia. Second, Macedonia, Albania, Roumelia, the greater part of the Archipelago with the seaward countries of Asia Minor, would form a kingdom which should have Constantinople as its capital, and the investiture of which should belong to Russia ; Russia would keep for herself the greater part of the territories on the left bank of the Danube, the shores of the Black Sea—with the exception of the Crimea, which should remain independent under a Russian protectorate—and the two Kabardas ; Austria would take Wallachia, between the Danube and the Aluta, Servia, Bulgaria, and Herzegovina ; the Morea would form an independent State under an Austrian Archduke, or would be handed to Venice, which in that case would cede Istria and Friuli to Austria, and would form a league with the allies against the Turks. The third scheme was more modest ; it assumed that the Turks should retain possession of the left bank of the Danube ; Servia, Bosnia, and Herzegovina should go to Austria ; Russia should keep her conquests on the Black Sea ; the Tartars should be independent ; Prussia should indemnify herself in Poland, and the Poles in the Danubian principalities. The three last schemes only treated of a partition of Poland between Russia and Prussia, and offered Austria the choice of taking her share either in Poland, or in Silesia, or in Germany.[4]

While these singular proposals were finding their way from Florence to Vienna by the byways which secret diplomacy is wont to follow, official diplomacy was all for war. The Russians declared so at Berlin ; the Austrians gave it to be understood in very clear terms. For a moment Frederick felt disturbed. Was success going to escape him ? Had he been wrong in his conjectures ? Had he been so much mistaken in the thoughts and passions of the people whom he thought he knew so well ? He wished to partition Poland, but he saw in that partition only a means of restoring peace ; if the partition was to lead to war, or to be a result of war, he preferred to abandon it. The Russians, who were decidedly out of breath in Poland, were imploring him to take possession and to come to their aid. He had no idea of doing so ; it would have been to unchain the storm. ' Van Swieten,' he wrote to his brother, on August 14, 1771, ' spoke to me to-day in such a way that I am compelled to believe that war will be declared at the beginning of next year. Saldern[5] sends

---

[4] Kaunitz's Report to the Empress, January 17, 1772 : Arneth, vol. viii., pp. 339-343 ; Beer, vol. ii., p. 130 ; Duncker, p. 252.

[5] Saldern was directing the Russian army and Russian diplomacy in Poland.

me an officer to beg me to extend the sanitary cordon,
which I broke a week ago, up to the Wartha and Posen.
All Lithuania is in insurrection. I refused.' His anxieties
show vividly through a letter which he wrote to his Minister
Finkenstein on September 13 : ' I am leaving nothing
undone to prevent a rupture between the two Imperial
Courts by every imaginable means, and I shall even attempt
impossibilities to stifle the fire of the general war which
would be its unhappy result. But I wish, more than I
can hope, that my pains may be attended by a fortunate
success.'

Thus the aspect of affairs seemed to be reversed. Fortune
seemed to be abandoning the King of Prussia and to be
serving the Austrian Chancellor, to be failing the calcu-
lator and favouring the visionary. But it was one of
those side-scenes which, in a well-conceived piece, cross
the action of the play only to reawaken interest, and to
lead up to the final issue. Frederick had seen aright, and
Kaunitz had omitted to take his Sovereign into account.
While the King of Prussia was showing so much uneasiness,
a courier was bringing him a despatch which would, in a
few moments, allay all his anxieties and renew all the
springs of his activity. Rhode, the Prussian agent at
Vienna, could understand half-utterances, and could put
what he had understood into plain language. On the
evening of September 6, he had gone to pay his respects
to the Queen-Empress. Maria Theresa spoke to him at
length of the difficulty in which she was placed. She told
him ' that her sole wish was to find a solution without
having recourse to arms . . . that she would willingly
lend herself to all reasonable expedients that could be
found ;' that, moreover, she would certainly not go to war
without consulting the King of Prussia ; that the Turks
would heed nothing that was said to them, and that she
prayed the King of Prussia to bring them to reason ; that

she did not see how war could be avoided unless Russia
would relax her demands, and unless the King of Prussia
would see his way to speak plainly; that, for the rest, she
would not prevent the Russians from exercising authority
in the Crimea, but that she would not allow them to do
the same in Moldavia and Wallachia. This was a ray of
light to Frederick; he knew Maria Theresa, and was well
acquainted with the hidden conflicts which divided the
Court and the Imperial family at Vienna. He calculated
that all Kaunitz's warlike demonstrations were only made
with an eye to his fellow-players, and to induce them to
compound; that the Empress would not go to war; that
Kaunitz, to get out of the deadlock in which he was
enclosing himself, would consent to everything, and that
Austria, placed between the alternatives of a humiliating
retreat and an advantageous treaty, would decide for the
treaty, and would accede to the partition of Poland.
Convinced that from thenceforth he might advance without danger, Frederick showed himself by so much the more
warlike as he saw less probability of war.

He sent for Van Swieten on September 18, and told
him that he had been informed of the Empress's real views,
that he approved of them greatly, that he was delighted
to know Austria's ultimatum, that he was about to inform
the Turks of it, and to do his utmost to induce the Russians
to abandon the independence of the Principalities; but
that he did not see what inconvenience there would be for
Austria in granting them the independence of the Tartars;
that even if, as a matter of fact, he had not guaranteed
the Principalities to Russia, he yet could not allow his
ally to be attacked with impunity. He begged Van Swieten
to inform Kaunitz of their conversation as soon as possible.[6]
Having thus warned the Austrians, he turned his attention

[6] Frederick to Solms, September 25, 1771, *Correspondance de
Solms*, p. 523; Martens, vol. vi., pp. 69, 70.

back to the Russians, and sent a plan of partition of
Poland to the Czarina on October 1.   He pressed Catharine
strongly to give up the Principalities in view of Austria's
animosity.   He added that he had made preparations to
agree with his ally, for furnishing her with military assistance in the event of the Austrians attacking her.   He was
only awaiting a reply from St. Petersburg before setting
to work.   'To give the more weight to this declaration,'
he says in his *Memoirs*, 'the cavalry was increased and
entirely remounted.   The orders given to this effect were
executed promptly, and in every quarter.'   They had the
more effect in that Frederick, for reasons of economy as
well as for reasons of policy, saw fit to carry out this
operation in Poland.   He reformed the sanitary cordon,
which had been broken, and sent a corps of 4,000 cavalry-
men into Poland to protect a remount of 6,000 horses
which he had decided to make.[7]   'This is a fine business
of sending-off,' he wrote to Prince Henry on September 27,
1771 ; 'but man is made for work, and is but too happy
when he can work for his country's good.'   And he added,
on October 2 : ' Yesterday I sent off the courier with all
that relates to the Russian convention.   I have made an
attempt to try if we can put Danzig into the portion which
falls to us.   It is certain that if we do not obtain it in the
present circumstances, we must never think of it again ;
now is the time to end our treaties with Russia, because
the impression made by the Austrian armaments is, at
present, at its strongest in St. Petersburg, and because
probably the arrival of 50,000 Russians in Poland will
make the Austrians more circumspect.'

[7] The French Agent's Report, September 24, 1771 : Boutaric,
vol. i., p. 167.

CHAPTER XV.

(October, 1771—January, 1772.)

With a stroke of the pen Frederick had upset the sapient edifice erected by Kaunitz. Austria's difficulties were even greater than he could suppose. The Emperor Joseph wrote to his brother Leopold: 'If we are to talk of war, we ought not to be in the melancholy circumstances in which our countries Bohemia and Moravia are. The King of Prussia, with 20,000 men, can conquer them without a battle, and our whole army, from lack of supplies, and owing to the impossibility of collecting them, will have to escape over the Danube. That, upon my honour, is the situation in which the fairest kingdom of the monarchy is placed, and it seems to me to be no time for big words. This risk alone is quite as great as the injury which would accrue to us if Russia gained the Crimea; thus it must be peace if possible, and, above all, no war for us.'[1] Such was the reality; Kaunitz had vainly striven to hide it under the tangle of his diplomacy. 'Kaunitz,' says the eminent historian of the House of Austria, 'was, as it were, thunderstruck when he learnt, from Van Swieten's report, of the tenour of the Empress's

[1] Joseph to Leopold, October 27, 1771.

interview with Rhode.'[2]   ' Her Majesty has done him a fine
turn,' wrote Joseph ; ' in an interview which she has had
with Rhode, the Prussian Minister, she has upset our
whole system. . . . We look pretty foolish at present,
but it will have to be seen what line can still be taken to
get out of it ; briefly, my feeling is that, by acting firmly,
either everything will be restored as it was before the war,
or if either of the two parties gain, ourselves and the
King of Prussia will have to gain also in proportion.'
That was precisely the point to which Frederick wished
to bring them ; there was no other solution, for the
Emperor knew better than any man that there could be
no question of firm action.   Kaunitz was soon to arrive
at the same conclusion ; but he felt a first prompting of
anger and vexation which he was unable to hide.   ' Baron
de Rhode attributes remarks to Your Majesty which are
quite incredible,' he wrote to the Empress on September 20 ;
' they destroy in a moment what has been the work of three
years. . . .   Your Majesty can easily imagine what was my
consternation when I read this despatch, and I cannot con-
ceal from Your Majesty that, did I not discern some remedy
in the conviction I must needs hold, that it is impossible
that M. de Rhode could have understood rightly, I should
lose courage for the first time in my life.'   The Empress
replied that the Prussian Minister had given a faulty
rendering of her views on the subject of the Crimea, that
he had pressed her to make that concession to the Russians,
that she had committed herself to nothing, but that it was
quite true that she had no wish for war, because she felt
repugnance to it from principle, and because Austria was
in no condition to go to war.   ' Accordingly,' she added,
' it behoves us to think seriously of a means of issuing
from the whole business with as little damage as possible.
The Turks and this convention embarrass me more than

<hr />

[2] Arneth, vol. viii., p. 325.

all the rest, and it is in you alone that I place all my
confidence, to relieve me, and to save from total ruin this
monarchy, which has cost us so great anxieties and so great
pains.'

This last sentence sufficed to calm the self-esteem of the
susceptible Chancellor. In reality, his one wish was to
begin the game again, and to take his revenge. If there
were few Statesmen so infatuated with their own genius,
there were few of such mental activity, so supple, and so
fruitful in expedients. The Emperor considered that there
were three alternatives :[3] the first consisted in waiting until
the war should exhaust the belligerents, and should compel
them to treat on the basis of the *status quo ante ;* the
second consisted in proposing to Russia to arrange her
differences with the Turks : the Russians would be persuaded to content themselves with moderate acquisitions,
and Austria would offer to unite with them to prevent the
partition of Poland. Turkey, saved by Austria, would
throw herself into her arms, and would cede her the territories promised by the treaty of July 6 ; Austria would
renounce the territories which she had occupied in Poland,
and would confine herself to ordering the matter of the
ancient rights in agreement with that republic, and to
depledging Zips. Poland, left to herself, would fall back
into her traditional anarchy, that is to say, under Russian
supremacy ; the King of Prussia would lose all credit at
Constantinople. While Russia was acquiring Turkish territories, while Austria was *depledging* Zips and receiving a
portion of Wallachia, he would be compelled to go away
empty-handed, and to abandon his designs upon Polish
Prussia. By so doing, Austria would remain faithful to
her engagements to the Turks ; but it was necessary to
foresee the contingency of it being to her interest to
break those engagements ; and this was the object of the

[3] Memorandum of September 26, 1771 : Beer, *Documents,* p. 26.

third hypothesis laid down by the Emperor. If Russia could not be persuaded to moderation, if she sought to effect vast conquests and to make the King of Prussia share in them, the equilibrium must be maintained, and Austria must have her share.   Austria had then no better course to adopt than to come to an agreement with Russia and Prussia, but what should she ask of them ?   At the expense of which of her two neighbours—the Turk her ally, or the Pole her friend—would Austria think fit to indemnify herself ?   Should she take Bosnia, Herzegovina, and Turkish Dalmatia; would she prefer Moldavia and Wallachia; or, lastly, Cracow with the surrounding palatinates ?   The first course, that of waiting, Joseph considered chimerical; the second, the agreement with Russia, he thought the wisest course ; the third, that of partition, the most risky.   Maria Theresa unhesitatingly pronounced for the second plan; she saw in it the triple advantage of tricking the calculations of the King of Prussia, of restraining Russian ambitions, and of carrying out the engagements which Austria had entered into.   Kaunitz yielded to his Sovereign's opinion, and agreement between the three Powers of the Austrian monarchy seemed for a moment to be restored.   'It is a great consolation to me that you also are for Number Two,' Maria Theresa wrote to Kaunitz, 'and I hand over the whole matter into your hands with all my heart and with much contentment.   I have always been well pleased with the result of so doing. No war, no defection from our system, no total abandonment of the Turks, and no money.'

Maria Theresa thought and wrote like a good Austrian; but would she have succeeded in saving the Turks and in avoiding the partition of Poland by this policy, which was at once prudent and honourable ?   We may be allowed to doubt it; certainly Austria would have avoided great difficulties in the future and cruel weaknesses in the

present. But simplicity was by no means one of Kaunitz's
characteristics, and the Emperor had learnt the law of
nations in the school of the King of Prussia. They agreed
to use strategy with the Empress, and to lead her subtly
towards their plan. But while fixing upon ' Number Two,'
they had every intention of having an eye to the chances of
' Number Three '; their diplomacy set before it the remarkable object of combating the partition of Poland, and at
the same time of reserving for Austria the best share in it,
should it take place. Hence the perpetual equivocation
of their language, and the duplicity of their behaviour.
If they had sincerely followed the plan approved by Maria
Theresa, they would have cordially ratified the treaty of
alliance concluded with the Turks on July 6, they would
have induced the Porte to resist, they would have given
firm counsels of moderation to the Russians, and would
have excluded even the hypothesis of the partition from
their combinations. They did none of these. They were
found at one and the same time supporting the Turks
and retaining the means of deserting them; repudiating
Russia's conditions of peace in their official despatches,
and making proposals to the Russians to come to terms
on these same conditions in secret interviews.

It was with the Turks that the negotiations were of
the greatest delicacy. The Turks had scrupulously fulfilled their engagements. On July 25, 1771, a first
convoy of two millions had left Constantinople, and the
Austrian commissioner had received it at Semlin. The
Turks naturally demanded the ratification of the treaty.
Kaunitz made no haste to satisfy them. In his view, the
Turkish alliance had never been anything more than a
scarecrow. If Russia yielded to Austria's advice, and
abandoned the partition of Poland, the treaty, though
still unratified, would have produced its effect, and would
be duly carried out; the Turks would have nothing to

complain of. If, on the contrary, drastic measures had to be resorted to, and Poland had to be partitioned, it would be agreeable to the Court of Vienna to avoid the pain of breaking a solemn engagement. Kaunitz retained the means of replying to the Turks that, according to all the doctors of the law of nations, a treaty not ratified is a treaty without value. And yet, imperfect as it was, the Turks had carried it out ; they had paid. Austria had need of two millions, were it only to persuade the Russians by threats of war to make peace at the expense of Turkey. It was important, moreover, that the Turks should believe that the promises of July 6 still held good, for Austria might be led to fulfil them, and it would have been imprudent to send back the money. Kaunitz adopted an expedient and gained time. He did not send the asked-for ratifications, but he wrote to the Kaïmakan on October 14, 1771, saying that the Empress remained faithful to the alliance, and especially to Article V. of the treaty, by which she had undertaken to procure an acceptable peace for the Porte.

Kaunitz laboured to this end, if not with great loyalty, at all events with much activity. He held frequent interviews, in this month of October, with the Russian Minister at Vienna, Galytzin. Both were equally afraid of committing themselves, and they long fenced with skilful feints before coming to close quarters. Was Kaunitz already acquainted with the great schemes which Count Massin had been charged to whisper at Florence ? It does not appear that there was any question of these schemes between him and Galytzin. What most engaged the attention of each was to know what the other thought about Poland. Galytzin urged Kaunitz to complete the occupation of Zips, and to move forward the Austrian eagles, so as to include Cracow within the cordon. Kaunitz replied that the occupation of Zips was a matter of principle, and that, for the rest, he could make no pronouncement until he had particular information about the plan of partition which was attributed to the Courts of Berlin and St. Petersburg. On October 13 Galytzin declared categorically that all these reports were false.[4] Kaunitz thereupon took up a defensive attitude, which he maintained till October 24.

On the latter date, considering no doubt that the hour was come, and that time pressed, he requested Galytzin's presence at his chancery. He communicated to him an official despatch, which he was sending to Lobkowitz. It was to the effect that Austria could not accept the mediation on the conditions laid down by Russia; she considered that the Porte could make peace only upon the following conditions : namely, the annexation of Azof and of the two Kabardas, the commerce of the Black Sea, and a war indemnity; Russia would have to renounce the conquest of the Principalities and the independence of the Tartars. Such was the programme of Austrian diplomacy, a programme not to be departed from unless the Court of St. Petersburg showed itself inclined to enter upon a confidential exchange of views with that of Vienna of such a character as might notably modify the relations between them.[5] It was the moment for compromising confidences; before entering upon them Kaunitz took precautions. 'I can only resolve on taking this step, if I am certain that your Court will keep what I am about to confide to you the most profound secret, that this secrecy shall be absolute, and that neither friend nor enemy, nor any Court in the world, shall have the least revelation of it. The secrecy must even apply to our own Minister at St. Petersburg, M. de Lobkowitz. And if

[4] Martens, vol. ii., p. 16.
[5] For details, *vide* Kaunitz's account of this interview : Beer, *Documents*, p. 32, and Arneth, vol. viii., p. 330.

your Court, against our expectation, opens its mouth on
the subject, I must warn you that we shall deny all the
statements as inventions, and that we shall give you yourself, M. le Prince, a formal denial.' After this significant
exordium, he set forth the first peace scheme, whose object
was to spare Poland, to isolate Prussia, and to arrange
everything between Vienna and St. Petersburg ; then he
added : ' There might be another means of pacification,
if Russia were disposed not only to enlarge her borders on
another side, but to procure also on the same side an
enlargement for her ally, and provided that we arrived at
an agreement and mutual accommodation of such a
character that our Court should obtain proportionate
advantages in territory and population, so that the
equilibrium should not be disturbed, but, on the contrary,
maintained. Although this means of pacification must
not be deemed impracticable and inadmissible, and though,
for that reason, our Court ought not to obstruct the
execution of a plan of partition so prepared and debated
in common, I must confess to you, in all sincerity of heart,
that we consider it a work of the greatest difficulty, and
that, no less in our own interests than in those of Russia,
we should prefer the other means.'

Kaunitz fully realized that the Russians would find it
difficult to reconcile this offer of a partition of Poland and
of abandoning Turkey with the French alliance. He felt
that it was necessary to reassure the Russians upon this
delicate point. ' The report has been spread abroad,' he
said, ' and has found credit, that everything that we have
done in Turkey and Poland has been in agreement with
the French Court. Nothing is further from the truth,
inasmuch as, though, in truth, we hold that Court in all
the just esteem and consideration in which it is fitting that
an allied Court should be held, we are so far from having
entered into a concert with that Court on the subject of

Turkey and Poland, that we have up till now communicated to it none of the documents which have been exchanged on this subject between ourselves and Russia.' Kaunitz thought to produce a great effect upon the Russians by this last confidence. It produced at least an effect of surprise; and, indeed, it was an odd way of proving Austria's sincerity. Galytzin knew his rôle; he sustained his character, and showed great politeness. 'The Russian Minister was not a little astonished,' says Kaunitz in his report, ' but he assured me at once that he gave entire credence to my assertions.'

Thus, by devious ways and along hidden paths, Austria was journeying insensibly towards the partition of Poland. The Empress disliked the idea, but her son and her Minister led her to it without her suspecting it; and while she thought that she was faithful to the French alliance, her chancery was treating the ally at Versailles with the same freedom as the ally at Constantinople. Durand, the French Chargé d'Affaires, had a vague suspicion of the negotiations which were being disguised from him. He found Kaunitz much too composed when he denounced the King of Prussia's intrigues to him. Kaunitz asserted that he knew nothing of them. On October 26, two days after the interview with Galytzin, Durand again pressed him on the subject. Kaunitz replied: ' As for the engagements which the King of Prussia may enter into with Russia, we cannot suppose that Catharine II. is willing to labour for his aggrandizement; the engagements which that Prince has formally made known to us only apply to the settlement of the troubles of the republic, and to the guarantee of the King of Poland.'[6] Kaunitz had spoken the truth upon one point; he was very certainly unfaithful to the French Court, and Galytzin would have been wrong not to believe it when he assured him that it was so.

[6] *Vide* Boutaric, vol. i., pp. 170, 171, and Ferrand, vol. i., pp. 170-174.

The King of Prussia was less easy to persuade. Kaunitz
had no intention of telling him of the confidences he had
made to Galytzin, but confined himself to communicating
to him the official despatch addressed to Lobkowitz. He
hoped that, seeing Austria so determined, the King of
Prussia, from fear of war, would urge concessions upon the
Russians, and would thus facilitate the agreement between
Vienna and St. Petersburg which should turn to his confusion. It was too much to ask of Frederick the Great;
he was not at all the man to be caught in his own net.
He wrote to Finkenstein on October 18, 1771 : ' The
issue of the whole matter depends, in my judgment, on
the direction which is taken by our negotiation of the
secret convention with Russia. If it has the success which
I hope it will have, all the other difficulties which can
come in our way from the Court of Vienna seem to me
unimportant, and sufficiently easy to turn aside.' Austria
provided him with an unexpected argument for hastening
Russia's decision. Lord Murray, the British Ambassador
at Constantinople, who was watching Thugut's manœuvres
with jealous solicitude, had learnt of the despatch of the
convoy of silver into Austria on July 25. He informed
his colleague at Paris, who hastened to hand on the information to the Prussian representative, and Frederick sent
on the news all hot to St. Petersburg. He calculated that
the Russians would be alarmed, that they would throw
themselves into his arms, and that, in order to avoid war
with her two neighbours, Austria would not hesitate to
betray Turkey and to dismember Poland ; by this skilful
manœuvre the King of Prussia would destroy the credit of
Austria at Constantinople, while forcing that Court to
become his accomplice at Warsaw. He wrote to Zegelin,
telling him to show the Turks how chimerical were the
hopes which they based on Austria. The Turks, he
thought, had but one course to adopt, namely, that of

direct negotiation with Russia.[7]   Finally, convinced that
in the whole of this matter Austria was acting behind the
back of France, Frederick took care not to lose so fair an
opportunity for arousing ill-feeling between Versailles and
Vienna, and to lay the burden of excluding the French
from the negotiation on the shoulders of Kaunitz himself.
He instructed Sandoz, his agent at Paris, to express to
M. d'Aiguillon, Choiseul's successor, the desire which the
King of Prussia felt to see the negotiations for peace set
on foot at Constantinople in the form of a Congress, and
to beg the French Minister to procure the assent of Vienna
to this overture.[8]   We see that Frederick the Great was
merely being candid towards himself, when he confessed
in his *Memoirs* that it was 'by dint of negotiating and
intriguing' that he managed to incorporate Polish Prussia
with his States.

The Russians were at the last extremity in Poland;
they pressed Frederick to come to their aid.   The King
of Prussia announced that he was ready to occupy the
palatinates which he had assigned to himself.   He insisted
that he should take possession of Danzig; the Empress
objected that it was a free town, and that she had guaranteed
its independence.   'This matter appears to be absolutely
trivial,' Frederick wrote.   'The Pope had Avignon; the
French took it.   Strasburg was a free town; Louis XIV.
made it his own.   How many like cases does not history
show us!   I should not, however, trouble about a mere
trading town.   But . . . it cuts into all my possessions. . . .
In recompense for the risks to which I am going to expose
myself for Russia, I must at least obtain the continuity of
my possessions. . . .   And what is more, I shall take good
care not to mobilize even a cat before I have some security
that I shall be indemnified. . . .'   They might take it or

<hr>

[7] Beer, vol. ii., p. 146.   [8] Boutaric, vol. i., p. 168.

leave it : ' No taking possession, no troops.'[9] ' If they want to set me in motion,' he added, ' I must be on a sure footing.' He was but little disturbed, however, by Russia's delays. ' It matters little,' he wrote to Finkenstein, on December 6, 1771, ' whether this convention is signed a few weeks sooner or later ; quite the contrary : the more it drags out its length, by so much will Russia's difficulties be increased. Perhaps, indeed, she will only lend herself to our conditions when she feels the urgent necessity of granting them to us, and the extreme need which she has of our alliance.'

On the very day on which Frederick was writing this letter Russia was justifying his conjectures. The Russians were victorious, but exhausted. They had no more money, men were beginning to fail them, soldiers were deserting, officers were asking for leave. The war in Poland had weakened and worn them even more than the war in Turkey. A German diplomatist wrote from St. Petersburg on December 14, 1771 : ' In spite of the brilliant successes which the army has gained wherever it has had an opportunity, in Turkey and in Poland, its present circumstances are far from favourable. The Russians have lost large numbers from exhaustion, and especially from the bad organization of their ambulance. Since the beginning of this war five levies of 50,000 men have been made ; but scarcely half the recruits reach the theatre of war ; the rest die on the way or desert. . . . They are feebler than can be imagined. False statements are given to the Empress. According to those statements, the principal army numbers 60,000 men ; it is certain that, apart from the irregulars, there are not more than 20,000. Count Panin has only 12,000 men.'[10] Under

[9] Frederick to Solms, October 30, November 6, November 11, 1771 : Solms's *Correspondence*, pp. 547, 554, 558.

[10] Sacken's Report : Herrmann, vol. v., p. 702.

these circumstances, if the war were to continue, and if
Austria were to take part in it, armed assistance from
the King of Prussia would become indispensable to
Catharine. Peace appeared preferable ; but, in order that
it might be signed with advantageous conditions, Frederick
had still to be satisfied. Catharine wrote to him on
December 6, 1771, saying that she renounced her claims
to Moldavia and Wallachia, but that the Turks would
have to cede Bender, Otchakof, or, at the very least,
Kinburn. The King of Prussia would get Polish Prussia
and Warmia, but he would not take possession of them
immediately; as for Danzig, Russia's engagements to the
maritime Powers forbade her granting it. The King of
Prussia was to march 20,000 men into the Principalities
if Austria declared war, and was also to create a strong
diversion in Poland. If the Austrians attacked the King
of Prussia, Russia would provide him with 6,000 foot-
soldiers and 4,000 Cossacks, and would support him with
all her strength after the signature of the peace with the
Turks. These proposals were still far from answering to
Frederick's wishes ; they left him many risks to be run,
and gave him no right to take his securities immediately
after the signature of the treaty, as he would have wished
to do. As a matter of fact, the Czarina meant to make
sure that the treaty would be carried out ; she had no
intention of allowing the King of Prussia, once established
in Poland, to confine himself to keeping what he had
taken, and to leave Russia struggling with the Turks and
the Austrians.

While taking her precautions on the side of Prussia,
the Czarina was trying to win over the Austrians, and to
induce them to come to terms. Kaunitz had sent an
official declaration and also some confidential communi-
cations to Russia ; Panin replied in the same form. On
December 5, 1771, he wrote Galytzin an official despatch ;

he repudiated the conditions of peace proposed by Austria, and then passed to the affairs of Poland. Prince Kaunitz, he said, is appropriating districts of Poland; he protests against any idea of partition ; he asserts certain ancient rights, it is true, but he will not deny that there is no State which has not certain 'open rights' with regard to its neighbours ; such is the case with both Russia and Prussia with regard to Poland ; these rights are indisputable, and an agreement has been arrived at to give effect to them. If Austria will accede to the negotiation, and join her claims to those of the two allied Courts, there is a disposition at Berlin, as at St. Petersburg, to make common cause with her. The confidential instructions which accompanied this despatch replied to Kaunitz's suggestions, and made it clear that they had not deceived the authorities at St. Petersburg. ' He has played a double game,' wrote Panin ; ' he wished to frighten Russia, but he has made a mistake. It is known at St. Petersburg that he has concluded a treaty for subsidies with the Turks. It is known that, sunk in the rut of his perfidies, devised the better to blind and deceive his own Court, he has understood neither the fundamental interests nor the dignity of a Christian Power.' It is his own business ; but Russia has taken steps in consequence ; she has reinforced her troops in Poland, and extended her alliance with Prussia to meet ' all possible cases of rupture.' This rupture, however, she prefers to avoid, and the means are very simple. The Czarina, in agreement with the King of Prussia, ' has resolved to bring upon the heads of the Poles the consequences of their ingratitude, and to make certain convenient acquisitions at their expense, to the advantage both of the frontiers of her empire and of those of her ally, the King of Prussia, *following in this the example of the Court of Vienna.* It is at the present time indispensable,' Panin continued, ' that Prince Kaunitz be

brought to realize that we have settled everything already,
and that it would therefore better repay the Court of
Vienna also to make acquisitions, and, rather than expose
itself to the uncertainties of a war, to enlarge its territory
at the expense of Poland without further delay, a course
to which no opposition will be offered either by the King
of Prussia or by ourselves, if only the Court of Vienna
will refer to us and to the King at a convenient time.'[11]

All Kaunitz's artifices were recoiling on himself. He
was struggling in the net of subtilty which he had so
laboriously woven. His tottering policy was now nothing
but a series of feints, evasions, misconceptions and contradictions. Durand called his attention to the King of
Prussia's behaviour in Poland. 'We cannot suppose,'
Kaunitz replied, 'that Russia can consent to the aggrandizement of a Prince whom she has been endeavouring,
till now, to exclude from the affairs of Poland, nor that
she can engage herself in a dismemberment which would
bring about a general war in Poland.'[12] Durand was
continually urging the danger of this dismemberment.
Kaunitz adopted a very lofty tone with the French:
doubtless Durand *ventured* to speak to him of Zips; for the
Chancellor wrote to Mercy on December 4: 'Our behaviour
towards the King of Poland is too high, too honourable,
and too reasonable to be able to give pleasure where you
are; but I suppose, nevertheless, that they will be prudent
enough not to show it. In any case, we have done as
we thought fit, and we can very easily dispense with
their approval. However, I share your opinion of
M. d'Aiguillon's habit of mind and of his character;
he is playing a double game, and may very well break
his own head in the process, and may probably land his
Court between two stools, as the saying is, into the

[11] Martens, vol. ii., pp. 16-18.
[12] Durand's Letter, November 6, 1771.

bargain, unless he speedily changes his behaviour towards ourselves and Spain.   I told M. Durand casually, in a contemptuous and sarcastic tone, that I knew from Berlin that M. d'Aiguillon was treating M. de Sandoz with much cajolery, and that the King of Prussia asserted that he had positive assurances from the Duke that France would in no way obstruct such schemes of aggrandizement at the expense of Poland as he might entertain . . . that, considering this, I could not help being a little astonished whenever he, Durand, thought fit to express his fears to me on the subject of the King of Prussia's views on Poland. . . .'

Durand's reception was no better when he brought Kaunitz the proposal for a Congress, which had been suggested by Sandoz at Versailles.   Kaunitz replied, on December 11, 1771, that the Congress was impossible, since the Czarina would have none of it, and since her especial aim was to exclude France from the negotiations; that the King of Prussia was deceiving everyone; that Austria could not implicate herself in these intrigues; 'that an assembly, formed before a plan of pacification had been sketched out between the different parties, offered no hope of success; that that was all he could say on the subject . . . that it was to be feared that an interview would only result in the establishment of peace to the detriment of a third party, and that a dismemberment of Poland could not fail to change the system of Europe." Nevertheless, Kaunitz thought it well to show rather less assurance on this last point than he had formerly affected. Durand wrote on December 14: 'One thing alone mitigates his uneasiness, which is, that he does not imagine that the Russians can support the ambitious views of a monarch who, by the acquisition of Danzig and Polish Prussia, would speedily become the rival both of their commerce and of their power.'   Very different language was used by Kaunitz to the Prussians, and Frederick's agent, Rhode, was able to write to him on December 1 : 'The Queen-Empress, as well as the Emperor, have slightly suggested, though in general terms and in hints only, that they would like to have their share, in the event of there being a question of a dismemberment of Poland, and that mutual explanations should be given on the subject.'

Austria was soon to be compelled to give this explanation, for which she hinted her desire. On December 20, 1771, Kaunitz learnt the substance of the answers which Panin had addressed to Lobkowitz. At the same time Austria heard that the Russians had finished the campaign with some decisive successes ; that the Turks were demanding the ratification and execution of their treaty more vigorously than ever ; that they were, moreover, but little averse to a partition of Poland, if they could regain the Danubian principalities at that price ; finally, that Russia and Prussia had tightened their alliance, that they had agreed upon the partition, and that Austria had to choose between a more than perilous war, and a peace fruitful in advantages. Maria Theresa's first movement was one of consternation. 'I am in great agitation . . .' she wrote, when sending for Kaunitz on December 30. The deliberation began.

Kaunitz set forth the state of affairs in a memorandum dated January 17, 1772.[13] He had too much political wisdom to halt between the war and the partition. The only matter which seriously engaged his mind was to know whether the partition was to be effected at the expense of Poland, or at the expense of Turkey, or at the expense of both. 'The Russians,' he says, 'hinted through Count Massin that there were several plans to choose between.' He summed up the proposals of the Russian agent, and discussed them with entire freedom of

[13] Arneth, vol. viii., pp. 336-346.

mind. The question of the treaty of alliance with the
Porte appeared to him merely a matter of form. The
Turks had been very free in their observance of it towards
Austria; Austria might act in the same way. Kaunitz
left to the Empress the duty of choosing between the
different proposals which he set before her; but he, nevertheless, seemed to prefer that the operation should be
carried out at the expense 'of the barbarian, the
hereditary enemy' at Constantinople, rather than at that
of 'innocent Poland.' Maria Theresa sent on Kaunitz's
production to the Emperor. Joseph gave his voice for the
continuation of the war.[14] Austria, he opined, could only
gain by it; the two adversaries would mutually exhaust
each other. They themselves would take possession of
the territories in Poland, with the reservation that they
should restore what they had occupied if the partition was
generally abandoned, and should take a compensation in
Turkey, in agreement with the Russians, whenever peace
should be made. Kaunitz replied to the Emperor's
observations on January 20, and had no difficulty in
showing that, in view of the alliance between Prussia
and Russia, the prolongation of the war would turn
to the detriment of Austria.[15] Joseph yielded to the
evidence. 'It only remains,' he wrote to the Empress
on January 22, 'to decide which of the schemes of compensation is to be chosen. *Militariter, politice et camera-
liter*, nothing would suit us better than Glatz and Neisse;
Bayreuth and Ansbach, at all events; if that is deemed
impossible, as, unfortunately, I doubt not that it is, the
most advantageous course would be to take Belgrade with
a portion of Bosnia up to the gulf of the Drina. That is
my poor opinion; but as Prince Kaunitz does not reveal

[14] Joseph's Memorandum, January 19, 1772: Beer, *Documents*,
p. 39.
[15] Kaunitz's Memorandum: *ibid.*, p. 42.

his own, and gives no indication as to which of the seven proposals he prefers, I have thought it necessary to ask him.'

Kaunitz made his opinion known on the following day; but simplicity was not his strong point, and he applied himself to marking out 'the progressions' which he thought fit to establish between the 'different proposals.' The Emperor and Empress accepted the 'graduated proposals' which he presented to them. In the first line Austria placed the county of Glatz and a portion of Silesia; in the second, Belgrade, with a piece of Bosnia; in the third, Ansbach and Bayreuth; then, finally, on the line of retreat, the suggestion of a cession of Wallachia, and, in default of anything better, the partition of Poland. It was decided that Van Swieten should be informed of these resolves, but with the proviso that he should leave it to the King of Prussia to make the first advances, and should only indicate 'the graduated proposals' in the form of purely personal suggestions. The reason for this was that, before committing herself and revealing her covetousness, Austria wished to be sure that the affair in which she was engaging was to be meant seriously. The instructions sent to Van Swieten on January 25, 1772, showed this very clearly: 'It would be horrible to be willing to draw down on ourselves the greatest possible calamity, which is war, when the proposed end can be arrived at without risk or danger, and in much greater security; we therefore think that the moment has arrived when good friends owe it to themselves to speak with open hearts. . . . That enlightened Prince (the King of Prussia) will feel that, to avoid all jealousy, and that we may not thwart each other's measures, it will be indispensable to begin, at the first and as soon as possible, with a solemn promise on the faith of a King, that *the most perfect equality* shall be observed in the acquisitions which may be in question for him and for

ourselves, and that at once, as not a moment is to be lost
in affairs of this sort, the desires of either party should be
mutually confided without delay. We shall proportion
our demands to those which the King thinks fit to make.'

Having sent Van Swieten this catechism, Kaunitz himself undertook the task of conversing with Galytzin. He
saw him on January 27, 1772. Galytzin laid before him
the conditions propounded by Panin in his two despatches
of December 5, 1771. The Russian diplomat had not to
expend any great eloquence to convince the Austrian
Minister. Kaunitz had already determined on his line
of action. ' I saw clearly,' Galytzin reports, ' that the
Prince, contrary to his usual habit, was all ears ; that he
shied at nothing, ultimately confessing that I in no way erred
in thus reasoning ; and that he, too, could hardly accustom
himself to the notion of a fresh war, which might easily
become general.' He declared that having received some
' elucidations' of ' the details and circumstances,' which he
had till then lacked, he *now* considered the demands made
by Russia against the Porte to be entirely just. On the
following day, January 28, he gave Galytzin a formal
declaration in writing that Austria agreed to the principle
of the respective enlargements laid down by Panin in his
despatch of December 5. Austria, he said, would have
preferred that there should be no partition of Poland ;
but if there were one, she could not remain indifferent
either to the increase in her neighbours' power, or to the
overthrow of the balance of power in Europe, and she was
disposed to enter into negotiations concerning the share
which should accrue to each. Kaunitz even added, in the
course of the interview, that, the principle of the partition
of Poland once laid down, ' there would be means for taking
away some more land, from someone who had enough and
to spare, and who would be obliged to yield on that point,
when he found the three Courts in agreement upon it.'

Galytzin observed that that remark could only apply to
Turkey. Kaunitz did not deny it.[16]

Thus it was that Austria, after having promised on
July 6, 1771, to bring about, *either by the way of negotiation or by that of arms*, the restitution to the Porte of the
territories invaded by Russia, and to cause peace to be
concluded without the slightest injury being done *to the
independence and the liberties of Poland*; after having
received an advance of 2,000,000 florins by way of earnest
money, had, in January, 1772, reached the point of making
proposals to Prussia and Russia for the dismemberment of
Poland and for the partition of Turkey. A sad result for
so many subtleties! Kaunitz might shut his own eyes to
the value of his work, but all his art could not disguise
the cruel truth from the eyes of Maria Theresa, and the
judgment which she passed upon his policy will continue
to be that of history. 'It is not possible to retrace our
steps,' she wrote.[17] 'The too-threatening tone used to the
Russians, our mysterious behaviour both towards our allies
and towards our adversaries—this has all come from having
laid down the principle of profiting by the war between
the Porte and Russia to extend our frontiers. . . . *We
have wished to act in the manner of the Prussians, and at
the same time we have wished to retain the appearance of
honesty*. Acting in this light, we have created illusions in
our own minds as to our means, and are still trying to flatter
ourselves over appearances and events. It may be that I
am wrong, and that these events are more favourable than
I can see them to be; but should they secure us the first
sketch of the partition . . . should they secure us the
district of Wallachia, even Belgrade itself, I should still

[16] Martens, vol. ii., pp. 18, 19.

[17] On January 22 or 25: Arneth, *Joseph II. und Marie Therese*,
vol. i., p. 362 ; vol. viii., p. 594, note.

deem them too dearly bought, being, as they are, bought at the price of honour, at the price of the glory of the monarchy, at the price of the good faith and religion which are our peculiar possession. . . . I confess that I can with difficulty endure it, and that nothing has cost me more than the loss of our fair fame. Unhappily, I am bound to confess that we deserve it.'

CHAPTER XVI.

THE PRINCIPLE OF THE TRIPLE ALLIANCE—THE EQUALITY OF
SHARES.

(January—February, 1772.)

FREDERICK THE GREAT gave his contemporaries lessons in
the Prussian practice of statecraft; but he did not trouble
to teach them how to retain the appearance of honesty.
He did not waste time over such 'trifles.' He was not
satisfied with the Russians' reply; they asked too much,
and did not promise enough. He peremptorily refused to
send his army to the Danube; but, by way of a set-off, he
gave up the idea of annexing the town of Danzig, holding
'that the possessor of the Vistula and of the Port of
Danzig would gain possession of this town in course of
time, and that so important a negotiation ought not to
be stopped for the sake of an advantage which, properly
speaking, was only postponed.' He added as a condition
sine quâ non, that he should put himself in possession of
Polish Prussia and of Warmia as soon as the treaty was
signed. This ultimatum was sent to Solms on January 4,
1772. It was only with great reluctance that he had
promised to support Russia with all his strength, in the
event of Austria attacking her. All his energies from that
time were devoted to making that clause inoperative, and

to making Austria decide for peace and partition.   Austria
anticipated his wishes.

Van Swieten received the instructions which Kaunitz
had addressed to him on January 25, and he waited on
the King of Prussia on February 4, 1772.   Frederick had
not expected the march of affairs to be so quick and so
prosperous.   'You will be as astonished as I was,' he wrote
to his brother, 'when you know Van Swieten's proposals.'
The Austrian diplomatist first propounded the question of
principle, that is to say, that of perfect equality in the
respective acquisitions of the three Courts.   'This proposal, *which was just,* met with no opposition,' Frederick
says in his *Memoirs.*   It was the moment for 'each to
confide his desires to the other with open heart.'   Frederick
spoke first, and declared what his share would be.   Austria,
he added, can find an equivalent portion in the palatinates
bordering on Hungary, including Cracow.   Van Swieten
objected that between Hungary and Poland there lay the
Carpathians, and that those mountains would prevent
Austria from extending herself upon that side.   And yet,
said Frederick, you would be very annoyed if anyone tried
to take the Milanese from you, in spite of the Alps which
separate them from your States.   Van Swieten rejoined that
there would be a better way of satisfying his Court, which
would be an exchange.   'And what exchange?' the King
inquired.   'We would give you all our share of Poland
for the county of Glatz and Silesia.'   'What?   What?'
Frederick cried.   Van Swieten had to repeat his proposal.
He endeavoured to show that Prussia would 'round herself off' much better by doubling her acquisitions in
Poland.   'No, sir,' said Frederick, 'that does not suit
me at all.   I have the gout in my feet, and you might
make me such a proposal if I had it in my head.   Poland
is the matter in question, and not my States.   I ask and
stipulate for nothing more than Polish Prussia.   Take the

share which is yours in Poland or elsewhere, but not in my States.' Upon this Van Swieten was led to set forth the 'graduated proposals' of Prince Kaunitz ; he spoke of Belgrade, of Bosnia, and of Servia. Frederick allowed him to talk, and even encouraged him ; he was not sorry to know what was at the bottom of Kaunitz's mind. Knowing of Austria's treaty with the Turks, he derived much satisfaction, as a good Prussian, from establishing the duplicity of the Court of Vienna. 'I told him in joke,' he reports, 'that I was very glad to learn that the Austrians were not yet circumcised, as they had been accused of being, and that they wished to take their share at the expense of their good friends the Turks.' 'I must say,' he wrote to his brother, 'that it is perfidious conduct on the part of that Court to try to take territory from those who have put their trust in it, and have chosen it as the mediator for peace ; and to seek to impose cessions of territory upon the Turks, which would weaken them as much on the side of Hungary as the conquest of the Crimea will weaken them on the side of Russia.'[1]

Austria had given in. Frederick had found out Kaunitz's game. 'I see how much troubled the latter must be at seeing his plan upset,' he wrote to Finkenstein on February 7, 1772. 'But whatever be the schemes which he is revolving in his head, I yet think that I can see pretty clearly that he does not mean to fight for them, and this conviction is enough to set me at ease. . . . And, indeed, provided we stand fast, Russia and I, and provided my treaty with the last-named is signed, the Court of Vienna will have to adapt itself to circumstances, and in the end content itself, willingly or unwillingly, with the share which will be allotted to it in Poland.' It was

[1] Frederick to Prince Henry, February 8, 1772 : Duncker, p. 249 ; Frederick to Solms, February 5, 1772 : *Correspondance de Solms*, p. 639 ; Swieten's Report, February 5 : Beer, vol. ii., p. 154.

evident that Austria would have preferred not to be implicated in the matter of Poland, to take her acquisitions at the expense of the Turks, and to leave all the odium of the partition upon her two neighbours. But Frederick did not mean this to be. Austria must be an accomplice. 'If Austria gets no part of Poland,' he wrote to Solms on February 16, 'all the hatred of the Poles will be turned against us. They would then regard the Austrians as their sole protectors, and the latter would gain so much credit and influence there that they would have thousands of opportunities for raising all sorts of intrigues in the country.' If Austria had respected Poland in 1772, she might in the future have made herself that country's protector. Frederick, who foresaw that one partition would necessarily lead to another, did not wish to leave this encumbrance to his nephews. History proved only too clearly how sagacious this reasoning was. In the meantime, sure that Austria 'would not fight for it,' and that she would let her hand be forced, Frederick no longer hesitated to promise the Russians a military assistance which he knew would be useless, and wrote to Solms on February 16, telling him to hasten on the conclusion of the treaty. His wishes coincided with the Czarina's, and the courier who was carrying these orders to Solms met on his way the courier who was carrying the instrument of the treaty to Frederick. On January 16 Panin and Solms signed two conventions at St. Petersburg; by the first, Russia and Prussia, in view of 'the general confusion in which the republic of Poland lies, owing to the dissensions among her leaders and the perversity of mind of all her citizens,' declared the necessity for 'joining to their States certain districts of that kingdom'; they defined those districts; they promised mutual support against Austria, in case of need; and, by the second convention, they settled the conditions of their respective supports. But

Frederick was fully convinced that the need for this would not arise. ' I think,' he wrote to Solms, ' that we should confine ourselves, after taking possession, to declaring to them dryly that it has been done for such and such reasons. . . . This tone of firmness would impose upon the Court of Vienna, and I would wager my head that no war would arise from it.'[2]

At Vienna the perplexities were redoubled. When Maria Theresa heard of the interview which the King of Prussia had had with Solms on February 4, she was at first very distressed. She protested her integrity and invoked Public Law. ' I do not understand,' she said in a writing to which she herself gives the name of ' Jeremiads'—' I do not understand the policy which, when two parties use their superiority to oppress the innocent, allows and enjoins the third party, in the name of mere precautions for the future and of convenience for the present, to imitate and perform the same injustice. . . . A Prince has no rights other than those possessed by any private individual ; the greatness and the maintenance of his State will not enter into the balance on the day when we shall all have to appear to give our accounts.' The Empress's conscience condemned these inequitable speculations ; they offended her political sense of shame. ' What will France, Spain, England say, if we suddenly establish an intimate connection with those towards whom we have taken up such a high attitude, and whose conduct we have declared to be unjust ? . . . Let us rather be held weaklings than knaves.' This was no doubt fine language, and no Sovereign could set more noble resolutions before him. The difficulty lay in bringing her conduct into line with them, and here it was that policy began to taint morality.

---

[2] Martens, vol. vi., p. 70 *et seq.*, text of the two conventions ; Frederick to Solms, December 8, 1771, January 4, 1772 : *Correspondance de Solms*, pp. 569, 597.

'Let us endeavour,' the Empress continued, 'to lessen the pretensions of others, instead of thinking of *sharing* with them on *such unequal conditions*.' These last words formed the channel by which sophistry gradually worked its way into the Empress's mind, and urged her unconsciously towards compromises. She tended to confuse the equity of the partition with the equality of the parts; she began to think that justice would be satisfied when the needle of the balance stood upright, and the two sides of the scale weighed evenly. 'We are bound to the Porte,' she said; 'we have even received money from it; the pretexts which we could or would find to make the Turks the first defaulters, in order to profit by their spoils afterwards, do not agree with entire integrity or with true principles. I could never submit to that; so there can be no question of Servia and Bosnia, the only provinces which would suit us. There remain only Wallachia and Moldavia, unhealthy, wasted countries, open to the Turks, Tartars, or Russians, and possessing no town—countries, indeed, in which we should have to use many millions and many men to keep our hold on them.' What, then, was to be done, and what means were there to maintain the precious equilibrium of the scale without offence to justice? One only; the King of Prussia had pointed it out long ago, and the Empress was brought to it in her turn. It was Poland; but it was unfair to despoil a third party without indemnifying him. Maria Theresa considered that 'the unhealthy, wasted countries, open to the Turks, Tartars, and Russians,' would do excellently for the Poles. 'It would be necessary,' she continued, 'to have recourse to Poland, and to assign Wallachia and Moldavia to her by way of indemnity; this would, moreover, be the sole means, and the least evil, to which I could lend myself.' As a matter of fact, the Turks would have nothing with which they could reproach their ally, Austria, since she would take nothing from

them, and it would ill become the Poles to complain of
the expropriation which they would be made to undergo
when they were given so fair a recompense in exchange!

The outcome of these struggles, at once tragic and
subtle, which rent the soul of Maria Theresa, and to
which history bears such singular testimony, Frederick
had only too precisely foreseen, though he was perhaps
incapable of realizing their cruel course. The philosopher
of Sans-Souci, who derived so refined a pleasure from the
spectacle of human contradictions, who was so ready to
smile at the weaknesses in others from which he himself
was exempt, and who so strangely enjoyed laying bare the
hearts of men, would doubtless have paid some thalers out
of his treasury for the privilege of reading the letter which
Maria Theresa addressed to Kaunitz when sending him her
' Jeremiads.' The pious Sovereign of Austria arrived at
the same conclusions, couched in almost the same terms,
as those reached by the complete sceptic who ruled at
Potsdam. A year before, on January 21, 1771, Frederick
had written to his brother concerning Warmia : ' This
share is so slender that it would hardly be worth the
clamours which it would arouse.' On January 13, 1772,
Maria Theresa wrote to her Chancellor : ' One ought to
know *how* to yield, and not, for a slender profit, to lose
one's reputation and integrity before God and man.'

Kaunitz had imagined, from Van Swieten's report, that
the King of Prussia would readily lend himself to an
enlargement of Austria in Turkey ; he had taken
Frederick's questions for offers, and his curiosity for
assent. He much preferred this line of policy, and proposed, on February 13, to take all Wallachia and the
southern part of Moldavia and of Bessarabia ; the rest of
these two provinces should be allotted to the Poles. By
thus recompensing the Poles for what others took from
them, by avoiding asking anything from them for Austria,

and by taking nothing from the Turks except what they had already irrevocably lost, Kaunitz thought that the Empress 'would satisfy the demands of the most scrupulous delicacy, and at the same time would fulfil the sacred duties of her sovereign estate.' Joseph thought quite differently. 'What can Poland demand from us,' he wrote on February 14, 1772, 'when we take nothing from her? Are our consciences so tender that we are to recompense her for the injustices (if such they are) committed by the Russians and the King of Prussia in taking a few morsels? I conclude, in short, by saying that we must have all Moldavia and Wallachia. . . .' The Danube and the Pruth would be the frontier of Austria. Joseph even claimed that they should have Belgrade and Old Orsowa on the right bank of the Danube.

Deliberations went on without much progress being made. Joseph sketched out scheme after scheme; Kaunitz prepared erudite despatches for Berlin and St. Petersburg. The Empress rejected one day what she had resigned herself to accept the day before. She could come to no determination either to take from the Poles, or from the Turks, or to take anything from anyone. 'I confess,' she said, in a note dictated to her secretary, Pichler[3]—'I confess that at no time of my life have I experienced so much anxiety. When all my States were threatened, I leant upon my good right, and on the help of God. But to-day, when not only is right not upon my side, but when obligations, equity, and good-sense fight against me, I have no rest left. I have only the uneasiness of a heart which has accustomed itself neither to shutting up its ears nor to making duplicity pass for candour. Confidence and faith are for ever lost, and, with them, the purest jewels and

[3] This note is in German. *Vide* Arneth, vol. viii., p. 365, and Chapter XIII., for the account and the text of the deliberations of the Court of Vienna.

the true force which a Sovereign has against her fellow-rulers. What will all the Powers think of us? how will they judge us when they see us risking our reputation for so miserable a gain as Wallachia and Moldavia? Two provinces? which *as regards material interests* are injurious to the monarchy, *as regards policy* will, perhaps, conduct us to our ruin after having made us lose our credit. . . . I am no longer strong enough to manage affairs alone, so I let them, to my greater sorrow, go their way.' What most wounded and humbled her, was Frederick's raillery on the subject of the unhappy scheme for partitioning Turkey, which they had been so rash as to communicate to him. 'The King could not quit the subject of our baseness,' she wrote; 'our despatches have earned me that, which makes it the more deplorable.'

In the end, however, Kaunitz won the day. He laid down that, while reserving the right to propose other combinations in the future, it would be well to take official note of the partition of Poland, to take possession of some territory in that country by way of security, and formally to establish Austria's right to an indemnification. The equivocation which this proposal contained, and the deceptive influence which the fine phrases of equilibrium and equality exercised over Maria Theresa's mind, combined to conquer her scruples. On February 19, 1772, she placed her signature at the foot of the following draft declaration, which was countersigned by the Emperor:

'Her Majesty the Empress of all the Russias, and His Majesty the King of Prussia, having rights and claims to certain palatinates and districts of Poland, as we have on our side, to obviate all difficulties which might arise on this subject, and all that might weaken the friendship and good harmony now happily subsisting between us, we mutually promise on our sovereign faith and word, by the present Act, signed by our own hand: That, whatever may be the extent or the limits of our respective claims, the acquisitions which may result from them shall be perfectly equal ; that the share of one shall not exceed the share of another, and that, very far from opposing obstacles to the measures which each of us shall see fit to take to realize his or her claims, we will aid each other as need may arise, mutually and in good faith, to facilitate our success, binding ourselves, at the same time, to the most complete secrecy upon the subject of the present reciprocal engagement.'

This declaration was first despatched to Berlin.   If the King of Prussia signed it, Van Swieten was to send it to St. Petersburg.   He would then add that Austria was waiting, before disclosing her claims, to know those of Russia.   The King of Prussia signed it on February 28, 1772 ; the declaration at once left for St. Petersburg, and the Czarina signed it, in her turn, on March 5.   Austria had now no hope of evading the difficulty and of escaping complicity in the partition.   On January 15, Prussia and Russia had agreed at St. Petersburg to partition Poland and to invite Austria to accede to the partition, and on February 19 Austria, who was still ignorant of this treaty, declared herself ready to give her consent to the partition, on the condition that equality should be observed in it. Accordingly, when Galytzin communicated the St. Petersburg treaty of partition to Kaunitz, the Austrian Chancellor realized that the matter was irrevocably decided, and that, whether she would or no, it was in Poland that Austria must take her share.   He laid it before the Empress on March 8 ; Maria Theresa gave in.   ' I imagine,' she replied to Kaunitz, ' that from now there is nothing else to be done ; but this consideration does not console me either for the aggrandizement of these two Powers, or still less for the necessity which is laid upon us of sharing with them.'

Pending the conclusion of an agreement about the respective shares, all parties seized securities. The Russians had been in occupation of two-thirds of Poland since 1768; the Austrians and the Prussians had drawn cordons along the frontiers of the republic in 1769 and 1770, and these cordons had been gradually extended so as to include the greater part of the lots which both these two States claimed as their shares. The three armies which were thus invading Polish territory paved the way, each in its own manner, for the authority of the States to which they belonged. Before becoming their neighbours' subjects, the Poles learnt to know their manners, their habits, their traditions, and their characters.

The war which the Poles were waging amongst themselves and also with the Russians was one of atrocity and savagery. Catharine's soldiers rivalled the confederates in violence; soon they surpassed them. On either side slaughter, pillage, burnings, violation, and holding to ransom were practised in the name of religion; they converted each other mutually with sabres and whips. 'The confiscations,' Herrmann says,[4] 'brought more than a million ducats into the Russian Treasury.' 'Poland is to-day precisely what Germany was when Faust-Recht obtained there,' wrote the Saxon Resident at Warsaw. Dividing parties, exciting them against each other, sowing discord, fomenting hatreds within the nation, crushing those whom they could not corrupt, artificial and fanatical, using guile and violence in turn, the Russians behaved like the Tartar conquerors. Their Minister at Warsaw, Baron Saldern, was, according to one eye-witness, 'a madman with a sword in his hands. He breathes forth continually burnings, hangings, and degradations. He talks folly and foulness to all the foreign Ministers.'[5]

[4] Herrmann, vol. v., p. 496.
[5] Report of the Saxon Resident, Essen, May 25, 1771.

The Austrians, more cultivated, were inspired by the examples of the Byzantine Empire. They marked out boundaries with gravity and minuteness, planted, took up, and replanted their eagles, rummaged archives, compiled and placarded methodical recitals of their titles and 'ancient rights,' verbalized, drew up protocols, signed passports, issued instruments, dealt out justice, and bestowed a lengthy title, in Law-Latin, upon the agent whose duty it was to levy contributions, and to apply to the 're-incorporated' and occupied districts the rough and rigorous government of the hereditary States of Austria.

Frederick the Great behaved quite crudely, in the Prussian manner, and wasted no time uselessly in giving himself the exteriors of legality. While reserving it for a later time to organize his Polish possessions with as much art as he had brought to the assimilation of Silesia, for the present he treated the territories enclosed in his cordon as conquered country, taxable and corvéeable at will. He formed magazines there, replenished his supplies of provisions and forage, remounted his cavalry, made his troops live on the country, and paid for all that he took with a debased coinage which he afterwards refused to receive into his coffers. The Royal Philosopher reproduced in Northern Poland the proceedings which the Tartar Krim Gueray, who also prided himself on his philosophy, had formerly followed in the South. The Tartar Khan gave up the male slaves, but took away the women, in order to convert them, to people the harems of the Crimea with them, and to raise up a stock of Mussulmans from them.[6]

----

[6] 'My religion,' Krim Gueray said to the French envoy, 'allows me to give male slaves to the Christians, and enjoins me to keep the females, to make proselytes of them.' 'I suppose,' replied the Frenchman, 'it is because you like pretty women best.' 'Not at all; I follow the most reasonable law. . . . The conversion of a man is always a miracle; that of women, on the contrary, is the

'The King of Prussia,' the Saxon Resident wrote on March 18, 1771, 'has caused to be taken from Poland nearly 7,000 girls of from sixteen to twenty years of age, and he demands that, from every tract of so many acres, there shall be delivered to him a maiden or girl with a cow, a bed, and three ducats of money.' The bed was to be a feather-bed, with four pillows; two pigs completed the dowry.[7] These Polish damsels, with their baggage, were transported and married in Prussian Pomerania, where the growth of population and the propagation of the porcine race left, it appears, something to be desired. 'This rigour,' the Saxon diplomat concluded, 'has driven the people to despair.'

'The bulk of our work, my dear brother, is now done,' Frederick wrote. . . .[8] 'This will unite the three religions —Greek, Catholic, and Calvinist; for we shall partake of the same eucharistical body, which is Poland, and if it is not for our souls' good, it will assuredly be a great object gained for the good of our States.' This great object was not the acquisition of some few provinces, a rather secondary object in itself, and one not worth so much trouble; it was the securing solidarity of interests and political complicity, and the establishment of an alliance between the three Northern Courts; and it was, lastly, the putting Prussia in the first place in this alliance, less from the extent of her territories and the potency of her resources, than from the position in which she had managed to place herself between Austria and Russia. 'If all this leads to a durable alliance between the three Powers,' Prince Henry had said, 'that alliance will dictate to Europe.'[9] Europe has since learnt it to its cost.

---

most natural and simplest thing in the world; they are always of their lovers' religion.'—*Memoirs of Baron Tott*, vol. i.

[7] Ferrand, vol. i., p. 129.   [8] To Prince Henry, April 9, 1772.

[9] Letter to the King, March 5, 1772.

So great results obtained at so little cost ought to have satisfied the King of Prussia; he might have contented himself with expounding this masterpiece of intrigue and diplomacy to posterity in his *Memoirs*. But the cynical element in him, which had too often tarnished the heroic, must always come forward to depreciate his statecraft. The three allied Sovereigns were constrained to stamp even their private occupations, in this great crisis of European history, with the mark of their singular characters. While Catharine the Great was striking medals in honour of Alexis Orlof, and elaborating a code of laws destined to enlighten the human race in general and the Russian nation in particular; while Maria Theresa was beating her breast and striving to allay the pangs of her conscience by subtle distinctions of intention, Frederick the Great was twitting the victims of his iron policy, and distilling the biting raillery with which he loved to cover his vanquished adversaries, in little pamphlets, parodied from Voltaire. 'To give you an account of my occupations,' he wrote to Voltaire on November 18, 1771, 'you must know that I had scarce recovered the use of my right hand (he had had a violent attack of gout), when I betook myself to scribbling, not to instruct the public of Europe, whose eyes are very well opened, but for my own amusement. Catharine's victories were not my theme, but the follies of the confederates.' Not content with spoiling the Poles, he must needs take from them the kind of prestige which always attaches to the unfortunate, and he sought to make them ridiculous.[10]

The picture of them at the beginning of his poem is only introduced to justify the remarkable discourse

---

[10] ' Enfants bâtards des discordes civiles,
 Quoique hautains entiers dans leurs débats,
 Ils n'étaient point a vaincre difficiles,
 Et préféraient le pillage aux combats. . . .'

which Peace addresses to them at the end of the sixth canto.[11]

Such is the moral of the *War of the Confederates.* In Prussia, later on, a whole system of historical philosophy was drawn from it; Frederick contented himself, and it is more than enough, with producing a dilution of this idea in a ponderous medley, entitled the *Civil War of Geneva,* an insipid production worthy in every respect of the second-rate inspiration which dictated it. The King's wit is restored, on the other hand, in full force in the *Dialogue of the Dead* between the Duc de Choiseul, Count Struensee and Socrates, which Frederick wrote, also for his own amusement, in February, 1772, that is to say, at the time when the bearers of the treaty of partition were posting between Vienna, Berlin and St. Petersburg. It is useless to dwell upon the offensive aspect of this satire. Struensee had been imprisoned on January 17; he was lying under the threat of a sentence of death. 'The Duc de Choiseul,' said the King, 'may be considered as civilly dead since his exile, and Master Struensee may be considered as already condemned to death by the sentence which will be passed on him. Nothing, then, need prevent an author with few chronological scruples from treating them as defunct ancients.' Frederick the Great here gave too much consideration to chronology, and such scruples as he might have laid on himself should have related to other chapters. It was easy enough to deal with the man

[11] ' Vous avez à vos puissants voisins,
        Sans y penser, longtemps servi la nappe.
        Vous voudrez donc bien trouver bel et beau
        Que ces voisins partagent le gâteau
        Tels sont les fruits de votre extravagance.'

The expression in the last line but one, ' partager le gâteau' (literally, ' to share the cake '), is that alluded to in Voltaire's letter (see p. 220).—TRANSLATOR.

whom he contemptuously called 'Master Struensee'; that Danish Ruy-Blas was indeed a conspirator of very pitiful stuff. Frederick also acquits himself tolerably well with Socrates; he makes him into a sort of dried fruit of the encyclopædia, a disciple of Wolf and Puffendorf mixed, whose man-of-the-world smile routs all systems; but with Choiseul the royal pamphleteer is generally reduced to abusiveness. And, moreover, the force of logic defeats his hatreds, and in the end it can no longer clearly be seen whom the author wishes to deride. Herein lies the piquant interest of the work, and it is also its lesson. How can we admit that the Prince who quotes the dismemberment of Poland with pride in his *Memoirs* as 'the first instance which history furnishes of a partition peaceably ordered and concluded between three Powers' is not searching his own heart when he puts this maxim into the mouth of Struensee : 'A vast genius makes himself known by bold enterprises; he desires novelty; he performs things hitherto unprecedented; he leaves petty scruples to old wives, and marches straight to his end without troubling himself about the means which conduct him thither.' The daemon of literature is a traitor by nature, and a great stripper of consciences; he cannot keep secrets confided to him, and only those have been able to dissemble all their lives who have been devoid of wit and have not felt the prick of talent. This was not the case with the King of Prussia, and no one who has studied him at all closely can help thinking that he is pleading his own cause, when he makes Choiseul say, when Socrates calls him a villain : 'Teach your bald head to know that *coups d'état* are not crimes, and that everything which brings glory is great. . . . Master Philosopher, know that a man must not have a strait conscience if he would rule the world.'

CHAPTER XVII.

THE DISTRIBUTION OF THE SHARES.

(January—May, 1772.)

The Declaration, which was signed at Vienna on February 19, at Berlin on the 28th, and at St. Petersburg on March 5, 1772, sanctioned the principle of the partition of Poland, and, though it omitted to define the shares which should be allotted to each of the three co-parceners, decided that those shares were to be perfectly equal. The partition resolved upon, equality being established as its basis, it remained to draw the frontiers, and to prepare Europe for the news of this strange touching-up which its map was to receive. This gave rise to a double negotiation just as thorny as the first. It was difficult to carry out the partition; it was still more so to explain it. Austria worried herself greatly over this explanation; Russia was a trifle uneasy about it, Prussia not at all. Frederick's wish was that each party should take possession as quickly as might be, reserving it till later to draw out frontiers, and to inform Europe of the treaty when it had been carried out. Russia was not in such a hurry; she was occupying much more territory than she meant to keep, and she had therefore no need to take more as security. Catharine also hoped to lead the Court of Vienna into temptation in the direction of the East, to make it her accomplice at once in Turkey and in Poland, and thus to pave the way for an alliance which should one day solve the Eastern question by the partition of Turkey in Europe between Austria and Russia. Austria sought to justify the partition, and to make it as advantageous as possible for herself; to make it an enterprise of less injustice and less inequality; and it was for that reason that, while very backward in making her own wishes known, she had asked for preliminary information of Russia's intentions.

Russia was not slow to reply. Panin drew up ' a plan of concert' between the two Courts, and communicated it to the Austrian Minister towards the end of March, 1772. Panin allowed it to be understood that, besides her share of Poland, Austria might procure the cession of Belgrade to herself by the Turks, with a part of Bosnia and Servia, during the negotiations for peace. ' No doubt,' he added, ' Austria would thus obtain an enlargement superior to those of Prussia and Russia; this would modify the principle of equality; but this opportunity would nevertheless be eagerly seized in order to show goodwill towards the Court of Vienna, and to pave the way for a *triple alliance* between Austria, Russia, and Prussia.'[1]

In the interval Kaunitz had reflected that it was better worth while to abide by the principle of equality pure and simple; that that principle had been laid down, and that it had better be applied with all its consequences; that by mixing up a scheme for partitioning Turkey with the carrying out of the partition of Poland, Austria would run the risk of losing the substance for the sake of the shadow. Since she could provide for herself at the expense of the Pole, it was there that she should make a beginning. Kaunitz, then, made it known at Berlin and St. Petersburg what the share was that Austria claimed; it was the county

[1] Lobkowitz's Report, March 30, 1772 : Arneth, vol. viii., p. 599.

of Zips, of course ; then the greater part of Red Russia,
including Lamberg and Little Poland up to the Vistula,
which included the salt-mines of Wieliczka. 'The Court
of Vienna,' Kaunitz wrote to Lobkowitz on April 12, 1772,
' holds to its determination to do nothing prejudicial to
the Porte unless the latter furnishes *just* and well-founded
motives for the contrary.' If the Porte furnished *just*
motives, Austria reserved the right of settling the matter
at Constantinople, and of demanding *just* indemnification ;
but the matter would lie between Austria and Turkey ;
the partition of Poland would be entirely dissociated from
these fresh proceedings. The particular advantages accruing
from this operation would in no way affect the *just* principle
of the equality of shares. In this same month of April
Joseph wrote to his brother Leopold : ' Russia is reassured
as to our intentions ; she has ceased to trouble herself about
making peace with the Porte, and who knows whether the
latter may not yet give us a *just* cause for joining in, by
its false behaviour, and that in the coming year we may
not pocket Belgrade and a part of Bosnia, just as we shall
this year pocket the palatinates of Poland ? It is no longer
a secret that a corps of troops will enter Poland from our
side in June ; but upon the subject of the partition, the
most absolute secrecy must be maintained, though it has
begun to leak out, and though the French have already
got some scent of the business at Berlin.'

Sure of the complicity of the Court of Vienna, the King
of Prussia, who lost no opportunity of sowing discord
between France and Austria, had revealed the proposed
dismemberment of Poland at Versailles, and had hinted
that Austria was to share in it.[2] Louis XV. made these
hints known to Mercy, who hastened to warn his Government, though the matter gave him no uneasiness. ' As
the motions of intrigues absorb all men's minds here, and

[2] Louis XV. to the Comte de Broglie, January 12, 1772.

divert them from outside affairs,' he wrote to the Empress
on April 15, 1772, 'there is the less reason to fear the
steps which the French Government might have taken, at
any other time than this, to hamper the operations which
will arise from the approaching establishment of peace,
and the arrangements which will be made relating to
Poland.   All that the Duc d'Aiguillon has said to me on
the subject up to the present has given me but very little
trouble.   This Minister handles affairs without energy,
without nerve, and without ideas.   His bent leads him to
employ petty methods of duplicity; but this system can
never be very formidable, and only entails a little vigilance
and observation.'

The Ambassador whom Louis XV. had just sent to
Vienna ought not, it was believed, to prove more far-
seeing and exacting than the Ministry of Foreign Affairs
on the subject of the alliance.   D'Aiguillon wrote to this
Ambassador: 'The resolutions of the Court of Vienna will
decide the condition of the eastern part of Europe and the
fate of Poland.   A passive part is the only one which will
be in harmony with the King's wishes and sentiments.'[3]
The Court of Vienna asked nothing more.   This declaration reassured it, and the man who made it expressed in
his own personality the sentiments of those who drew it
up.   This was Prince Louis de Rohan, the coadjutor of
the Bishop of Strasburg, a Court prelate, ostentatious,
prodigal, ambitious, brilliant, witty, restless; in other
respects, an aristocratic libertine, but a mediocre diplomatist, though at bottom he had more penetration than
he allowed to appear.   He presented his credentials to the
Empress on January 19, 1772.   He displeased her from
the first.   His behaviour revolted her.   'It is a very
worthless fellow, wanting alike talents, prudence, and

[3] Austrian Instructions, d'Aiguillon to Rohan, February 6, 1772,
p. 447.

morals ; he ill sustains the character of a Minister and an ecclesiastic,' she wrote to Mercy. ' Rohan is still the same ; but almost all our women, young and old, beautiful and ugly, are none the less bewitched by this original but very evil compound of extravagance and folly.' If Maria Theresa the devotee was scandalized by the Ambassador's licentiousness, the prudent ruler of Austria was none the less reassured for her political enterprises. ' The Emperor,' she wrote to Mercy, on March 18, 1772, ' likes conversing with him, it is true, but only to hear his follies, his twaddle, and his sorry jokes. Kaunitz appears to be fairly well pleased with him, because he gives him no trouble and shows him every kind of deference.' Louis XV.'s ally, like his worst enemies, had arrived at congratulating herself upon the weakness of his Government and upon the incapacity of his agents. After shedding a few tears over Choiseul's ' civil decease,' and scattering the flowers of German rhetoric by handfuls over the entombment at Chanteloup,[4] Maria Theresa had promptly consoled herself with the reflection that a friend of such a character would have given her a great deal of trouble. ' The solution of the drama will certainly not gain the applause of our allies,' she wrote in April, 1772. ' If the Duc de Choiseul were still in office, he would doubtless take advantage of the opportunity to strip us of some part of the Low Countries, where we should not be in a condition to offer the slightest resistance.'

Nevertheless the struggle between conscience and interest in the Empress's soul was still unassuaged, and the thought of France reawoke all the anxieties which stirred her. At war with herself, she still repeated, with the Apostle :

' What I would, that do I not ; but what I hate, that do I.'

She continued to examine into the origins of the

---

[4] Choiseul's country seat.

evil which she hated, judging and condemning, with
singular sagacity, 'these measures, false, ill-arranged,
inconsequent, dangerous, and in scanty conformity with
rectitude and honour,' which, leading Austria from error
to error, from blunder to blunder, had brought her to
the humiliating extremity of 'finding herself rightly
accused of falseness and duplicity, and that by the King
of Prussia himself.' If the accomplice at Berlin could
justly give this description to Austria's conduct, what
would be the righteous indignation of the ally at
Versailles? And yet dissimulation towards the latter
was a necessity; that attitude could not now be departed
from, and this was the strange conclusion to which the
Empress's searchings of heart led her :[5] 'For what remains,
as we have up to this point used so much reserve with
France, it will be necessary still to continue upon the
same footing until peace is concluded, and our engagements with Russia and Prussia are carried out; after that
specious reasons must at the least be given in justification.'

It cost Kaunitz no great struggle with himself to
accomplish the delicate task of deceiving Louis XV.'s
Ambassador with forms. Rohan pressed him with questions. His answers would worthily serve as commentaries
to the *Lettres Provinciales*. 'As regards Poland,' he said
in April, 1772—that is to say, when he had just sent his
proposals for partition to Berlin and St. Petersburg—'as
regards Poland, we have resolved, as have the King of
Prussia and the Empress of Russia, not to allow our neighbours to secure any territorial increase in that country
which could disturb the equilibrium, or lessen the even-
ness of the political balance in the North. It is in pursuit
of this principle, from which we shall never depart, that
we have resolved to send an army immediately into

[5] *Vide* Arneth, vol. viii., p. 601, *Pièces Justificatives*, for the text
of this remarkable self-examination.

Poland. . . .' Rohan was not a profound politician;
but, though a Court prelate, he had some tincture of
casuistry, and had at least dipped into those studies of
moral theology which, according to Talleyrand, are the
best schooling for diplomacy. Butterfly as he was, he saw
through Kaunitz's words, and perceived that if Austria,
Prussia and Russia had resolved not to allow *the neighbours*
of Poland to enlarge their borders at the expense of the
balance of power in Europe, it must mean that they had
resolved to enlarge their own borders at the expense of
their neighbour, the Polish Republic. He wrote to
d'Aiguillon on April 13, 1772, declaring that, in his
judgment, the partition was already a settled affair.[6]

Frederick, however, who had formerly brought such
vigorous pressure to bear on Austria to gain her consent
to the partition, now thought that she was putting too
much heartiness into the business, and that the share
which she assigned herself was out of proportion to those
of Prussia and Russia. ' Allow me to say,' he said
smilingly to Van Swieten, on April 28, ' that your
appetite is a good one.' The Russians shared the impression, and, from the first words that Lobkowitz spoke to
him on the subject, Panin did not attempt to disguise the
fact.[7] The annexation of Lemberg and of the salt-mines
of Wieliczka he thought excessive. The Court of Vienna
had another pretension which offended him no less; it
affected to take this immense share only upon compulsion
and against its will. ' As Russia and Prussia have already
concluded a convention of partition between themselves,'
Lobkowitz said, ' the very essence of the matter demands
that Austria shall only accede to the definite treaty in the
quality of *pars principalis contrahens*.' Like the King of

[6] *Vide* Rohan's Reports in Saint-Priest, *Le Partage de la Pologne,*
chap. v.
[7] Lobkowitz's Reports of April 28 and May 1, 1772.

Prussia, Panin insisted that Austria's complicity should be open and duly certified in diplomatic instruments. He said as much to Lobkowitz, in courteous but plain language, in a conference which they had on May 28, 1772. He added that Austria's plan tended towards the complete annihilation of Poland.

The Czarina and her Minister only consented to allow others to eat into the frontiers of Poland, and to do the like themselves, with the reservation of keeping the heart of that republic at their own disposal. This was the bottom of the 'observations based upon friendship and good faith' which Panin communicated to the Austrian Minister in this same interview. Poland, he said, must for ever remain an intermediary Power destined to prevent any collision between the interests of the three Courts ; there must, then, be left to her 'such strength and intrinsic consistency as shall harmonize with such a destination.' It was for the maintenance of this just balance between their interests that the three Sovereigns had laid down the principle of equality in the partition which they proposed to accomplish. But, pursued Panin, 'an equality of such a character could not be so perfect and so strict in every respect that each of the three shares should comprise the same extent of country, the same fertility of soil, the same population, or, in a word, *the same political value.*' The meaning of these last words may appear sufficiently vague ; but it was not so for the Chancery of Vienna. They are consecrated terms. Metternich, who prided himself more than any other man on his jurisprudence, undertook the task of defining them half a century later, and that with great clearness. 'The valuation of terri- tories shall be made according to population,' he wrote on December 24, 1814, in his scheme of organization for the Statistical Commission ; 'the valuation of the popula- tion shall not be made *simply with regard to numbers ; it*

shall also take into consideration the kind or quality.' It
was thus understood by the Congress of Vienna, and Panin
gave it the same meaning. He laid it down that, Prussia's
share being taken 'in sandy and uncultivated country,'
and Russia's consisting only of 'woods, marshes and sandy
lands,' there existed, both in respect of productions and of
population, 'a prodigious difference between those shares
and that which Austria assigned to herself.' Consequently
he came to the conclusion that, to restore the equilibrium,
to maintain the principle of equality, and to preserve a
sufficient 'intrinsic consistency' for Poland, it behoved
Austria to give up the salt-mines of Wieliczka—'the King
of Poland's only sure means of subsistence'—and the town
of Lemberg, which 'from time immemorial has been, and
must be, the general rendezvous of the Polish nation.'

The Court of Vienna had foreseen these objections.
Joseph thought that it was expedient to take precautions,
and to make himself secure against every contingency.
He wrote to Kaunitz on May 2: 'The taking possession
of a greater or lesser part of Poland than would remain in
our hands would lead to no consequences and would
establish no right; the Russian and Prussian troops are
at the present moment in districts which they do not
expect to keep. . . . Could not we enter into possession
of some palatinate, take an arbitrary extension of territory,
positions advantageous from a military point of view and
convenient for our subsistence—in a word, reconnoitre the
country well, and afterwards arrange the demarcation of
our boundaries, according to the advantages which the
ground, the country, and our convenience shall demand,
and upon which a mutual agreement shall be made?'
This was done; Kaunitz approved the plan, and Maria
Theresa accorded her *placet*. On May 25 Marshal Lacy
received an autograph order from the Emperor, instructing
him to enter Poland, to take possession of Lemberg,

'especially the two salt districts,' to continue to exploit the country, but to keep what it produced in a 'separate treasury,' and to allow nothing more to go to the King of Poland, 'in order,' said the Emperor, 'that these two places (the salt-mines and Lemberg) may be in our hands before we are prevented by representations, or are hampered in carrying this out.' The troops marched, and the Minister of State, Count Pergen, was ordered to undertake the government of the occupied Polish territories, with the title of Commissary Plenipotentiary.

CHAPTER XVIII.

THE CONSECRATION OF THE ALLIANCE—THE TREATY OF PARTITION.

(May—August, 1772.)

'I CAN well believe,' Maria Theresa wrote to Mercy, on June 1, 1772—'I can well believe that the line which we have lately adopted with regard to Poland will have made some sensation in France. However convinced I may be of the King's feelings, I could not bring myself to write to him on this subject; but I give you entire freedom to say to him whatever you may think fitting about the matter on my behalf.' Kaunitz had taught Mercy his lesson. Austria had done everything to avoid the partition of Poland, but she had been alone in her resistance; all the Powers, especially France and England, had abandoned her. She had been compelled to resign herself to letting things take their own course. Then it was that she had learnt of the treaty of partition concluded between Prussia and Russia, and that, to maintain the equilibrium, she had resolved to enter Poland, and to give effect, in her turn, to such *ancient rights* as she might possess over certain provinces of that kingdom, which provinces were, however, very inferior in extent to those which Russia and Prussia had assigned to themselves. It would be well, Kaunitz said, to lay stress upon the treaty concluded between Hungary and Poland

in 1412, for it was upon that treaty that Austria's claims
to Red Russia and Podolia were based.[1]   It was the last
word upon the matter of Zips, and it may be seen that,
however *poor an opinion* Austria had of her title to that
country, she yet deemed it solid enough to be extended to
the whole of Galicia.

D'Aiguillon appeared to be but moderately moved by
these 'erudite deductions,' and showed some inclination
to resist. He even tried to stir up the English and to
induce them to protest. 'Vanæ sine viribus iræ !' Kaunitz
replied, when Mercy informed him of the French Minister's
ill-humour.[2]   And, indeed, France could do nothing. She
would assuredly not seek a means of salvation for Poland
from the King of Prussia. Whether she would or no, as
regarded her alliance, she was forced to fill the very clearly
defined part which Austria so cleverly assigned to her.
Vioménil was recalled. 'France,' Vergennes wrote in 1775,
' has ceased to trouble herself about the welfare of Poland ;
she has even ceased to give advice to the patriots, not
being in a position to give them support, whether by her
influence or by the force of her arms.'[3]   Louis XV., moreover, had chosen his part. 'I see clearly,' Mercy wrote to
the Empress on May 15, 1772, ' that the projected dispositions in Poland have in no way affected the King
personally ; that he believes that Your Majesty could not
help subscribing to the aforesaid dispositions, and that
they incontestably proceed from the circumstances of the
case. The only thing which could pain the King would
be being led to conclude that Your Majesty's friendship
towards him had cooled.' The Duc d'Aiguillon, ' dis-

---

[1] Kaunitz to Mercy, April 29, May 15, May 31, 1772 : Arneth,
vol. viii., pp. 428, 429 ; Mercy's *Correspondance*, vol. i., p. 315, note.

[2] Mercy to Kaunitz, May 15 ; Kaunitz to Mercy, May 31, 1772.

[3] Vergennes to M. de Pons, Resident at Danzig : *Instructions de
Pologne*, vol. ii., p. 310.

trustful, ignorant of affairs, confounding his ideas,' was
totally unable to judge of the actual circumstances, and,
failing to understand, blamed and criticised. But it
appeared that all his efforts to move his master only
tended to his own destruction. 'The Most Christian
King,' the same Ambassador wrote a month later, on
June 15, 'regards this object with an eye of justice and
moderation, which fully reassures me as to the stability of
his sentiments and of his attachment to the alliance. . . .
It will remain for us only to mitigate the effects arising
from the self-esteem of the Duc d'Aiguillon, who is
personally irritated at the melancholy part which he is
playing at the outset of his ministry. I flatter myself
that effective means may be employed to bring him back :
that of the good offices of the Favourite appears to me one
which should not be neglected.'

Maria Theresa had been much exercised before deciding
for the partition ; but, the decision once taken, she gave
effect to it without stopping at 'trifles.' Rohan slandered
her to d'Aiguillon ; the latter, moreover, passed for a
'good Prussian.' She thought it necessary to prove to
the King of France that her friendship was warmer than
ever, and to cut short the opposition, excited in a Minister
without enlightenment, by the hints of an Ambassador
devoid of scruples. She could not choose the means of
her defence ; as she had sacrificed her principles when it
was a question of taking, now that it was a question of
keeping she did not hesitate to sacrifice her prudery.
She appealed from Rohan to the Du Barry, from Frederick
the Great to the King's mistress, and charged her daughter
to plead her cause. She wrote to Mercy on July 5, 1772 :
'To prevent these evils and this unpleasantness for the
monarchy and the family, all means must be employed,
and my daughter the Dauphiness alone, with the aid of
your counsels and your local knowledge, can perform this

service to her family and to her country. Above all, she must cultivate the good graces of the King by her assiduity and tenderness; she must try to divine his thoughts; she must shock him in nothing, *and she must treat the Favourite well.* I do not demand any degradations, still less intimacy, but *such attentions as are due in consideration for her grandfather and master*, and in view of the good which may result for us and for the two Courts; perhaps the alliance hangs on it. . . . I look to your duty and to that of my dear daughter, that you may use all your care and she all her graces, detaching herself from such prejudices as may prompt her to a contrary course. None such can be weighed against the good that she can do.'

We must not smile when we read this strange production. It would be to ignore the habits of the age and the characters of the persons. Maria Theresa here spoke of the family as she did elsewhere of right. She invoked the respect due to an old man to conquer her daughter's prejudices, with the same melancholy gravity with which she elsewhere invoked the respect due to her subjects to conquer her own scruples. Fate willed it that, from the invasion of Zips down to this cajoling of the Du Barry, she should imitate the King of Prussia's conduct point for point; but she had no suspicion of this, and continued to regard that Prince as a scandal to Kingship. The fact was, Frederick prided himself on his duplicity, and gloried in his trickery. Maria Theresa, on the contrary, condemned her own conduct, and asked pardon of Heaven and earth for each of her deficiencies. She thought Frederick impudent; she judged herself weak. She saw in him a libertine glorying in his vice and proud of it, in herself the deplorable victim of the misfortunes of the times and of the evil passions of men. Frederick's intriguing was cynical; Maria Theresa's was bathed in tears. These fair and wise tears, destined to deceive the world, blinded herself first of all. ' My maxim is honesty and candour, no duplicity or guile towards others,' she wrote in January, 1771, when the partition was first spoken of. The partition decided upon, she certainly thought herself no less sincere when she said to the Prince of Saxe : ' My sole consolation lies in the uprightness of my intentions, in the constancy of my endeavours to prevent a result in which I have been forced to take part.'[4]

Kaunitz wept not at all, and belaboured himself with no reproaches. At ease with respect to France, he knew that he had nothing to fear from England. The English Ministers entirely disapproved of the partition of Poland ; but, as they neither could nor would do anything, they gravely declared that, ' *although this extraordinary and unexpected event* gave rise to plausible apprehensions for the future of European commerce, His Majesty did not, any more than did the other commercial Powers, regard the matter as of such actual importance as to require direct opposition from him, or any active measures for its prevention.'[5] Kaunitz, then, could push his point boldly. For the first time since the beginning of these slippery negotiations he found himself on the way to success. His plans were prospering.

The Austrian troops advanced in Poland. ' General d'Alton has occupied the salt-mines, and has made the men employed take an oath that they will make no more returns to the King,' Joseph wrote on June 17, 1772. Esterhazy was marching on Lemberg. Austria was invading, taking, keeping. Kaunitz was arguing, measuring districts, numbering populations, discussing the ' political value ' of the shares, and demonstrating that Austria's was indisputably the least advantageous of the three. He

[4] Rohan's Report, May 28, 1772 : Saint-Priest, vol. i., p. 286.
[5] The Secretary of State for Foreign Affairs to the British Ambassador in Turkey, July 24, 1772.

took high ground with the two allies, and lectured them roundly. He wrote to Lobkowitz on July 5, 1772 : ' Russia and the King of Prussia treat the negotiation of this partition as though it were a question of three private individuals with landed property to divide, while we have here to deal with three great Courts, one of which has adopted the arrangement proposed to it by the other two, prompted in no way by covetousness or a need of extending its rule, but solely to save all three from the calamity of an appalling war. . . . Both at St. Petersburg and at Berlin they might, I should have thought, do us the honour of believing that we have some knowledge of the nature of a political calculation. . . . They should tell themselves that, for the Court of Vienna, all these arrangements are a question, not *de lucro captando*, but solely *de damno vitando ;* and in view of this they should, as it seems to me, instead of making great ado about a trifle more or less, take a large view of the matter, for all matters of this nature should be so treated. . . .' In the meanwhile, the Austrian troops were still marching. ' Our operations in Poland are going on fairly well,' Joseph wrote on July 9 ; ' we have got beforehand with the Russians at Tinietz ; they will be in a temper. It remains to be seen what they will do.'

The Russians might perhaps be annoyed, but, fortunately for Austria, Frederick the Great was there. ' Arguments fortified by guns and bayonets' were in his eyes logical and much to the point. ' I see,' he wrote to Prince Henry on June 18, ' that the Empress of Russia is not as pleased with the Austrians now as she appeared to be at first ; but then Prince Kaunitz is putting as much chicane into these negotiations as they are capable of containing. This maddens me, because it stops our taking possession, and exposes us to every kind of unpleasantness, both from the questions of the Poles and also from those of other foreign

Powers to which one knows not what answer to give in this state of uncertainty.' The King of Prussia was the more 'maddened' by these delays, as he had personally visited the *morsel* which was to fall to his share, and had found it excellent. 'Convinced of the importance of hastening the conclusion, and that by using too much precision in the valuation of the different shares, opportunities would be given for foreign interference, and the risk would be incurred of losing the fruit of such great labours, he advised the Russians to accept Austria's ultimatum.'[6] The Czarina saw the justice of his reasoning. Kaunitz, when the share which he demanded was allowed, ceased to discuss the form of the documents. Austria's scruples were removed by the advantages which she gained, and she no longer hesitated to accede to the partition on the same footing as Prussia and Russia. The treaties were signed at St. Petersburg on July 25, 1772.

In the name of the Most Holy Trinity, whereas the spirit of faction which maintained a state of anarchy in Poland gave grounds for fearing the *total decomposition of the State,* which might disturb the interests of the neighbours of that republic, affect the friendly harmony existing between them, and ignite a general war, Austria, Prussia, and Russia, having, moreover, certain claims and rights no less ancient than legitimate with respect to Poland, had decided to give effect to them, to restore order in the interior of Poland, and to give that State a political existence more in conformity with their interests as her neighbours.[7] The theory of the partition thus laid down, the partitioners passed to its application. Austria took Zips, nearly the whole of Red Russia with Galitch, Lemberg, Belz, part of Podolia and of Volhynia with Tarnopol, the southern part

[6] *Mémoires, Œuvres,* vol. vi., p. 46.
[7] Preamble of the three Treaties of Partition : Angeberg, pp. 97, 100, 103 ; Martens, vol. ii., p. 24.

of Little Poland on the right bank of the Upper Vistula,
with the salt-mines of Wieliczka and Bochnia.   Zips was
reincorporated with the Crown of Hungary; the rest formed
the kingdom of Galicia; the whole gave Austria an increase
of 2,600,000 inhabitants.   Prussia gained all Polish Prussia,
that is to say, the bishopric of Warmia, the palatinates of
Pomerelia, Culm, and Marienburg (except the two towns
of Thorn and Danzig), the northern districts of Greater
Poland and of Cujavia with Bromberg: in all 600,000
inhabitants.   Russia annexed the whole country of the
Dwina, the Dnieper, and the Drusch, that is to say, the
palatinates of Polsk, Witepsk, Mohilef, and Mcislaf, containing about 1,600,000 inhabitants.

Austria had got a medicine for her scruples.   The
Empress, while continuing to deplore the means, could
not help rejoicing at the result, and the feelings which
divided her mind appeared in her style of writing in
cleverly balanced propositions.   She wrote to Marshal
Lacy on August 23, 1772: 'The St. Petersburg courier
has brought back *the unhappy partition*, signed.   It is still
to you that I owe *this great advantage, if such it be*.   But
what is certain is that you formed the plan and *were able
to demand so much* and so *to procure this gain for the State*,
without being implicated in the question, whether it was
just or not.'

The Czarina knew no such mental restrictions.   She
possessed an impassive mind, and reasons of state swayed
her conscience.   Rulhière had published an account of
the revolution of 1762.[8]   He had disguised nothing—
neither the Czarina's conspiracies, nor her intrigues, nor
her amours.   Catharine greatly wished to see the book,
and begged Diderot to get it for her.   The request was
embarrassing, and the philosopher took precautions.   ' As
for what concerns yourself, madam,' he said, ' if you care

[8] *Anecdotes sur la Révolution de Russie en l'Année* 1762.

greatly for decorum and for the virtues, the worn rags
of your sex, this work is a satire against yourself; but if
large views, if masculine and patriotic ideas, rather interest
you, the author shows you here as a great princess, and,
taking it altogether, he does you more honour than
injury.' 'You increase my wish to read this work,'
Catharine replied.[9] These treaties *à la* Semiramis delighted the encyclopædists. It may be imagined that
no secret qualms disturbed the Czarina's joy after the
partition. 'Never have I signed a document with so
much satisfaction,' she said to Lobkowitz.[10] She wrote
to Maria Theresa on September 15 : 'I view with the
most lively joy the establishment, through the concert
upon Polish affairs, of a new interest, and one which may
so fitly be joined to those which permanently subsist
between our monarchies.' The contentment was appropriate, but the laughter was forced, and there is a ring
of affectation in the tone of levity which Catharine II.
adopts when telling her friend Voltaire the good news :
'We have found no other method of protecting our
frontiers from the incursions of the so-called confederates,
commanded by French officers, than that of extending
them. The course of the Dwina and of the Beresina, of
which I am just now taking possession, will have that
effect. Do you not think it reasonable that those who
shut their ears to reason should pay the piper ? I have
sent for the comedian you tell me of. Apropos, what do
you think of the revolution in Sweden ?'[11]

Voltaire thought that it was just, and that the work
was a good work. 'Assuredly it is a truly kingly cake,'[12]

[9] Durand to d'Aiguillon, November 9, 1773 : Publications of the
Historical Society of Russia, vol. xvii., p. 288.

[10] Lobkowitz's Report, September 24, 1772 : Beer, vol. ii., p. 198.

[11] September 12, 1772 : text published by the Historical Society
of Russia.

[12] *Vide* p. 200.

he wrote to Frederick on October 16, 1772, quoting the
sorry verses of the *Guerre des Confédérés;* 'it has always
been your destiny to astonish the world. I know not
when you will stop, but I know that the Prussian eagle
flies very far.' It was enough for the moment for Frederick
the Great that that eagle had lit on Polish Prussia.
'Thank Heaven,' he wrote to Finkenstein on August 22,
'that business is ended ; it was fully time, for the blow
would have missed its mark.' He replied to Voltaire's
compliments on November 1 in the tone which fitted the
learned levity of their correspondence. 'Happy,' he said,
praising the perpetual youth of the hermit of Ferney—
'happy the man who can thus wed imagination to reason!
That far excels the acquisition of some few provinces,
whose existence is not discernible upon the general globe,
and which from the celestial spheres would appear hardly
comparable to a grain of sand. Such are the paltry
matters over which we politicians are so strenuously
busied. My excuse must be that when a man has entered
a certain body, he must adopt its spirit. I have known
a Jesuit who solemnly assured me that he would expose
himself to the cruellest martyrdom could he but convert
an ape. I would not go that far, but when it is possible
to bind up and join intersected territories, to make a
whole of one's possessions, I know no mortal who would
not joyfully labour to such an end. Always bear in mind
that this affair has passed without bloodshed, and that
the encyclopædists cannot exclaim against mercenary
brigands, and use other fine phrases whose eloquence has
never moved me. *A little ink, with the aid of a pen, has
done it all*, and Europe will be at peace, at all events
from the last troubles.' Frederick was beforehand with
criticism. Precautions being bootless, criticism laid down
its arms. 'It is asserted,' Voltaire replied on November 17,
'that it is yourself, sire, who imagined the partition of

Poland; and I believe it, for there is genius in it, and
that the treaty was made at Potsdam.' Flattering as was
the praise, the King of Prussia refused it. ' I know of no
treaties signed at Potsdam or at Berlin. I know that
some have been made at St. Petersburg.' ' I know that
it is pretty generally believed in Europe that the partition
which has been made in Poland is a result of political
manœuvres which are attributed to me. Nothing, however, is further from the truth. After different treat-
ments had been vainly proposed, recourse had to be had
to this partition as the only means of avoiding a general
war.' There had been in it no concerted plan, no design
matured for long or pursued from afar. It was only an
expedient, and he had adopted it because there was no
other. ' I played the part of an extinguisher; I put out
the fire.'[13] If Frederick declined the credit of the invention, it was assuredly not because he saw any reason to
blush for his conduct, but his exchange of letters with
Voltaire was for him a sort of semi-official correspondence.
In them he presented matters, not as he saw them, but
as it was to his interest that the public should see them.
Opinion, in his eyes, was not a judge to be bowed down
to; it was a means of government, a weapon against
which a man must arm himself when he could not use
it. ' I keep silence about such recent events, of which it
would be indiscreet to speak,'[14] he said. But in the meanwhile he very skilfully adapted truth to the needs of his
policy. He kept his revelations for his *Memoirs*, and his
confessions for intimate conversations. He treated Voltaire
as a diplomatist; he behaved to his familiars as to posterity,
and in the free discussions at the Potsdam soirées he
related events and passed judgment on them as nakedly

[13] Frederick to Voltaire, December 6, 1772, October 9, 1773,
September 19, 1774.

[14] To Voltaire, September 19, 1774.

as it was his pride to do in his *Memoirs*. D'Alembert called on him after the partition, and, says a contemporary,[15] 'spoke frankly to him of this violation of the law of nations and of sovereigns.' Frederick did not attempt to justify himself. ' The Empress Catharine and myself,' he replied, ' are two brigands ; but that devotee the Queen Empress, how has she settled it with her confessor ?'

As for Prince Henry, he wrote to Solms, reminding him that he had ' set the affair going ': 'I demand no recompense for that ; my only ambition is for glory, and I confess that I should think myself fortunate in receiving it at the hands of Her Majesty the Empress of Russia. This might be brought about if she would deign, on the occasion of the taking possession, to honour me with a public letter to show me her satisfaction, which might serve me as a proof that I have contributed to this great work.' 'It is my gossip the Man in a Hurry,[16] and that is all about it,' Catharine said of him.   It is not known whether she gave him any other testimonial ; but it is certain that the Prince continued to boast of having woven this web of perfidy, that the philosophers were very indulgent to him on that score, and that he inherited the same credit with the revolutionaries as he had enjoyed with their predecessors.   He presented the Institute of France with the manuscript of *Jacques le Fataliste* in the year 5 ; the Directory sent him arms of honour in return, with bound copies of Diderot.[17]

---

[15] *Essais de Mémoires sur Suard*, Paris, 1820, p. 153.

[16] *C'est ma commère l'Empressée.*

[17] Letter from Prince Henry : Martens, vol. vi., p. 68 ; *Segur's Account, Mémoires*, vol. i., p. 145 ; Procés-verbaux du Directoire, Vendémiaire, an V.

CHAPTER XIX.

THE CONGRESSES OF FOCKTCHANY AND BUCHAREST.

(May, 1772—March, 1773.)

The negotiations which had just been concluded at St. Petersburg had affected the course of affairs in the East. The *just* and tutelary principle of equality in the partition of Poland once laid down, it was suddenly found that the most cordial agreement was established between the Prussian and Austrian representatives at Constantinople. On January 22 Kaunitz informed Thugut that, the King of Prussia having sided with Russia, Austria could not dream of fighting both her neighbours at once; that consequently the best thing the Porte could do would be to sign an armistice and to negotiate a peace. The Prussian Minister, Zegelin, held the same language. Informed by the mediators that Russia gave up her claims to Wallachia and Moldavia, the Turks inclined towards peace; their strength was exhausted. To bring them to a decision, it needed only that Austria should declare, in good set terms, that she abandoned them. It was on such slippery occasions as these that Kaunitz's genius appeared to the best advantage. For a long time, and with consummate art, he had prepared the way which should lead Austria in the guise of honesty from the Turkish to the Russian alliance. He had had his reasons

for not ratifying the treaty of July 6, 1771 ; as Austria
had not sent the ratification, the Turks had suspended
payment of the subsidies.   Kaunitz had not failed to take
note of the fact.[1]   On April 8, 1772, he wrote to Thugut,
telling him to come to a clear explanation with the Ottoman Ministry.   Austria had promised to assist Turkey by
negotiation or by war ; she had been faithful to her
engagements ; she had armed, she had negotiated, she
had induced Russia to give up the principalities ; she
could do no more.   Prussia had, in fact, allied herself
with Russia, and that alliance modified the conditions of
the treaty.   Austria had promised to support the Turks
against Russia ; she had made no engagement to support
them against Prussia.   The Turks had, moreover, placed
themselves outside the terms of the convention, in that
they had ceased to provide the subsidies.   As for the
clause which guaranteed the liberty and independence of
Poland, it did not apply to present circumstances ; the
treaty of 1771 had not foreseen that Austria would, in
1772, have claims to prosecute against that republic.   In
these circumstances, Thugut was to ask the Turks whether
they still held themselves bound by the Convention of
July 6, 1771 ; he was to declare that Austria, 'in her
most high magnanimity,' was disposed to annul that Act
and to restore the instrument of it ; that she would so far
extend her greatness of soul as not to demand the overdue
subsidies, and that she would even have been disposed
to reimburse the money received, had she not already
expended between 6,000,000 and 7,000,000 of florins on
armaments, so that on the whole account the credit of
generosity would still be on her side.[2]

Thugut saw the Sultan's Ministers during the night of
May 8-9, 1772.   The infidels had at first some difficulty

[1] Despatch to Thugut, January 21, 1772.

[2] Arneth, vol. viii., pp. 444-448 ; Beer, vol. ii., pp. 250 and 252.

in grasping the arguments of Maria Theresa's representative, and in appreciating their delicacy. But on reflection,
as they were too weak to be angry, they chose the wisest
part, which was to accept Austria's declarations for what
they were worth, and to extract all the advantages which
they could from them. They replied to Thugut, in the
night of June 6-7, that they now expected but one thing
from the Court of Vienna, which was that it should aid
them in the negotiations which were about to be opened,
and should endeavour to obtain an honourable peace from
Russia, and that, if Austria could not succeed in this, they
would consider the convention of July 6 annulled. They
had, in fact, resolved to negotiate. On June 10 the
armistice was signed, and it was decided that a Congress
should be held. 'These people have acted very sensibly,
very amicably, very suitably,' Kaunitz wrote on July 7.   As
the Turks had left to him the care of deciding in what
direction he should use his influence with the Russians on
their behalf, he naturally thought that it behoved him to
use it in the direction of Austrian interests, that is to say,
in such a way as should induce the Russians to subscribe
to the Austrian pretensions in the partition of Poland.

He would have wished to avoid all mention of Turkey
in the treaty of partition; but the Russians insisted, and
Kaunitz was compelled, in order to get his share, to
acquiesce. The treaty of July 25 consequently set forth
(Article IV.) that, the Russians having communicated the
conditions of peace to Austria, and having, out of regard
for Austria, renounced all claims to the principalities, the
Court of Vienna promised 'to continue to apply itself
sincerely to the success of the Congress, and consequently
to use the *good offices* which it has undertaken to give
to the two belligerent parties.' The treaty spoke of *good
offices towards the two belligerent parties,* merely out of
respect for the forms of diplomacy. In reality, it was

solely a question of supporting Russian claims, and Russia
in very explicit terms informed Austria of the fact. On
the very day on which the treaty of partition was signed,
Panin sent Lobkowitz a '*confidential declaration*,' in which
the Czarina demanded a *prompt and satisfactory* answer to
this question: Will the Austrian Plenipotentiary support
the Russian Ministers at the Peace Congress, and, in the
event of the Turks refusing the Russian ultimatum, will
Austria threaten to leave the Turks to their own devices?[3]
Until Kaunitz should be in a position to reply, and in case
his reply should not be '*satisfactory*,' Russia took precautionary measures. She put herself in such a position
as should give Austria every opportunity of carrying out
her promises to Turkey.

The Plenipotentiaries met at Focktchany on April 19,
1772. Catharine thought to do the Turks great honour
by confiding the negotiations to Count Orlof; he was
assisted by Obreskof, whom the Turks had consented to
set free several months before. 'My angels of peace are
now, I suppose, face to face with those villainous Turks,'
Catharine wrote to Mme. de Bielke. 'Count Orlof, who,
without exaggeration, is the handsomest man of his time,
must indeed appear an angel opposite those boors!'
Thugut and Zegelin presented themselves to take part in
the conferences, but the Russians objected; they declared
that their powers said nothing about *mediation*, that it
was only a question of *good offices*, and that, under those
circumstances, the admission of the Prussian and Austrian
Ministers to the conferences would be contrary to public
law. Zegelin accepted the decision as final, and did not
insist. Thugut, who knew about the negotiations for the
partition, saw that it was no time for raising a dispute
with the Russians; he wrapped himself in extreme
reserve, and awaited instructions. The Turks and

[3] Martens, vol. ii., p. 33.

Russians remained alone and undisturbed. They came
to an understanding without much difficulty upon the
secondary conditions, but found it impossible to agree
about the independence of the Tartars. The Russians
wished it to be absolute; the Turks replied that the
Sultan, as head of the religion, could renounce neither
the nominal sovereignty, nor the investiture of the Khan,
nor the nomination of the judges. That was their ultimatum. The Russians took them at their word. Orlof
had no wish for peace; he expected great advantages for
Russia, and great gains for his family, from the coming
campaign. Also he was impatient to get back to
St. Petersburg, where he had reason to fear that he
would be supplanted. 'The Congress has been broken
up, solely by Orlof's fault,' Joseph II. wrote;[4] 'his credit
is diminishing, and, as his duties demanded residence, he
is almost certain that another has taken them up in the
interim.' He replied to the Turks that their conditions
were incompatible with the independence of the Tartar
peoples. 'Can a people,' he said, 'be considered free
when its chief, its Prince, is subjected in his title, in his
dignity, to the confirmation of another Power?' The
Turks had formal instructions to refuse this concession.
They withdrew, and the Congress was broken up. It had
lasted for twenty days. Thugut had every reason to
applaud his own prudence. Kaunitz had, as a matter of
fact, addressed a reply to Russia which it was impossible,
says a Russian historian, to regard otherwise than as
entirely satisfactory; Austria undertook to use her
influence on Russia's behalf.[5] It would have been hard
for the negotiator of the Austro-Turkish alliance of 1771
to be reduced to this extremity; the rupture of the
negotiations freed Thugut from that necessity.

   [4] To Leopold, October 8, 1772: Frederick, *Mémoires, Œuvres*,
vol. vi.   [5] Martens, vol. ii., p. 34.

It was once more Poland that paid the costs. The time had come to carry out the treaty of July 25. The business now in hand was to get the Polish Diet to ratify the partition, to justify it in the eyes of Europe, and to map out the new frontiers as advantageously as possible. This threefold duty—of diplomacy, of jurisprudence, and of geography—absorbed all the attention of the Court of Vienna. 'After carrying out our arrangements,' Maria Theresa had said, 'reasons of at least a specious character must be alleged for our justification.' Kaunitz devoted all his energies to so doing. He wrote to Van Swieten as early as April 12, 1772 : 'Try to find out from the King of Prussia what steps he and the Russians mean to take concerning the King and the republic of Poland, for informing them the good tidings of the dismemberment, and making them consent to it, of their own accord or on compulsion ; as, for instance, whether they mean to publish a manifesto, and whether they propose to set forth in it the titles and rights on which our acquisitions will be founded. . . .' The King of Prussia was in no great hurry to give Poland and Europe *an abstract of his claims.* 'You understand,' he wrote to his Agent in Poland on April 21, 'when the rights are not over-good, they should not be detailed.' The fact was enough for him. Kaunitz found the Russian diplomatists more inclined to understand his point of view. Not without reason did they style themselves the sons of the Doctors of Byzantium ; they have possessed at all times a taste for subtle distinctions, and they readily confound, in their practical mysticism, principles with facts, justice with success, rights with laws, and jurisprudence with casuistry. So it was decided that a manifesto should be composed. The Russians drew one up. It was clear enough. Joseph thought it *awkward ;* Kaunitz thought it *too explicit.* He manufactured another, which left nothing to be desired, and it was adopted and

published in solemn form.   It is a masterpiece of political
Pharisaism which deceived nobody, least of all those who
signed it.   It deserves the ironical disdain with which
Frederick the Great judges it in his *Memoirs*; he signed
it, but he took care not to appear to be taken in by it.
'We would not,' he says, 'here detail the rights of the
three Powers; singular conjunctures were needed to lead
men's minds to this point, and to unite them for the
partition . . . .'

The conjunctures were singular indeed, and the most
sadly singular of all was the impotence and effacement of
France.   Austria would have displayed less audacity in
her logic if she had had to give an account to her ally.
Unfortunately she felt only too independent.   'The settlement of the arrangements relating to Poland is a fresh
mortification for the French Ministry,' Mercy wrote on
September 16, 1772; 'but I think I may assert that the
Most Christian King regards these same arrangements with
more reason and justice, and that they will in no way
modify his sentiments towards the present system.'   Mercy
had adapted reason and justice to the tastes of the King
of France.   Madame du Barry, who was wont to receive
foreign Ministers only on Sundays, had granted Maria
Theresa's Ambassador admittance to her more intimate
circle, and even received him in the King's presence.   'The
access which I have secured to the Favourite,' Mercy wrote,
'enables me to enlighten her upon the great truths of
politics.'[6]   While Mercy hinted *the truth* on this wise at
Versailles, Kaunitz proclaimed it proudly at Vienna.   In
proportion as the Austrian Ambassador advanced in the
good graces of the King's mistress, the Austrian Chancellor
redoubled his insolence towards the Ambassador of France.
He even went to the extent of throwing the responsibility for the partition on the shoulders of the French.

[6] Mercy to Mary Theresa, October 16 and November 14, 1772.

'*It is France*,' he said one day to Prince de Rohan, '*that has been the primary cause of these events.* Perhaps we are more afflicted than she ; but she it is who has willed what has taken place.'[7]

Mounted on that high horse, the Austrians had now no uneasiness in talking with the King of Prussia. They did so in the freest possible manner. 'Prussia and Austria,' says a celebrated German historian, 'had been placed, as a result of this event, in a fraternal relationship, and they had, before all, a civilizing mission to fulfil.'[8] The *civilizing mission*, agreeing upon this point with the famous *patriotic German system* which had been so fairly spoken of at Neisse, willed it that the demarcation of the Prussian and Austrian frontiers in Poland should include the largest possible extent of territory to be *civilized*, and that, if need were, this great task should extend even outside Poland. The Russians also kept the cause of civilization in view, and Panin thought it a convenient moment for talking once more of the *Triple Alliance.* It had just been consecrated by certain seemly operations. Why should it not be made a principle of public law ? Before pronouncing an opinion, Prussia and Austria wished to know how they were to stand with regard to their respective ambitions. There was one point on which they agreed at once, namely, the exclusion of France from all their combinations. 'As for the precaution which the King thinks it necessary to take,' wrote the Austrian Chancellor, 'to wit, that this alliance shall not be extended further, and shall never become a *quadruple alliance*, we are entirely of your opinion in this respect.'[9]

In the midst of these confused negotiations the news was received of the revolution in Sweden. By a *coup d'état*,

[7] Saint-Priest, vol. i., p. 273.
[8] Ranke, *Die Deutschen Mächte*, vol. i., p. 21.
[9] Secret instructions to Baron Van Swieten, January 21, 1773.

boldly conceived and boldly carried out, Gustavus III. had
preserved the independence of his country, and had snatched
the Swedes out of the jaws of that fate which the Poles
had brought upon themselves by their civil discords and
by the feebleness of their government.   It was an annoying
discomfiture and a notable check for the Czarina.   It also
gave the King of Prussia matter for serious uneasiness.
If Russia went to war with the King of Sweden, his treaties
obliged him to take part, a course for which he had no
desire.   Louis XV. would perhaps intervene in favour of
Gustavus III. ; Austria might be led to side with France,
and the system whose erection had cost so much art and
so great pains would be all upset.   It was therefore necessary that Russia should be kept busy with the Turks, and
that the Czarina should not make peace in the East in
order to throw herself upon Sweden.   Frederick the Great
extricated himself from this difficulty with his wonted
dexterity.   He found means of keeping the Russians in
Turkey while apparently helping them to get out of it,
and of preventing the Czarina from going to war with the
Swedes while he appeared to be helping her to make peace
with the Turks.   'The motions of wrath and vengeance,'
he says, 'would, however, have gained the day in the mind
of the Empress of Russia, had not the Turks displayed
great firmness in resisting the hard and grievous conditions
which it was sought to lay upon them.'   The King of Prussia
thought these conditions *exorbitant*, *onerous*, humiliating ;
but this was in his eyes only a reason the more for using
his influence with the Turks in their support.   He gave
his Minister, Zegelin, formal instructions on this point.
He knew that the Porte would not give in ; that France
was encouraging it to hold out ; that the more exaggerated
the Russian claims were, the more the Turks would be
stubborn to resist ; that the negotiations would drag
lengthily on ; that the Czarina would forget Sweden, and

that he would once more save his States from the danger of a general war.[10]

The events in Sweden had, in fact, decided the Czarina to renew the negotiations. A suspension of hostilities was arranged, the Russian and Turkish Plenipotentiaries met at Bucharest, and an armistice was concluded to March 21, 1773. Matters were taken up at the point where they had been left at Focktchany. This time an agreement was arrived at, more or less, as to the independence of the Tartars, and the ecclesiastical relationship with the Sultan which that people should maintain. But hardly had the Turks yielded this point, when the Russians put forward a new claim. This last had nothing to do with questions of religion, and it is not very evident how it could be reconciled with the absolute independence which Count Orlof had formerly claimed so haughtily for Russia's new clients. The Russians wished to keep for themselves the two fortresses of Kertch and Yeni-Kalé which commanded the entrance to the Sea of Azof, and gave a footing in the Crimea. The Turks, in their turn, invoked the principle of the independence of the Tartars, and demanded that these two places should be given up to the Khan. The Russians insisted. As no more arguments could be provided on either side, the Congress separated at the beginning of January, 1773, and was prorogued until the middle of the following month. Nothing could be more in harmony with the King of Prussia's schemes. His policy had been successful, and Russia was forced to postpone the execution of her plans against Sweden.

Austria, as her manner was, continued to minister unwittingly and unintentionally to Frederick's interests.

[10] Frederick, *Œuvres*, vol. vi., pp. 49, 50, 54; Prince Henry to the King, October 14, 1772: Arneth, vol. viii., p. 454, Thugut's Reports, November.

Kaunitz had instructed Thugut, on December 22, 1772, to keep quiet during the Congress, to remain at Constantinople, and to abstain from interfering in any way. Placed as she was between Turkey and Russia, each of whom had the right to count on her good offices, Austria thought it the part of prudence to keep in the background, preferring to an intervention which might in the end irritate both Russia and the Sultan, a wise reserve which should enable her later on to secure a fresh gain from one side or the other, perhaps even from both. The Court of Vienna also knew that a certain coolness had arisen between Berlin and St. Petersburg in consequence of the Swedish affair, and more especially owing to the claims which the King of Prussia still raised to Danzig. And, finally, the execution of the partition was going very haltingly. However skilfully the rights of the three partitioning Governments had been ' deduced,' the Poles refused to appreciate their cogency, and showed more stiffness than had been expected. ' These heads empty of logic,' as Frederick styled them, flattered themselves that the affairs in the East would divide the three allies. It was a very gratuitous illusion.

The three allies might, indeed, squabble over the application of the principle of the equality of shares, but they were entirely resolved not to give up the game, and, so far from regarding their differences of opinion and the Polish resistance as reasons for limiting their claims on Poland, they looked to a fresh partition for the means of reconciling their rivalries, and of compelling the Poles to submit. ' I suppose,' Frederick wrote on November 4, 1772,[11] ' that by dint of a few threats and certain sums of money judiciously applied, these people may be made to subscribe to our wishes. . . . But if it were necessary, contrary to all expectation, to adopt this last alternative,

[11] To Benoît, his Agent in Poland.

and to resort to force to bring them to reason, the worst that could result would be that we might be obliged to have recourse to a fresh partition, and still further to extend our respective shares.' This was Kaunitz's view also, and he based his conviction upon an argument in which we may fathom the depth of the artificial genius with which Heaven had endowed him. 'There is,' he said, 'probably no Polish seigneur who, owing to the advantages which, to the detriment of the State, private individuals find in being the subjects of an ill-ordered Government, would not rather remain a Pole than become the subject of one of the three Powers. It is therefore probable that not one of these individuals will be found who will not set his private interest before his patriotism, and who will not warmly devote himself, for that reason, in the approaching Diet, to securing the accordance of the cessions and renunciations demanded by the three Courts, in order that he may not find himself compelled to come under another sovereignty by a wider extension of the dismemberment of Poland.'[12] He therefore proposed to Russia that the Courts should make a declaration to the Poles to the effect that unless, in the month of March, 1773, they had satisfied the demands of the three claimants, the latter, who so far had given effect to only a part of their claims, were resolved to extend them 'to all the other Polish provinces with respect to which they had rights of the most legitimate nature.'[13] The Russians did not altogether share this view. They wished to keep what remained of Poland at their own disposal. It suited them neither to hand over Danzig, nor to swell Austria's share indefinitely. But their chief concern was to keep Austria in suspense for as long as the affairs in the East should be undecided. In Panin's opinion they should

[12] Kaunitz to Lobkowitz, November 16, 1772.
[13] *Referat* of September 25, 1772.

confine themselves to showing the Poles 'the astonishment and indignation' which the three allied Courts felt at 'the seductions and intrigues' by which the Government of Poland sought to retard 'the establishment of peace, and of the security of their possessions which was so much to be desired.' The three Courts could not allow them ' to endeavour, by insidious delays, to expose the legitimacy of their rights to all the vicissitudes of events.' They had therefore resolved to be no longer impeded by the objections of the Poles, and 'to employ such means as they should deem most prompt and most expedient to do justice to themselves.'[14]

Austria signed this declaration on January 20, 1773, but she was only half satisfied with it. She felt that the Russians were offering a dumb resistance to her ambitions. The King of Prussia was advancing claims, both to Danzig, and also to the margraviates of Ansbach and Bayreuth, which the Austrians thought inacceptable. They also coveted Bavaria. Frederick suggested that they should dismember Venice,[15] which they had no desire to do—at all events, for the present. 'Things must be arranged,' said Kaunitz, ' in such a way that we may all live, as the saying is.'[16] The Court of Vienna thought that there was too much arguing, and that its appetite was being too long exposed to the classic trials of Tantalus.

In these times of fasting the Empress's conscience tormented her more than usual, and while exposed to these irritating uncertainties, she wrote this inimitable letter to Mercy on February 1, 1773: 'The King of Prussia's allurements are only too clear. He will not now relax his grip on Danzig and Thorn . . . even Russia has agreed to it, which is incomprehensible. He has made us lose valuable time, in which some remedy might have been

[14] Martens, vol. ii., p. 35.   [15] Van Swieten's Reports.
[16] Instruction to Van Swieten, January 21, 1773.

devised, by dallying and cajoling us. They have fairly
led us by the nose; I am inconsolable about it. If I
could console myself, it is by the thought that I was
always opposed to *this iniquitous partition, which is so
unequal,* and to binding ourselves to these two monsters. . . .'
Maria Theresa was willing to talk of the *iniquitousness* of
the partition, but she did not mean that others, the
French especially, should echo her words. A general
outcry had arisen at Paris against the Austrian alliance,
to which public opinion universally attributed the
humiliations endured by France since 1756, and more
particularly this last check, which was less calamitous
perhaps, but more offensive, than the others.[17]   A
pamphlet on the partition of Poland went the round of
Paris ; that act was styled a work of brute force, of
crying injustice, of manifest usurpation.[18]   'The pamphlet
which has been issued on the subject of the partition of
Poland has made a very ill impression,' the Empress wrote
in this same letter of February 8, '*and it will not be easily
forgotten.   France goes beyond every other nation* by these
petty vengeances.'

What exhausted the Austrians' patience far more than
did this unfortunate pamphlet was the incoherent and
vain efforts of the French Ministry to stir up the Turks.
The Court of Vienna had fully realized that, as long as
the peace remained in uncertainty, the settlement of the
partition would make no progress in Poland. Panin had
not accepted Kaunitz's plan for bringing the Poles to
reason. So far from meditating a fresh partition, he proposed that means should be concerted for re-establishing
'the Government of Poland in its true principles,' that is

---

[17] *Vide Le Secret du Roi*, vol. ii., p. 399.

[18] *Observations sur les Déclarations des cours de Vienne, Berlin et
Petersbourg sur le démembrement de la Pologne*, London, January,
1773.

to say, in anarchy. Instead of conquering, he offered to
corrupt her, and the same Minister who, in the declarations of January 20, protested against ' the seductions and
intrigues of the Poles in the neighbouring Courts,' proposed to the allies on February 26 that corruption should
be added to threatening, that *a fund for seduction
should be secured*, and that there should be ' formed from
henceforth a treasure to be devoted to the success of the
present operations, for which it is estimated that the first
sum for each Court cannot be less than from 150,000 to
200,000 crowns.'[19] On this were pinned the hopes of the
Russians for persuading the Polish Diet. But it was not
the Austrians' business. They sought not so much to
seduce men as to take territory. Checked on this side,
they turned again to the Turks. At Kaunitz's suggestion,
the Empress decided to offer the Porte 5,000,000 or
6,000,000 florins to help it to gain better terms from
the Russians, if it would in exchange cede Little Wallachia to Austria ; that is to say, the territory between
the Danube, the Aluta, and the Austrian frontier, of
which Austria had already secured a promise by the
Convention of July 6, 1771. It was hoped at Vienna
that this enticing offer, presented at the time of the
Congress, would captivate the Turks. But when Thugut
received these new instructions on March 10, 1773, the
Congress was once more on the point of breaking up, and
all that the Austrian Minister could do was to abstain
from interference.

The negotiations had been renewed at Bucharest on
February 15, 1773. The Russians persisted in their
claims, and even enlarged them. They demanded, besides
the free navigation of the Black Sea, the cession of
Kertch, of Yeni-Kalé, and of Kinburn, the dismantling of

[19] Scheme of a plan for the conduct of the three Ministers in
Poland : Beer, *Documents*, p. 143.

Otchakof, the recognition of Russia as guaranteeing the independence of the Tartars, and a right of protection over such subjects of the Sultan as professed the Greek religion. The Turks resigned themselves to everything, except to the cession of Kertch and of Yeni-Kalé, which would place the sea in the hands of Russia, and would enable them to construct a fleet and to hurl it against the capital of the Empire. 'The Porte,' the Russian Minister wrote, 'sees very clearly that the Russians aim at the conquest of Constantinople, and that they wish for Kertch and Yeni-Kalé in order to prepare the execution of this scheme.' Resolved not to yield this point save at the last extremity, they offered to pay the Russians 70,000,000 piastres if they would renounce their claim to these two places and to the navigation of the Black Sea. Obreskof replied that, so far from accepting 70,000,000 piastres as a compensation for Kertch and Yeni-Kalé, Russia would pay that sum to get those two places, and that, moreover, the freedom of navigation was a condition of peace *sine quâ non*. Agreement on these two principles was impossible, and the Congress was once more broken up on March 22, 1773. War began again. The Czarina was ready for it; she had no fears for her success, having no opinion of the support which the French Ministry announced for the Turks, and the hope of which had notably strengthened their resistance. 'If the Turks continue to follow the good advice of their so-called friends,' she wrote to Voltaire,[20] 'you may be sure that your wish to see us on the Bosphorus will be very near its accomplishment.'

[20] On March 3, 1773.

CHAPTER XX.

THE   TREATY   OF   KAINARDJI.

(June, 1773—September, 1774.)

The Czarina had decreed victory. She ordered Roumanzow to cross the Danube, to march on the enemy, and to beat him wherever he found him. Roumanzow vainly tried to show his Sovereign the danger of the undertaking; the Czarina would hear nothing of it. On June 13, 1773, the Russian army crossed the Danube and moved on Silistria. The Turks attacked the Russian rear-guard, beat it, and occupied a defile, which enabled them to take the enemy in the rear and to cut off his retreat. ' If the Grand Vizier had known how to take advantage of the opportunity,' says Frederick, ' there is every probability that this Russian army would have been destroyed.' The Grand Vizier remained in his camp. The Russian General, Weismann, attacked the Turks in their defile, and, after mighty efforts, succeeded in dislodging them. The battle cost him his life, but the Russian army was saved. They could recross the Danube, and, as the Grand Vizier made no attempt to pursue them, they calmly prepared for another campaign later in the year.

The King of Prussia tried to take advantage of this, as it were, suspension of hostilities to renew the negotiations. But both sides refused every concession. The Czarina reassembled her forces, and fully counted on bringing the Turks to their knees.   It was the general opinion of enlightened men that the Turks could not resist a fresh effort of the Russians, and that, in the event of a disaster to their army, the same causes as had till then supported their resistance would compel them to sue for peace. Favier indicated as much in the memoranda which he had drawn up for the Comte de Broglie: 'The opposition of the lawyers and of the ministers of religion is formidable even to the Sultan himself, so long as the means of sub- sistence of a dastardly and fanatical population are not absolutely cut off; but once the convoys are intercepted, the Dardanelles well blockaded, and neutral bottoms either confiscated or stopped and made to go back, the Ulema will dread famine, the Divan rebellion, and the Sultan a revolution.   The people themselves will come and clamour at the doors of the Seraglio for peace and bread, and for the heads of the Generals and Ministers. . . .'   The French publicist was no less clear-sighted when he defined the policy of the three Northern Courts towards the Porte: 'Russia crushes her, Prussia betrays her, and Austria, after ransoming her, watches for the division of her spoils.'

'We must have the courage,' Joseph II. wrote, on June 19, 1773, 'to finish the business on the footing on which we began it.   Convenience, and, to a certain extent, necessity, have been the only springs of this partition; it must be concluded in the same spirit, with the reflection that, as so much has been done and taken, other things also must be taken, which are trifling, but essential in order that what has already been taken may have a true value, and that the step may at least be worth the trouble it cost to take it.   Otherwise it will be in every sense deficient, mean, and equivocal.'   The Emperor was at that time travelling over his new Polish territories, and, while looking out for the *trifles* which he might yet take from

the Poles to give the work of the partition its true value,
he did not forget those districts of Turkey which might be
handy for Austria.   After examining the places, he fixed
on the country lying at the sources of the Sereth and the
Pruth, which has Czernovitz for its capital, and which is
called Bukovina. 'I think,' he wrote, 'that, both from
the military and the political point of view, that would be
at least worth Cisleithan Wallachia.'

This Imperial journey in a country which had been
taken, but the cession of which had not yet been obtained ;
this haste to appear before people who had but just been
plundered ; this heat to covet fresh conquests, filled Maria
Theresa with woe. 'You think that I hesitate too much
as to what people will say?' she wrote to her son on
June 20, 1773. 'I gave evidence to the contrary in the
first twenty years of my reign ; but *you* think too little of
it ; you only follow your own ideas and wishes, which,
uncontradicted as they are, with all your gift of style and
language, helped by endless sophisms and irony, are for the
most part successful.' She foresaw that she would again
yield ; she lamented it ; but, as said the pitiless railer of
Potsdam, 'still she wept, and still she took !' She lectured
the Emperor on his insatiable ambition, but congratulated
herself that circumstances allowed it to be gratified.   She
wrote to Mercy on August 2, 1773 : 'In view of the present
state of affairs, I think that it is more to the advantage
than to the disadvantage of our interests that the Duc
d'Aiguillon should be at his present post, at any rate
until the restoration of peace between Russia and the
Porte, and until the affairs of Poland are finally settled.
Gifted with small genius and few talents, lacking credit,
and continually harassed by factions, he is hardly in a
position to put difficulties in our way.   Our task would be
far more difficult if the Duc de Choiseul, thoroughly well-
intentioned though he was, were still in power, and the

same might be the case if Broglie were to replace D'Aiguillon, which might perhaps be a great misfortune.' Maria Theresa did involuntary homage to the fallen Minister and to the secret counsellor, who had striven to re-awaken the wholesome traditions of French policy in the soul of Louis XV.[1] Poland and Turkey had, indeed, much to endure from this alliance of 1756, whose only object seemed to be the abasement of France and the ruin of the States protected by her King.

The Comte de Broglie and his publicist Favier had only too clearly seen through the designs of Austria. While they were busied with denouncing this equivocal behaviour to Louis XV., Kaunitz's sole occupation was to justify their conjectures. On August 20 and September 6, 1773, the Austrian Chancellor wrote to Thugut, telling him to prepare the Turks, as soon as they should have made their peace with Russia, for thanking Austria for her good offices by the cession of Bukovina. Pending the time when it could force the Turks to give this token of their grati- tude, the Court of Vienna continued the complicated task of making good its claims and ' rights' with the Poles. Austria considered the line of the Sbrucz necessary to her frontier system. There was no mention of this in the Treaty of Partition. Article I. of that treaty laid down that the frontier on the east side should follow the course of ' the little river named the Podorze to where it flowed into the Danube.' It was easily certified that Podorze was a small town, and not a little river; but, as the Sereth started not far from there on its course into the Danube, Austria thought herself justified in concluding that it was the course of the Sereth that had been indicated by the treaty. Kaunitz wrote to Lobkowitz to this effect on September 15, 1773, adding that Austria was most

[1] *Vide* the Memoirs above cited, Boutaric, vols. i. and ii. ; *Le Secret du Roi*, vol. ii.

intimately concerned to add to her share the territory
enclosed by the Sereth and the Sbrucz; that the Poles
refused to concede this; that Austria consequently intended
to occupy a certain number of Polish districts which were
not contained in her share, in order to compel the Poles to
cede the line of the Sbrucz *by way of exchange.*

This proposal was not at all to Russia's taste, and all
the less so, inasmuch as Frederick, who knew of these
Austrian claims, was always ready to take advantage of
them to complete his share, and was demanding Thorn
and Danzig.[2] Catharine wished for no more partitioning;
she wanted to place what remained of Poland under her
protection, and wished that republic to preserve, as the
treaty prescribed, ' the consistency of an intermediary
Power.' Panin replied to Lobkowitz that if Austria
extended her frontiers the King of Prussia would do
likewise; that he, too, had set up his ensigns far beyond
the limits of his share; that it had cost much trouble to
get his eagles taken up and withdrawn; that nevertheless
this had been accomplished, and that Austria, by her
claims, would put the whole affair again in dispute. ' It
is an unprecedented event,' he said, ' that three Powers of
superior order have been able to agree upon a point which
offered to each severally so many different views and
interests, and that a general policy, whose sole motive has
been humanity and the love of peace, has triumphed over
every partial policy, and, without a blow being struck, has
produced advantages for each such as long and murderous
wars could not so abundantly obtain.' Why should such
fair results be jeopardized ? If the river Podorze did not
exist, that was ' a physical condition which it was not in
the power of any of the three Powers to change'; but
their intention was clear: it was, to draw a line from

2 Conversation between Frederick and Tchernichef, August,
1773: Martens, vol. vi., p. 98.

Podorze to the Dniester. The Sereth fulfilled this object ; there was no reason why the Austrian frontier should be carried further, or should swallow up the territory enclosed by the Sereth and the Sbrucz. ' There exist,' Panin said in conclusion, ' points of no less interest to which the convenience of the Imperial and Royal Court might be directed, and on which the Empress would find her hands freer.' That Austria might not mistake the meaning and scope of this hint, Panin coupled it with a request for friendly intervention with the Turks.[3]

The fact was that the autumn campaign, on which the Czarina had pinned such great hopes, was looking ill for the Russians. Two corps of Roumanzow's army had crossed the Danube and advanced on Varna. They were defeated and fell back in disorder on the Danube, which they only succeeded in ciossing with great loss. The Crimean Tartars were in commotion, and seemed inclined to return to the protection of the Sultan. The revolt of the Egyptian Mamelukes, to which the Russians were looking to create a diversion, had been suppressed, and the Czarina found herself threatened by an apparently formidable sedition in her own empire. This was the revolt of the Cossacks of the Don, commanded by Pougatchef. This adventurer passed himself off as Peter III. Raising the people on his way, he had just seized Orenburg, and was threatening to march on Moscow. Naturally, the Russians appealed to Austria's good offices, and showed a disposition to pay for her condescension with a strip of the Turkish Empire.

Kaunitz saw this. Without in the least abandoning his claims to the line of the Sbrucz, he wrote to Thugut on December 7, 1773, telling him to declare to the Turks that Austria could not regard the prolongation of the war with indifference ; that she expected the Porte to give Russia those political and religious guarantees which it was her

[3] Lobkowitz's Report, October 30, 1773.

right to demand. At the same time, and as it was one of
the principles of the Viennese Court to be on the safe side
against any event, the Austrian engineers were ordered to
plant the Imperial eagles along the line of the Sbrucz, and
to make a study of those places in Bukovina in which,
if need were, the same operation might conveniently be
performed. Kaunitz thought it prudent to come to an
understanding with the King of Prussia. On February 22,
1774, Van Swieten was ordered to place before that Prince
the system of precautionary invasions which was to facilitate the rectification of the frontiers by way of exchange.
Frederick pronounced the theory to be most expedient,
and in the spring of 1774 he ordered his troops to
move his ensigns forward in Cujavia. By this means he
took possession of about 200 villages. As the Austrians
had infringed the principle of equality, he says in his
Memoirs, 'the King thought himself justified in doing
likewise; he therefore extended his boundaries and included
the districts of Old and New Netze with the part of
Pomerelia which he already possessed.'

Russia was in no position to resist these manœuvres,
and her allies at Berlin and Vienna speculated on her
difficulties. They were serious. Forced by Pougatchef's
revolt to divide their forces, the Russians seemed to be on
the verge of a disaster. Count Solms wrote in March, 1774 :
' The effective forces are never at their full strength; the
generals are for the most part incompetent, and seldom
agreed amongst themselves; the officers and soldiers are
weary and disgusted; the country is exhausted by the
military charges and by the levies, which, in five years,
have exceeded 300,000 men; the Government bends beneath
its load; the whole world here is corrupted by license and
by the custom of obtaining everything by favour. An
important defeat might be very dangerous to this empire.'
If the Turks had known how to take advantage of their

victories, they might have made the Russians pay dearly
for the imprudence of a fresh attack. But their reverses
had taught them nothing, and their successes made them
forget the most elementary precautions.

Sultan Mustapha had died on January 14, 1774. The
one desire of his successor, Abdul Hamid, was for war ;
and he managed it even worse than his predecessor.
Roumanzow crossed the Danube, beat the detached corps
which the Turks opposed to him, defeated their vanguard
at Bazardjik on June 16, compelled them to move the
camp which they had formed at Kostidje, circumvented
the main body of the Grand Vizier's army at Shumla,
invested it, and proceeded to starve it out. The Turkish
troops deserted wholesale. The campaign was merely one
continued rout. The Grand Vizier, Muhsinrade, could only
throw himself upon the mercy of his conquerors. Turkish
plenipotentiaries appeared on July 10 at Roumanzow's
headquarters, who was encamped a few leagues from
Silistria. They were received in that General's tent, and
the peace was agreed upon then and there within four
hours. In less than a month Roumanzow's boldness and
constancy, and the Turks' incompetence and insanity, had
decided the issue of this war which had lasted for five
years.

Thus was signed, on July 21, 1774, the Treaty of Kust-
chuk-Kainardji, the first and the most famous of the great
transactions between Russia and the Porte. It was the
starting-point and the foundation for the lengthy process,
broken by sanguinary interludes, which was to bring the
soldiers of the Czar, after a century of efforts, to the gates
of Constantinople. The treaty conformed to the conditions which Russia had laid down. Russia took but
little territory ; excepting the two Kabardas, she restored
all her conquests ; she constituted herself the protector of
the Danubian principalities, and the guarantor of the

Tartars' independence; by keeping Azof, Kinburn, Kertch, and Yeni-Kalé, she paved the way for her future supremacy of the Black Sea, on which she secured the right of free navigation. The essential stipulations of the treaty were those which concerned religion. The Porte promised 'constantly to protect the Christian religion and its churches' in general, to 'place no impediment in the way of the free practice of the Christian religion, and to oppose no obstacle to the construction of new and the repair of old churches' in the principalities of Moldavia and Wallachia, in Greece and the islands of the Archipelago, in Georgia and Mingrelia.[4] It promised *to take into its view* the representations made by Russia on behalf of the Greek Church of Constantinople and its ministers, and to receive the steps taken by the Russian Ministry on behalf of the principalities of Moldavia and Wallachia *with the consideration which befits friendly and respected Powers.*

These stipulations, scattered over the various articles of the treaty in a disorder which does honour to the skill of the Czarina's diplomatists, formed the basis of the obligations from which Russian publicists have deduced Russia's *judicial right* to carry out her *civilizing mission* in the East, and *to interfere in the internal affairs of the Ottoman Empire.* This right was, as a matter of fact, nowhere written down. All the treaty did was to deal with the religious rights of the Christians. The Turks thought they might conclude from this that, outside the Danubian principalities, where the Russian right of representation applied generally, this right applied in the rest of the empire only to the use of the churches, to the maintenance of the hierarchies, and to the free practice of religion. Beyond this the treaty was silent. But the sense of these clauses had still to be interpreted, and this afforded a fair field for the display of that precious and

[4] Articles VII., XVI., XVII. and XXIII.

singular quality which is called in diplomacy the *judicial spirit*, and elsewhere, by an ingenious euphemism the art of 'search in original authorities.' 'Is it possible,' says an eminent Russian historian, 'to conceive of even the exercise of these *religious rights*, properly speaking, without a certain body of political *guarantees?* And must not the first of these guarantees be the liberty and the security of person and property? Is it possible, especially in the East, and in the ideas of Eastern peoples, to make a distinction between religion and politics, between law and morality?' Hence Russia's *obligation* to mix in the internal affairs of Turkey whenever the interests of the Christians demand it. And, 'as it is natural that Russia should feel the more sympathy for her co-religionists of the Greek rites in the East, inasmuch as strong links connect her with the Slavs of the Ottoman Empire,' Russian publicists conclude that 'if it is true, as Montesquieu has said, that law is the expression of the necessary relations that spring from the nature of things, moral and treaty law are binding upon Russia whenever their dignity and their supreme interests demand an effective intervention.'[5]

Such was, according to the Russians, the meaning of the Treaty of Kainardji. That treaty settled the spiritual relations of the Tartars with the Sultan, and those of the Greek Christians with the Turks. It made Russia the guardian of the political independence of the Crimean Mussulmans, and of the religious independence of the Christians of Turkey. The fact is that these arrangements strangely entangled things spiritual with things temporal, things sacred with things profane. They prepared a marvellous quarrel of investitures for such statesmen as should have the chance of profiting by them : an

[5] Martens, *Étude Historique sur la Politique Russe dans la Question d'Orient,* 1877.

inexhaustible store of negotiations for times of peace, and a standing pretext for declaring war.

Russia followed the same scheme of domination in Turkey as in Poland, and she prepared for its success by the same methods. To divide in order to rule, to trouble in order to conquer, to raise up a party of her own within the State, and to obtain from the State the right to intervene on behalf of that party, the policy was the same at Warsaw and at Constantinople. Russia had her Dissident Question in Turkey as in Poland. She became the guarantor of Tartar independence, and of Moldavian and Wallachian privileges, just as she had been the guarantor of the Polish Constitution and of the *Liberum Veto*. The confederations in Poland, the revolts in Turkey, did her the same service, and led her to the same end—namely, the dissolution of the State which she sought to dominate until she should be able to conquer, or compelled to share it with rival Powers. 'Every kind of reproach may be levelled against Russia,' a Russian has said, 'save that of lacking sequence in her policy.'[6] Russia's Eastern policy was in marvellously close connection with her European policy, and the men of that time were not blind to the fact. 'The whole erection of the stipulations of the Treaty of Kainardji,' Thugut wrote, ' is a model of skill on the part of the Russian diplomatists, and a rare example of imbecility on the part of the Turkish negotiators. By the skilful combination of the articles which that treaty contains, the Ottoman Empire becomes from henceforth a kind of Russian province. As Russia is able for the future to dictate laws to it, she will, perhaps, content herself, for some years more, with reigning in the name of the Grand Turk, until she thinks the time favourable for definitely taking possession. . . .

[6] Martens, *op. cit.*

Never,' he concludes, 'will a nation on the point of disappearing from the political scene have less deserved the compassion of other peoples than have the Turks. Unfortunately, events now passing in this empire will in the future exercise the greatest influence on the policy of all other States, and will give rise to endless troubles.'[7]

[7] Thugut's Reports, August 17 and September 3, 1774.

CHAPTER XXI.

THE ANNEXATION OF BUKOVINA.

(September, 1774—July, 1776.)

THE Treaty of Kainardji had hardly been signed when it was found to produce all its predicted consequences : a fresh conflict between the Turks and the Russians, and, as the recoil of that, a fresh crisis of interests and ambitions in Europe. As soon as the Turks had concluded peace, they began to reflect how they could free themselves from a part of the clauses which had been laid upon them. As soon as the Austrians and Prussians learnt of the treaty, they sought in it a pretext for fresh compensations and fresh conquests. ' It is easy,' said the Reis-Effendi to the King of Prussia's Minister[1]—' it is easy to judge whether engagements of such a nature can be stable ; but the circumstances may and must change. If, then, the Russians wish for a lasting peace and to establish a sincere friendship, their conditions must be softened and made endurable.' Those clauses in particular the Divan thought onerous which concerned the independence of the Tartars and Russia's interference in the relations of the Porte with the principalities. These stipulations, which were to give rise to more than one war, were thus disputed from the first. The Turks lost no time in interfering

[1] Note of September 3, 1774.

with the *prescription* of the treaty. They had not ratified
it ; they delayed the departure of the Embassy Extraordinary which was to convey the ratifications to St.
Petersburg, and asked the King of Prussia to intervene.

Frederick sent on their demands to St. Petersburg, but
carefully avoided compromising his friendship with Russia
by supporting them. His behaviour in the affairs of
Sweden, and more especially his claims to Danzig, had
somewhat affected the alliance. As for Austria, the
Turks had now nothing to look for from her. Kaunitz
did not even honour them with his compassion ; with the
same note of impertinence with which he had charged the
French with the responsibility for the partition of Poland,
he now reproved the Turks for their distrust of Austria.
'The Turks,' he said to the British Minister, ' have
deserved their fate, both for the softness and folly with
which they carried on the war, and for the lack of
confidence which they displayed towards Powers which,
like Austria, were disposed to pull them out of their
difficulties. Why have they not asked for the mediation
of Austria, of England, and of Holland ? . . .   That
nation is condemned to perish, and a good, small army
would suffice to hunt them out of Europe.' The Turks
would have had matter for a reply. From the
2,000,000 florins which they had paid in August, 1771,
down to Thugut's peculiar reserve during the two Con-
gresses, they could put forward more than one solid
argument to explain their lack of confidence in Austria.

Kaunitz was not a whit troubled by it. He was wholly
absorbed in his transactions with Russia. The Emperor
considered that the part of Podolia which reaches to the
Sbrucz ' was essentially necessary' to himself.[2] Austria
had occupied that territory, and had more or less explained at St. Petersburg that ' the river Podorze being

[2] Joseph to Leopold, October 3, 1774.

found not to exist, it had therefore been necessary to find another,' and that Austria's engineers had therefore planted the eagles along the Sbrucz.[3] For convincing the Czarina, the Court of Vienna relied upon the perfect harmony of views which tended to be established between the two empires on the subject of the East. Joseph, always inclined for great enterprises, leant towards the Russian alliance; he burnt to join the Czarina in the task, pregnant with glory and profit, which she was pursuing in the East: Austria's historic mission, according to him, harmonized wonderfully with Russia's mission of civilization. The Czarina was inclined for this alliance. She knew that Frederick was too prudent and too well-advised to second such vast designs; she remembered that in the winter of 1772 the highly sagacious Chancellor of the Imperial Court had judged Count Massin's proposals worthy of weighty discussion. The two States were thus marching towards the alliance which they were to conclude a few years later. 'Russia,' wrote Thugut on September 3, 1774, 'must expect that, when the Ottoman Empire is overthrown, the provinces which lie on the frontiers of the Hereditary States will become the share of the Imperial Court. The Russian Cabinet will the less think of resisting this acquisition, in that it will be unable to prevent it . . . and that the acquisitions which Austria will make of Bosnia, Servia, etc. . . . although of great importance in other circumstances, can be of no utility to Russia. . . .'

This was Kaunitz's opinion. He was labouring to secure a military position for the Imperial armies, which should enable them with equal ease to help the Russians in a joint campaign, or to threaten them, in the event of no agreement being arrived at. He wrote to Thugut on September 6, 1774, telling him that, as soon as the

[3] Despatch to Lobkowitz, July 16, 1774.

Russians were away, the Imperial eagles would be planted
in Bukovina. The order for occupation was given on
September 20. The Russians accepted it in the friendliest
manner. The Venetian Ambassador, Contarini, wrote on
December 10, 1774 : ' His Majesty the Emperor has sent
a very fine snuff-box to General Count Roumanzow, en-
riched with many brilliants, together with his portrait
and a purse of 6,000 ducats.'

This fresh annexation caused some outcry. ' People are
exclaiming greatly against this operation,' the Emperor
wrote,[4] ' but as we are undertaking the entire burden of
settling this difficulty amicably with the Porte, I do not
see how others should object to it.' And, in fact, no one
was very eager to balk Austria. Panin told Lobkowitz
that his Court would oppose the annexation of Bukovina
no more than it had opposed the annexation of the territory
between the Sereth and the Sbrucz, but that they must
realize that the King of Prussia would demand a compensation, and would wait for no man's leave before making
sure of it.[5] Clearly the friction had been quite temporary
which had for a moment troubled the friendship of the
King of Prussia and the Czarina. The annexation of
Bukovina gave Frederick a pretext for keeping what he
had occupied beyond his line of demarcation. Russia
shut her eyes, and, to show his gratitude, the King of
Prussia undertook to persuade the Turks to ratify the
treaty of peace. They were still postponing and protest-
ing. The Prussian Minister Zegelin used such diligence
that the ratifications were exchanged on January 24,
1775, and on February 2 an Embassy left to convey them
to St. Petersburg. The Turks, having now nothing to
hope for, resigned themselves to ceding Bukovina to the
Austrians. The treaty was signed on May 7, 1775.

[4] To Leopold, November 23, 1774.
[5] Lobkowitz's Report, December 13, 1774.

There was great joy at Vienna over this fresh success. As long as the matter was in suspense, the Empress had been continually torn by some scruples both as to the justice of the enterprise and as to its chances of success. She wrote to Mercy on February 4: 'Kaunitz appears to be very prejudiced against Breteuil,[6] and means to take a very firm attitude with him, especially if he opens the question of the affairs of Moldavia, in which we are entirely in the wrong. . . . I confess I do not yet see how we can solve the matter—hardly honourably. This distresses me more than I can say. . . .' Maria Theresa apparently thought that the treaty, however difficult to conclude, had an honourable ending, for she wrote to Kaunitz after receiving the news of it: 'I take a real interest in your satisfaction, and you do entire justice to my feelings towards yourself, which will end only with my life; I owe my entire gratitude to you, as I also owe my friendship and esteem. . . .' The Emperor, for his part, was triumphant. He had been told of a new libel against his policy. 'All this makes not the smallest impression on me,' he wrote to his brother on March 6, 1775, 'and my opinion is that we must let all men say what they will in peace, provided they let us do what we will.'

The Poles had behaved like the Turks, and had given in. The treaties of cession had been signed in March, 1775. In 1776 the three partitioners mutually guaranteed their new Polish frontiers. The demarcation of Bukovina was disposed of at the same time. 'Prince Kaunitz has just had the satisfaction of bringing the affair of the boundaries with the Turks to a glorious ending,' the Empress wrote on July 16, 1776. The great dispute which had begun in 1768 was now ended; for the moment nothing remained to be settled with the Turks. Accordingly,

[6] Louis XVI.'s Ambassador, and Cardinal de Rohan's successor since 1774.

Frederick the Great, who had no love for wasting his substance in vain displays, recalled the Minister whom he had at Constantinople, leaving there only a Chargé d'Affaires, Sieur de Gaffron, and reducing the salary accordingly. 'Am I not to be pitied,' said that unlucky diplomatist, on reaching his post,[7] 'in a country where I would not wish my worst enemy to be, if, apart from all the tedium of my stay, I am also obliged to run into debt?' 'The Russian Minister,' he wrote a year later,[8] 'has offered me his purse, that my distress may not be publicly known, though it is sufficiently apparent from my style of living.'

Thugut, on the other hand, increased in riches and honours. A strange comedy had been played between him and the French Ambassador. They found that they were collaborators and colleagues without knowing it. 'A despatch from M. le Duc de Choiseul opened my eyes,' Saint-Priest reports, 'and we had an explanation.' Saint-Priest had been merely mistaken. He became a dupe. Thugut dazzled him, and persuaded him that, thanks to him, the King [of France] viewed the policies of the Northern Courts 'as in a mirror.' The clearest vision which the King saw in that mirror was that of the deplorable figure which he cut in the world, and more especially at that time, when the three Courts were continually conspiring to surprise and befool him. The Court and State Chancellor was not the most betrayed of the two masters whom Thugut pretended to serve. Thugut was given the title of Internuncio, and was made a Baron in 1774. Vienna and Versailles were both equally pleased with him. But the game was a dangerous one, and the Internuncio trembled when the death of Louis XV. occurred to put an end to what remained of the Secret Diplomacy. Saint-Priest produced a fine memorandum as

[7] May 18, 1776.   [8] February 18, 1777.

an apology for Thugut's behaviour, and asked for a place at Court for him. Louis XVI. would have none of it. He had no liking either for that manner of man or for that mode of service. He refused to receive Thugut, but continued to pay him. Thugut remained at Constantinople. Austria was well satisfied with his position there, and the French Ministry continued to congratulate itself 'upon the zeal, the fidelity, and the superiority of the views which shone forth from Thugut, and by which France had profited so usefully for so many years.'[9]

[9] Note of March, 1777 : *Revue Historique, loc. cit.,* pp. 41, 42.

CHAPTER XXII.

THE TRIPLE ALLIANCE.

THUS ended the first episode in the modern history of the Eastern Question. That question had already assumed the nature which it was destined to retain; it was, in reality, a European question. Its solution had been found only in an upheaval of the European system. The Treaty of Kainardji was for Russia only a halting-place; the independence of the Tartars was but a step towards their annexation to the Russian Empire; the right of representation on behalf of the Christians was merely an instrument of propagandism and of domination, and the very clauses of the compact of 1774 contained all the motives for the fresh war upon which the Czarina was already preparing to embark. Fate willed it that the Russians' *civilizing mission* in the East should be fulfilled only at a heavy expense to the civilization of Europe; that every step which Russia took in the direction of Turkey should provoke a general crisis in European politics; that the establishment of Russia's *treaty right* should have, for its first result, the subversion of the public law of Europe; and that progress in the liberation of the Christians of Turkey should be achieved only through the subjugation of one of the most valiant nations of European Christendom. The partition of Poland was the necessary corollary of the Treaty of Kainardji, and these two acts, for a lesson and a warning to the European world, stand in complete solidarity on the pages of history.

The partition of Poland was not in itself an innovation in international relationships, as these were understood by the Chanceries of the eighteenth century. The idea of it was a very ancient idea, and in full harmony with the prevalent view of these relationships. It was a perfectly logical result of the system of the balance of power : to seek, in the dismemberment of a State impotent to maintain and defend itself, a means of reconciling ambitions, the rivalry between which threatened to embroil all Europe. Friends and foes of Poland alike trafficked with the Polish nation. That republic was, in a manner, for sale, and none scrupled to snatch a morsel to pay for the complicity of an ally, or for the acquiescence of an adversary.[1]

This explains the ease and tranquillity with which the partition was negotiated, and why, when it was consummated, so few protests were raised, although in reality it hurt so many interests.

But although this act sprang from the diplomatic habits of the Ancien Régime, it must be admitted that those habits had never been interpreted with so much logical cynicism, or pushed in their application to such excessive conclusions. Issuing from a rigorous application of the political usages of the time, prompted by motives of expediency, based on titles drawn from State Archives, explained by a declaration clad in all the forms of classical diplomacy, sanctioned by solemn treaties, the dismemberment of Poland was, in the eyes of the Chanceries, an act of perfect legality. It was the *summum jus* of the customs of the Ancien Régime ; it was also supreme injustice and the irreparable ruin of the ' law ' on which these customs were based.

[1] *Vide l'Europe et la Révolution Française*, vol. i., pp. 35-42 ; *Les Démembrements*.

By signing this partition, the monarchies of Divine Right themselves shook the edifice of their power. The example of former centuries, their own antecedents, all had prepared them for this act, and had led them insensibly to this abuse of their principles. Maria Theresa, the only person who felt any scruples at all, felt only those of a woman ; she felt, in point of fact, none of the scruples of a Sovereign ; she disliked taking the property of another under whatever form it was done, but she thought that by taking much she would lessen her guilt, and that the magnitude of the operation would cover its iniquity. The authors of the partition were the unsuspecting precursors of a revolution, and that revolution, to upset their thrones and to overthrow their empires, needed only to turn their own behaviour against themselves and to imitate their examples.

The partition, besides being a work of injustice, was also a work of bad policy. The historian must judge it no less severely than the philosopher. For those who achieved it, that act had but one reason for existence, namely, the need for preserving peace between three great empires. This is the excuse which Frederick the Great puts forward in his *Memoirs* ; he has himself shown its emptiness and sophistry at the end of his account. ' It follows,' he says, summing up the history of these years of intrigue and negotiation—' it follows from all that we have just set forth, that Europe was not in a stable condition, nor in the enjoyment of a secure peace ; fire lurked everywhere beneath the ashes.' In reality, the disturbed condition of Europe, and the revolutions with which she was threatened, sprang from ancient and deep-seated causes. So far from destroying these causes, the partition of Poland had been an effect of them. They were : the conflict between the aims and claims of Russia, Prussia, and Austria ; the interests which led Russia to advance in the direction of Europe and of the Black Sea ; those which led Prussia to extend and to concentrate herself at one and the same time, and those which led Austria to inflate herself indefinitely to avoid suffocation. A mission of civilization for the Russians, of history for the Prussians, of policy for the Austrians—by whatever names these rival ambitions were adorned—they compelled the three Northern Courts to annexation and conquest. The decay of Turkey and the anarchy of Poland opened to them a sphere of indefinite extent. They preferred agreement to strife, partition of the coveted territories to quarrels over them. Their rivalry caused their alliance, but their alliance in no way abolished the causes of their rivalry; on the contrary, it supplied it with fresh nourishment, and the whole effect of the treaties of St. Petersburg and of Warsaw was to add to the Eastern Question a question still more urgent, still more grave, and still more threatening, namely, that of Poland. If it had been possible to stop short at the treaties of 1772, the operation of the partition might be accounted not only a lucrative, but also an able and statesmanlike work. But history does not stop short. Facts, once established, carry their inevitable consequences, and, for the eternal revenge of right against might, ill-conceived enterprises and abusive treaties find their sanction in the hopeless entanglements which are their result.

The object which Prussia and Austria were really pursuing was that of the domination of Germany. To dispute the empire with the Hapsburgs, Prussia strove to strengthen her territorial consistency and to increase her forces. To counteract the growing power of the Hohenzollerns, Austria was perpetually drawn to fresh conquests. This effort, whose object was Germany, thrust Prussia and Austria inevitably beyond the limits of Germany. As they held each other in check within the empire, they sought elsewhere for the instrument of domination which

they needed; they sought outside Germany for the forces
which should give them the supremacy in Germany.   The
more these forces increased, the more they balanced.   The
only equality in the antagonism between the two Courts
lay in the inability of either to dominate the other.
Prussia pursued Austria in Poland, Austria pursued Prussia
in the East.   A fresh partition of Poland, a fresh plan of
conquering the Turkish Empire, were the sure result of
the treaties of St. Petersburg and Kainardji.   And while
the two German Powers, thus carried away by the impact
which each gave to the other, were letting themselves
drift, Prussia towards the Vistula, Austria towards the
Lower Danube,.they failed to see that they were being
dissolved in the midst of the Slavs, and that Germany was
escaping out of their hands, at the very time when they
were preparing to turn again to subjugate her.

Thus it was that Frederick the Great's successors in
Prussia, heirs of his vast ambitions, though not of his
genius, little by little falsified his work, led Prussia astray,
made her in less than ten years a State more Slav than
German, and prepared her for the prodigious catastrophe
of 1806.   Thus it was that Austria, losing the name for
honesty which she gratuitously gave herself, but which it
was so much her interest to deserve, was found wanting in
the rôle of a conservative and moderating Power which
history has assigned to her.   Wishing to outwit all men,
she was outwitted by all, and ended by forgetting her true
position in the multitude of her undertakings.   She lost
herself in the vague and vast schemes which she pursued
everywhere at once ; by continually exerting her strength
at the extremities of her empire, she weakened its heart
and loosened its foundations.   Thus it was, finally, that
when a common danger threatened them, and threatened
Germany, Prussia and Austria succeeded only in hamper-
ing and betraying each other.   Germany, abandoned by

them, abandoned them in return. When Napoleon marched on Vienna and Berlin, across a subdued and fascinated Germany, conquered Prussia and Austria had no means of opposing the French conqueror save the useless aid of the armies of Russia.

Prussia and Austria had an equal interest in keeping Russia away from Europe; instead, they invited her in. By inviting her, they raised up a rival to themselves. The needs of their policy willed that that rival should become their ally, that Prussia should open the road into Europe to the Russians, and that Austria should prepare their way to Constantinople. Russia alone seems, at first sight, to have gained everything in the game. But it must not be forgotten into what terrible difficulties she was thrown by the partitions of Poland. She has drawn nearer to Europe, no doubt; she has reached the Black Sea; but instead of a feeble and subjugated State, she sees a formidable empire extended along her frontiers; she has been forced to help to raise up in Germany, close to herself, a Power who is her rival from origin, from civilization, from traditions, and from interest, and who raises up against her ceaseless and terrible difficulties in her Turkish and Asiatic enterprises. That is not all; at the very time when she was boasting of the mission of humanity which she was fulfilling in the East, she condemned herself in Poland to the most bloody of contradictions: to restore Byzantine civilization in Turkey, she was compelled to enslave European civilization in the heart of Europe.

Thus, from the first, Eastern crises have become vital crises for the whole of Europe, and the Triple Alliance, begotten of the Eastern Question in 1772, and founded on the partition of Poland, has for more than a century formed the binding-knot of European politics. That alliance sprang, not from community of interests, but from the opposition of desires. Interests evidently con-

demned it; often its bands were severed, as often were
they renewed; jealousy dissolved it, greed still re-formed
it; it endured because covetousness is infinite, and because
the more it is fed, the more is its hunger increased. The
augurs of the Chanceries have always satisfied their own
minds with prophesying its end: The alliance was only
hypothetical, and the Duc de Praslin was assured that it
would never be realized, and that it would be embodied
only to vanish away. He reasoned out its motives in a
memorandum which is a monument of official fatuity.
' Each of the Powers bordering on Poland,' said that too-
witty Minister, ' has a direct and essential interest in
protecting her, because each would have everything to
fear from the Power which should be increased at her
expense. . . .   The concert established between the King
of Prussia and Russia for their aggrandizement could not
be of long life. That very aggrandizement, by making
them nearer neighbours, would also make them more
formidable to each other. It would sow jealousy between
them, and jealousy soon degenerates into hostility.'
Nothing could be more correct, as far as pure logic
goes; but events, during more than a hundred years, have
turned everything in the contrary direction. These events
began in 1774. The doctrine was not a whit disconcerted
by them, and Vergennes, who yet had a just and enlightened
judgment of things, consoled himself for the partition, at
all events from force of habit, by the same arguments
which led M. de Praslin to assert that it would not be
accomplished.   ' The partition of Poland,' he wrote,
' might in other respects interest the humanity of the
Princes of Europe, and the respect owed to the rights
of nations. . . .'   But ' by multiplying the objects of
jealousy and of discussion between the three Powers which
have taken part in it, it is probable that the consequences
of this partition will absorb and divide them when their

ephemeral union shall have attained its end.' That end
had been perceived by Favier at the first glance. This
political adventurer had seen further in this matter than
had professional philosophers, royal historiographers, or
experienced diplomatists. 'The extent of the objects
which this alliance may embrace,' he wrote in 1773, 'will
enable the allies to keep back or to throw down in turn
more than one victim.'[2]   After 1795 there was no more
Poland to partition ; it became the turn of Turkey and of
Germany. We may even now foresee the time when the
alliance, having devoured all around it, will turn against
itself rather than be dissolved, and, enduring to the end
the effects of the causes which founded it, will find the
material of fresh partitions within its own breast. Raised
by the Eastern Question, the Polish Question seems solved
since 1815. For a century men have been labouring to
solve the Eastern Question. On the day when that shall
be considered solved, Europe will inevitably see propounded
the 'question of Austria.'

   [2] *Le Secret du Roi*, vol. ii., p. 82; Breteuil's *Instructions*, 1774,
Austria, p. 487 ; *Conjectures Raisonnées*, by Favier, 1773.

INDEX

THE END.